Roger:

Here it is! I am not
sure whether it is better
late than never. But, at
least this gives me an opportunity
to thank you for all the things I
could add (pull in the Preface you may).
showing me that maybe I could
Christian then a atheist then you)
a theologian (that's the 'easy' for
Thank you for introducing me to
religion that is liberating — & for
all your help & encouragement in
writing the thesis — & for all the
damned commas that so I wrecked
in the editing. Cheers!

Patricia
(March 6th, 1994)

FUNDAMENTAL ETHICS:
A Liberationist Approach

FUNDAMENTAL ETHICS:
A Liberationist Approach

Patricia McAuliffe

GEORGETOWN UNIVERSITY PRESS / WASHINGTON, D.C.

To Mother,
who housed me during twenty-five years of my studies

Georgetown University Press, Washington, D.C.   20057–1079
© 1993 by Georgetown University Press. All rights reserved.
Printed in the United States of America
10 9 8 7 6 5 4 3 2 1   1993
THIS VOLUME IS PRINTED ON ACID-FREE OFFSET BOOK PAPER.

Library of Congress Cataloging-in-Publication Data

McAuliffe, Patricia.
    Fundamental ethics : a liberationist approach / Patricia
McAuliffe.
        p.   cm.
    Includes bibliographical references.
    1. Liberation theology. 2. Christian ethics. I. Title.
BT83.57.M225   1993   241--dc20   93-11108
ISBN 0-87840-541-0

Contents

v

Preface

While I have been teaching the contents of this book in courses in fundamental ethics at various theological schools in Manila, the Philippines, over the past two years, the source of my thought does not derive from this recent third world experience. My commitment to the view that what ethics must centrally be about is resisting suffering, especially oppressive social suffering, goes back to the 1970s, when I was teaching philosophy in Scotland. Involvement in an alternative trading co-operative and two sabbaticals in Asia led me to develop a course in practical ethics which dealt mainly with north-south relations, and which, I insisted, was not a fringe course.

Not only fond memories but my gratitude reaches back to this time to include my former colleagues in the Philosophy Department of the University of Stirling, Scotland. Although you did not know it, you were looking over my shoulder, as I wrote, demanding the same clarity, consistency and truth you also sought. I am grateful for this and for the encouragement you gave me to pursue my social ethical concerns.

In the 1980s, in Toronto, Canada, I expanded my intellectual and practical domain into the field of theology. It became apparent to me that the ethic implicit in liberation theology was both at the center of Jesus' life and responds to the urgent social needs of our world today. So I began to articulate this ethic as a fundamental ethic, *the* ethic which ought to be at the center, and which all of us ought to bring to the center, of our lives. That is the core of this book, the main body of which I wrote in the late 1980s.

In this context, I especially with to thank my teacher, Roger Haight, S.J., who introduced me to the liberationist vision in theology and shared his wisdom and good sense through his critiques of my text. And a special thanks to all my family who gave me constant support during my stay in Toronto, and especially to my parents, Billie and Newt, who housed me, and to Julia and Jonathan, who made me laugh and helped me to keep my perspective. Also, I am most grateful to the Social Sciences and Humanities Research Council of Canada which funded me during this period.

In 1990, I took the opportunity to come to Manila to teach. The experiences here, although too brief and too superficial, have both concretized and restructured various aspects of my thought. One thing that has impressed itself on me over and over is how important it is for the poor to take up their own cause, how considerable the extent to which they are doing just that, and how their liberation, and our humble attempts to participate in it, are both tied quite concretely to the salvation of us all. This is true of the relations between other oppressed and dominant groups among humans. Men are saved through women's liberation in which women must and do play the dominant role, whites through black liberation similarly realized, and so on. I have been made more acutely aware of these necessary relations in this land where the gap between poor and rich is shockingly, painfully, unhidden.

I am grateful to Maryhill School of Theology for giving me the opportunity to teach in this Third World context. And I am very grateful to the students of Maryhill, the Loyola School of Theology and the Institute of Formation and Religious Studies—all in Manila. While I gave you a systematic liberationist approach to fundamental ethics, you impressed on me, by your example and your examples which now liven my text, the importance of rubbing shoulders with the poor. I am grateful to Mario Bolasco who, on very short notice, read the revised version of this book and advised me on its Philippine content. I am sorry to add that this highly esteemed scholar has since died. I add a special thank-you here to Patricia Rayner, John B. Breslin and John Samples at Georgetown University Press who have been not only patient and encouraging but most cheerful in spite of delays caused by my heavy teaching load, constant eight hour brown-outs and the notoriously slow movement of Christmas mail in the Philippines. Finally, I thank the people in those oppressed and struggling groups with whom I have, just barely, rubbed shoulders: squatters, internal refugees, Mount Pinatubo victims, members of basic Christian communities, political prisoners, trade unionists, street children. . . . I hope to spend more time with you and to learn more from you before I have to leave these islands.

PATRICIA MCAULIFFE

Introduction

Our experience of the world is not one of harmony, order, a God-given plan. Rather it is overwhelmingly one of disharmony, disorder, suffering, oppression. People are being destroyed due to their class sex, sexual orientation, color, religion, language, because they are 'too' old or because they are 'handicapped' . . .; other species and the environment are being destroyed because they are seen as mere means to some people's ends. We are an "already damaged *humanum*" in an already damaged cosmos.

In a country as poor as the Philippines, many sympathized with the prostitutes who lost their livelihood when Clark U.S. military air base closed due to the eruption of Mount Pinatubo. But an angry American military wife protested to the press: "They are nothing more than little brown fucking machines," setting woman against woman, and race against race, as well as inadvertently capturing the exploitation of women by men, poor by rich, colonized by colonizer, civilians by military. Racism, whose most striking symbol and acute reality must still be centered in the apartheid of South Africa, is felt around the world. Not long ago, in "multi-cultural "Canada, a black mother desperately rang 911, the emergency police number, because her son was being viciously beaten—by the police. She could not think of anyone else to call on. Colonization has left in its wake inappropriate political boundaries, continuing economic dependence, obscured identity and damaged dignity. An exasperated Filipino student expressed in our ethics class last year: "When we (Filipinos) try to express important things in English, such as our feelings and values, we come across as superficial." The problem is reinforced, by a "banking" method of teaching and "textbook" learning introduced by colonizers. In recent years, we have witnessed nature's rebellion against our exploitation. Our future generations and the biosphere as we know it are under threat. In 1991, 8,000 poor people, mostly children and the mothers who were attempting to save them, were killed in the Philippines when flash floods ripped through their shanties along the riverbank. The cause of the floods was years of legal and illegal logging in the area. Political corruption, militarization, assassinations, and something akin to genocide of tribal peoples are interwoven with the logging in the Philippines. The situation is critical, with more than 20 other potential disasters pinpointed in this country whose rainforest is being destroyed at 3 times the rate of the average in the Third World. Nonetheless, the World Bank insisted in 1992 that new logging concessions be given.

The global situation depicted by these examples profoundly threatens and challenges theism and Christianity. It challenges those of us who are Christian to show how our religious lives can be meaningful, and how our religious faith can be true, in face of the tyrannous systems of disorder. But the excess of suffering and oppression in the world also threatens and challenges our very ethicity. *Unless resistance to suffering and oppression is at the center and core of our ethics, unless it is its raison d'être, then ethics, our ethical lives, ourselves as ethical beings cannot be taken seriously.* Our understanding of structurally caused suffering, such as that due to poverty, racism, and sexism, is relatively new and requires a paradigm shift in ethics. But suffering and resistance to suffering is very old. Indeed, this unitary experience is at the heart of human history and of life itself. From the beginning, poor and oppressed peoples have sought salvation by rebelling against their poverty and oppression. And from the beginning, there have been some who have joined in solidarity with them. This rebellion and solidarity are what ethical life and largely what religious life must be about.

There are, however, a number of paradoxes involved in how suffering and seeking salvation have related historically to ethics and religion. While suffering and seeking salvation have been at the center of people's ethical lives, they have not been at the center of classical western philosophical thought. Both Plato and Aristotle encourage us to seek the good by turning from negativity. Kant compels us to act out of duty to the law of our rational natures; neither suffering nor salvation are ethically important. Only the utilitarian, often thought to be an enemy of religion, has joined religion in making human suffering of central concern. Christianity's relationship to suffering, however, has itself been acutely paradoxical. On the one hand it has provided a sort of 'solution' to suffering by offering an extra-historical salvation and, on the other, it has introduced the seemingly insoluble problem of evil: in ordinary human experience, God is needed to respond to suffering, yet the fact of suffering appears to undermine the credibility of God.

Today this issue has taken an even more paradoxical twist. Atheists and liberation theologians point to the very same phenomenon of massive suffering in the world, the former to show that there is no God, the latter to show that this is where God is especially 'located.' Liberation theologians can say this only because they understand God's revelation in Jesus to involve the call to resist suffering, an ethical imperative. God reveals Godself especially in the poor and oppressed as a protest that humans must first direct themselves ethically to this place of greatest negativity because this suffering, this destruction of humans and of what it is to be human, must not go on. But this is to say that, in liberation theology, religion and ethics have come together in a new way. Jesus' revelation from God does not explain suffering but shows us what to do about it—to resist it. This is the only possible way to connect in a meaningful manner religion's concern about suffering and its commitment to a caring God. Thus liberation theology is fundamentally ethical. However, paradoxically, while critics charge that liberation theology is nothing but ethics, liberation theologians tend to avoid ethical language. And finally, while critics claim that, in reducing theology to ethics, liberation theology reduces out an extra-historical salvation, in fact, the ethic that it promotes cries out for God and final salvation.

My aim in this book is to take steps towards articulating a fundamental ethic which responds to the situation in the world of massive oppressive suffering and which captures what some people have been practicing all along. I do not describe and analyse at a practical level what are the social sufferings with which we are confronted, what are their causes, and what should be the policies for change. Rather, guided by liberationist thought, I try to get at something of what our ethicity and our ethical life must be if we are to be responders to massive world suffering and participators in the salvation of one another. This book operates on a level below social analysis where ethics meets anthropology, epistemology, religion and theology. While it relies most heavily on the liberation theology of the poor, it attempts to capture something of what the various liberation theologies have in common, indeed, of what it is, in part, to be human.

The sources and arguments of this book are multiple. It explores liberationist theologians' interpretations of Jesus and of church documents in order to draw out the implicit anthropology and ethic in them. It makes use of a variety of philosophical and theological sources as well as the evidence of experience in order to develop and justify the aspects of anthropology and ethics it has drawn out. And it integrates the aspects selected to form a constructive description. It insists, however, that the various aspects of the ethic not only cohere with one another but are required by the condition of world suffering. The ethic is a response to human and cosmic need before it is a system. Thus, this ethic is supported by the needs of the empirical situation, the possibilities and necessities of our anthropology, the Christian message, and theological and philosophical argument. But while it draws from the Christian liberationist vision, the ethic developed is primarily a human ethic, an ethic which should be accepted by all and for which Jesus is a paradigm example.

While I make use of a number of liberationist and other sources, I rely most heavily on Edward Schillebeeckx, Juan Luis Segundo, and to a lesser degree, Dorothee Soelle. Schillebeeckx's thought has provided the fundamental impetus for the entire project, and his negative contrast experience provides a foundation, a fundamental value and an imperative for the ethic. Segundo is perhaps the most creative and provocative exponent of the theology coming out of Latin America today. And his thought is remarkably "usable" for ethics. He has an important contribution to make to nearly every central topic I discuss, particularly the option for the poor, creativity, and the relationship between ethics and religion. Soelle is significant for her explicit concern for the poor, women, and the kinds of oppression suffered by middle class people in the north. She too has something important to say on nearly every central issue, including those of suffering, social connectedness, and eschatology.

A comment on my use of some key terms might be helpful. I use the terms "suffering" and "salvation" more than "oppression" and "liberation" because the former pair has a more universal ring, although I insist that the suffering caused by oppressive structures must be brought to the center of ethical concern and the salvation we must seek in history is best articulated as liberation. I use "liberationist" rather than "liberation" to describe the ethic I take steps towards developing because I intend it to be appropriate to the various liberation theologies that have emerged, I am strongly influenced by theologians who are not strictly liberation theologians and, while I draw heavily from the liberation theology of the poor, I also take the freedom to select and shape what I say to what ethics should be, whether or not most liberation theologians agree with it on every point. I use "anthropology," not normally to mean "theory of human nature" but non-static "human nature," fitting to Schillebeeckx's anthropological constants. Finally, because I refer to a number of oppressed and dominant groups, because my readers and I will not belong to all the same groups, and because my style uses "we" referring to my readers and myself, this essay would read more smoothly if I simply referred to all groups as "they." But, for the sake of concreteness, in select places, where I am discussing and not merely referring to particular groups, as, for example, when I discuss the option for the poor as an option of the poor and of the rich, I refer to the poor as "they" and to the rich as "we." I talk about women as an oppressed group in confined places and use "we." But when I talk about oppressed groups in general, I normally say "they."

The book is divided into five main chapters. The first two chapters discuss the negative contrast experience and the option for the poor as foundational for ethics. The following two chapters consider two fundamental elements of the ethic, social solidarity and creativity respectively. And the final chapter discusses the relationship between ethics and religion/theology. The various chapters attempt to balance the requirements of universality and historicity, the persona and social, practice and theory, what is Christian and human.

The first chapter argues that the universal experience of suffering and struggling for salvation is an experiential foundation for ethics and is captured by Schillebeeckx's notion of a negative contrast experience. The chapter explores and greatly develops this notion to show that it has a number of characteristics, such as being both concrete and universal, which make it an appropriate and fruitful foundation for ethics. Also, the contrast experience yields, in its productive force, a first ethical imperative of resistance to every threat to the *humanum*. Finally, the chapter shows that because Jesus provides a radical example of someone who lived out of the negative contrast, and because the negative contrast is implicit in the liberation theology of the poor, an ethic for which this experience is foundational is both Christian and liberationist.

The second chapter argues that the imperative rising out of the contrast experience, to resist every threat to the *humanum*, is too abstract; it must be concretized. We must give first priority to those who are most deprived of the *humanum*, the materially destitute. And to respond to the needs of the materially destitute requires that we make a paradigm shift in ethics which is captured in liberationist theologians' call to take up the option for the poor.

Chapter three develops a liberationist ethic as an ethic of social solidarity. It begins by exploring the central liberationist symbol of the kingdom of God in order to tease out the implicit social anthropology and ethic of this theology. It explores the anthropology and ethics of our relatedness to other humans and to social structures and institutions. This chapter deals with the task of relating the ethics of personal relations with the ethics of social transformation. It also considers what should be our ethical approach to other species and the environment.

The fourth chapter argues that a liberationist ethic is a creative, innovative ethic, for which practice is prior to norms for practice. This chapter thus applies to the ethical sphere the liberationist view of the priority of practice to theory. Following the pattern of chapter three, it begins with a discussion of Jesus' creative use of the Mosaic Law, relativizing its practical norms to its goal of human welfare. The anthropological problem that emerges is how to explain our creativity and the ethical problem that emerges is how, creatively, to find forms of practice which bring our fundamental value alive in a changing historical context. The chapter shows that a creative ethic is not anarchical but utterly responsible. It locates this ethic *vis-à-vis* natural law ethics, utilitarianism and proportionalism.

The fifth and last chapter once again applies the liberationist theme of priority of practice, this time to the relationship between ethics on the one hand and religion and theology on the other. It parallels the form of the two preceding chapters, drawing implications from their discussion of Jesus and developing our anthropology as evaluators of values. It argues that ethics is, in a number of ways, prior to and even foundational for religion and theology. The chapter goes on to explore how liberationist ethics discloses a religious dimension for some, a disclosure that affects the quality of ethics. The same pages argue that ethics logically cries out for heaven. Finally, the chapter draws from the whole book to describe aspects of a liberationist picture of heaven.

1

The Negative Contrast Experience Is Foundational for Ethics

INTRODUCTION

Our fundamental human experience is one of suffering and struggling against suffering for salvation. According to Schillebeeckx, the contrast between our experiences of suffering and salvation, which is too often a whole history of suffering and but brief moments of salvation, propels us to resist suffering and strive for salvation. He calls this experience, including its productive force of resistance, a negative contrast experience.

The following example is a slice of the story of one Filipino community's suffering and struggle against suffering, a sort of contemporary Exodus story in process.

> Elma is a sugar worker in Negros, with whom I had the privilege of spending a night. In the evening, the women and children of the little community met inside her nipa hut, the men remaining outside, while Elma told their story.
>
> Elma and many of the others were born on a nearby hacienda. Their parents were sugar workers and they became sugar workers. They were some of the first to join the National Federation of Sugar Workers' Union (NFSWU) when it was formed in 1971. They were locked out almost immediately, and to this day, more than twenty years later, they can get only temporary employment on haciendas, without benefits.
>
> During the next 15 years, however, Elma became a union organizer, was harassed, forced off and, after a court case, let back on her hacienda to live. When Marcos fled, so too did Benedicto, who owned much of Negros, including the hacienda on which she lived. With Cory Aquino as president and a new agrar-

ian reform law, Elma and the others assumed some of the land would become theirs. She and her husband were at the forefront of organizing protests and presenting court cases when they did not receive the land. They were harassed and, in 1987, arrested. Elma was beaten and her head banged against the bars until it bled profusely. She was threatened that if, by nightfall, she did not give the names of NFSWU and Basic Christian Community (BCC) organizers to the military, and did not admit that they were members of the New People's Army (NPA), "something bad would happen to her."

But their teenaged children had traveled immediately to Bacolod, the capital, and publicized their parents' arrest over the radio. Meanwhile, the NFSWU had organized a demonstration in front of the government offices, and the officer who had threatened Elma had been called away to attend to a shoot-out between two of his men. Elma and her husband were released. She spent three months recovering emotionally, but returned to her union work. She decided that she was poor, was of the poor, and must support the poor. Eventually, some 50 families on the hacienda won, through the courts, enough land and money to build their own huts and grow vegetables year round and even rice to last them part of the year. When I was with them, they were working on getting titles to their land.

In this chapter I shall argue that Schillebeeckx's negative contrast experience is foundational for ethics. When I speak of foundations, I mean something looser yet deeper than most foundationalists mean. What is at the starting point of ethics? What allows ethics to get off the ground? What makes it possible? Also, I mean what is at the core or center of ethics, what ethics and our being ethical beings are fundamentally about. What provides us with a first principle or imperative which guides right practice?

If we ask ourselves, Why be ethical; why ought we, why must we, be ethical?, it seems our response must be because there is need. Ethics is a response to need. And the overwhelming need in our world is that massive excessive deprivation, suffering, and oppression be alleviated. The situation of suffering in the world makes ethics necessary and the contrast experience which propels us to act against suffering makes ethics possible. Thus the starting point of ethics is found in the negative situation and our response to it. And if we ask, What is ethics fundamentally about; what is at its center and core?, surely it is to respond to the massive excessive suffering in the world. Finally, the imperative yielded by the contrast experience, to resist suffering and oppression, offers a first imperative or first principle for ethics.

To say the negative contrast experience is foundational in these three senses is not to utter a tautology or something which is incorrigible. It is not self-evident in either of these narrow logical senses. It is not, for example, reducible to the empty imperative to do good and avoid evil. While it does not tell us exactly what to do, it is substantive regarding what we ought to do, where we ought to direct our energies. To say that the negative contrast experience captures the starting point and core and first imperative of ethics is, in part, to appeal to intuition. But intuition is based on experience. It involves an appeal to self-evidency but a self-evidency which, I claim, makes the best sense of our experience of history whose movement can be defined in terms of suffering and seeking salvation.

This chapter will explore various features of the contrast experience in order to bring out its fittingness as a foundation for ethics. And while the next chapter will discuss the option for the poor as implicit in and a concretization of the imperative to resist suffering, that discussion will also serve to test the significance of the contrast experience. If we can see, on the basis of experience, that taking up the option for the poor is of central importance today, then we can ask, Does the negative contrast experience, at a more general and abstract level, show how this option is possible?

This chapter will show that an ethic which takes the contrast experience as foundational is a liberationist ethic, is appropriate to a religious and Christian ethic, and, in some fundamental ways, turns classical ethics upside down.

THE NEGATIVE CONTRAST EXPERIENCE IS FOUNDATIONAL FOR ETHICS

This section will explore and expand on Schillebeeckx's understanding of the negative contrast experience. It will pick out and discuss features of the contrast experience which make it a particularly appropriate articulation of what should be at the starting point and core of ethics. I will begin with a discussion of Schillebeeckx's understanding of experience in general to show that much of the ethical significance of the negative contrast experience is already contained in the nature of experience itself.

Schillebeeckx's Understanding of Experience

Experience[1] involves both subjective and objective dimensions; it involves givens from the side of the self as well as from the side of external reality. Indeed, only because it has a subjective dimension and never comes to us as "raw data" but is always interpreted, can experience be meaningful to us. And only because it is of an objective reality so that it sometimes conflicts with our interpretations and teaches us something new, does it reveal reality to us.

Because we cannot experience "raw" objective data but, in order to experience at all, we must *interpret* that data, then we must identify and so classify the object of experience according to images, concepts, models, and frameworks that we already know. And because the images and models we bring to experience are not, for the most part, innate, but are developed from previous experiences, the subjective element of experience changes in history. But while we interpret new experience in terms of a framework developed from previous experience, the reality we now experience may resist our interpretation. And when this happens it is important that we not force our interpretation onto reality but that we let ourselves be guided by reality.[2]

While the relationship between subjective and objective dimensions of experience is a dialectical one, "reality remains the final criterion" of the genuineness of experience. Ironically, reality is the final criterion precisely *because* it sometimes resists our interpretations and our projects. Only due to these occasions of resistance can we ever be certain that we are in contact with an independent reality, a reality which is not a mere product of our wants and expectations. Thus, *"the hermeneutical principle for the disclosure of reality is not the self-evident, but the scandal, the stumbling block of the refractoriness of reality."*[3]

This negativity, this critical quality of reality, is productive; it reveals the way things are by revealing the way they are not. And it reveals the way things ought to be by revealing how they ought not to be. In science, we interpret data in terms of established models and frameworks for as long as these models and frameworks account for our data, allowing us to predict and to control matter. But when our data begins to conflict with our framework, when reality thus resists our interpretation, we are forced to seek a new or revised framework and interpretation. Similarly, in ethics, we act according to established norms and theories for right practice for as long as they work. But when reality negates our best efforts, when we are confronted with massive excessive suffering and exploitation, we are compelled to revise our forms of practice and interpretation. The ecological crisis has, for example, forced us to change our interpretation and forms of practice with regard to nature. We can no longer understand nature as solely a means to our ends, and we are being forced to change our exploitative forms of practice.

Experience has a productive force, not only in terms of providing knowledge, but by compelling us to speak out and take action. We can communicate our experience, pass it on so that others can learn from it. By telling of our experience, by telling a story rather than by merely relating facts, we encourage others to use their imagination, to enter our experiential world, to expand their experience by sharing ours and so, finally, to speak and act for the same ends as ourselves. Thus experience makes us witnesses, messengers, narrators of what has happened to us. And *because experience, which we can pass on, challenges our established ways of thinking and acting, it is not innocent.*[4]

Finally, experience has a disclosive power. Ordinary empirical experience can open up something more or something deeper. A smile can invite relationship. An experience of joy, of momentary, partial salvation, can open up hope in God and total salvation.[5]

Contexts in Which Schillebeeckx Introduces the Negative Contrast Experience

In *God the Future of Man*, Schillebeeckx introduces the contrast experience in the context of a concrete problem: Can the church make an authoritative demand on Christians in political matters such as that of land reform?[6] The more fundamental issue being raised is: *Who has the epistemological privilege, therefore the primary authority, in moral matters?* And, lying behind this question: How do we know or come to know what we ought to do in concrete political matters? Schillebeeckx's view is clear:

> . . . long before the Churches had analyzed the social problems, there were people who, in their commitment and in a preanalytic dialogue with the world, had already reached the moral decision that fundamental changes were required. *New situational ethical*

imperatives have rarely or never been initiated by philosophers, theologians, Churches or ecclesiastical authorities. They emerge from a concrete experience of life and impose themselves with the clear evidence of experience. Theoretical reflection comes afterward, and so do the critical examination and rationalization, the philosophical or theological and official formulation. And so, after the event, such imperatives are put forth as "generally valid, abstract norms".[7]

These concrete experiences Schillebeeckx calls "contrast experiences." He describes them as the sorts of experience that make people suddenly say: "This should not and must not go on," experiences such as hunger, racism, and torture. But this protest would not be possible if these negative experiences did not "imply an awareness of values that is veiled, positive, though not yet articulate, . . . values still being sought, *and revealed in a negative manner.*"[8] In order even to recognize hunger, torture, and racism as negative, as what should not and cannot go on, we must experience them as in contrast with something else, something which is positive and good. But we experience positivity primarily as the negation of negativity, "peace," for example, as "not hot or cold war," depending on our experience of war.[9]

We can conclude that it is not church authorities but those who are directly experiencing social evils,[10] such as hunger and landlessness, who have an epistemological privilege regarding what to do in political matters. However, when it respects grassroots experience, church, especially due to its eschatological proviso, does have an important function to play in criticizing what negates humanity.

In *The Understanding of Faith,* Schillebeeckx asks what is the relevance of the Christian God today? In order to answer this we must ask, What do humans qua humans see as making life meaningful today?[11] We find that any common answer to the quest for meaning must be negative rather than positive. Why? If we asked a group of people what their positive utopian views are, we would receive as many answers as people asked. But if we asked what are the negativities which threaten us, we would find considerable agreement. *We agree upon the "search to realize the constantly threatened humanum" or, put negatively, a "resistance to every threat to the humanum." This constitutes the "universal preunderstanding of all positive views" of humanity.* Thus, seeking salvation by way of negating negation has a concreteness and a certainty that seeking positive utopias does not.[12]

This resistance to the threat to the humanum is, in the first instance, a practice and not knowledge.[13] The claim is that humans protest and act to change what is harmful to them first and reflect on it afterward. But this practice is only possible within a context of hope, a positive sphere of meaning which must be experienced and involves a call of and to the humanum. For example, we experience meaningfulness in terms of friendship and love. And "these human realities are sustained by a gratuitous meaning in itself, which communicates itself to us in them and takes possession of us."[14]

Resistance to every threat to humanity is not only the universal preunderstanding for all positive answers humans give to the search for meaning, but also it is the universal preunderstanding of talk about God and of the interpretation of the good news. If the Christian God and the good news of Jesus are to be relevant to Christians today they must be at least meaningful to everyone. And understanding the good news as the negation of negation fits perfectly Jesus' preaching and practice of the kingdom. It involves, primarily, the alleviation of suffering, resistance to oppression, inclusion of the excluded—the beginning, in history, of the wiping away of every tear.[15]

In *God the Future of Man*, and in *The Understanding of Faith*, Schillebeeckx introduces the negative contrast experience to solve a problem for church. In the former text, it is introduced to show that church can speak authoritatively on political and ethical issues only in a negative, critical way and only following grassroots experience. In the latter text, it is introduced as a publicly acceptable criterion for the interpretation of the good news, a means by which Christianity can offer a universal and religious answer to the human question of meaning. The appearance of the negative contrast experience in the *Jesus* books is very different. No longer is it treated as an almost logical construct, but it comes alive as an *experience*, a phenomenon, an empirical matter of fact. By means of narrative and description, more than by argument, Schillebeeckx tries to convince us that we really do experience in this way. All we need do is to look around us and at human history and we will see that, amidst all the suffering that human societies and individuals encounter, there are fleeting moments of joy, fragments of salvation, which are usually experienced as alleviation from suffering and which propel us to act against suffering. In the *Jesus* books, the issue of suffering and salvation is pervasive; and it is *one* issue. Here Schillebeeckx gets to the core of what the negative contrast experience is about: *the relationship between suffering and salvation and how it is that we can still have hope amidst all the suffering in the world.*

The following passages from *Jesus* and *Christ* show how, in these books, Schillebeeckx presents the negative contrast as an experience, a phenomenon, but also as a central and permanent element of our history, an anthropological constant. These passages demonstrate the relationship between suffering and salvation which the contrast experience expresses. They point out who experiences and lives out of the negative contrast most acutely, the poor, the oppressed, and those in solidarity with them.

> Ideas and expectations of salvation and human happiness are invariably projected from within concrete experience and the pondered fact of calamity, pain, misery and alienation—from within negative experiences accumulated through centuries of affliction, with here and there the fleeting promise of a happier lot, fragmentary experiences of well-being in a story, stretching from generation to generation, of hopes unfulfilled, of guilt and evil—the 'Job's problem' of our human history. Hence there eventually emerges an anthropological projection, a vision of what is held to be the true, good and happy mode of human life.[16]

> Ever since humankind has existed, among the oppressed and their prophetic spokespeople a vision has arisen which is opposed to what people really do. They were always the authentic bearers of the vision, but perhaps it had to be put in words by others, because oppression robbed them of the capacity for speech. As a vision it is generally vague and similar—though continually given different colouring in accordance with particular cultural, social and geographical situations; a 'damp' eschatology in dry desert countries, a 'dry' eschatology in constantly inundated lands; a kingdom of justice for oppressed peoples, and so on; at any rate, the same theme comes over time and again: not the existing wretchedness.[17]

Thus, because negative experiences help to delineate what is positive, happiness is inevitably experienced as deliverance from some suffering, such as dampness for desert people. So if we know what are a people's ideas of salvation we can deduce what are its sufferings. And the extraordinary thing is, it is those who are suffering most who keep the concrete vision of salvation alive for us all. Where there is a vision of salvation even amidst overwhelming suffering, there is a prodding at the causes and a confronting of the effects of the suffering;

there is the expectation that suffering and evil will be "unmasked." Indeed, there is the demand that suffering and evil be overcome, that "Enough is enough: The world must be changed—positively and radically changed!" But, in spite of our efforts, the human capacity for and experience of suffering are so great that humanity is compelled to "look for mercy and compassion at the very heart of reality, despite every contrary experience." Ultimately, salvation must be sought within a religious domain.[18]

In the *Jesus* books, Schillebeeckx consistently insists that *positivity*, an experience of joy or meaning, is an *actual element* of the negative contrast experience. In *Jesus*, he says that, experientially and linguistically, well-being

> . . . is brought to life and made intelligible only through contrasted negative experiences, *conjoined with* at least sporadic experiences of what 'makes sense'—whence there arises in hope an anticipation of 'total sense.'[19]

In *Christ* he tells us:

> What makes negative experiences of contrast in reality into productive experiences is *the meaning that can be found in them.* . . . Partial experiences of meaning and salvation are therefore had in practice; there is no question of a theory of salvation detached from any practice.[20]

Also, he is saying here, any hope of final salvation will be sheer illusion, perhaps impossible for us to conceive, except in the context of the experience and practice of partial salvation.[21]

Logical Mapping of the Negative Contrast Experience

It is appropriate here to tie together Schillebeeckx's rather scattered remarks by mapping out the logical relations of the elements of the negative contrast experience.[22]

The negative contrast experience is *passive*,[23] not in the sense of its being something we do not act on but in the sense of its being something that happens to us. It involves an external reality's impinging itself upon us. Although it is a concrete *occurrent* experience, it is also a universal tendency and value, an *anthropological constant*, as indicated by its being had and striven for by individuals and communities in different contexts down through the ages.

Figure 1-a. Negative Contrast Experience and Related Concepts

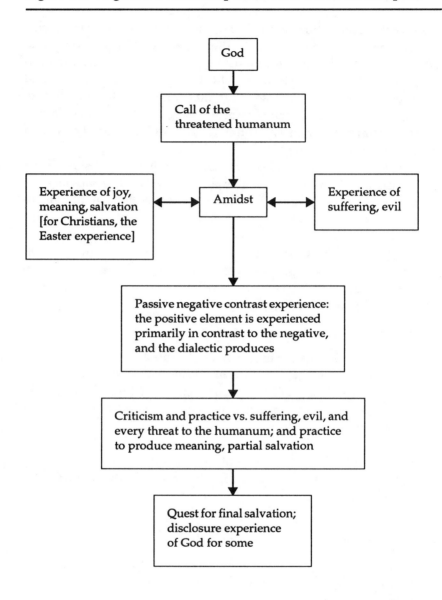

This diagram is schematic and does not show all the relationships that hold between the concepts mentioned.

The figure on the facing page, depicting Jesus' negative contrast experience, shows how the Easter experience, powerful ground for final salvation, is made possible.

Figure 1-b. Jesus and the Negative Contrast Experience

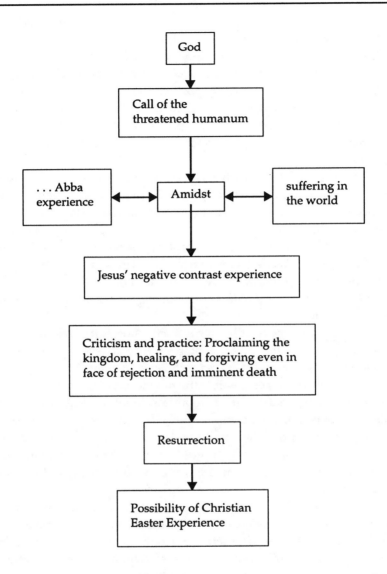

The negative contrast is not an experience of pure negativity but involves hope for deliverance or salvation, in the context of overwhelming suffering. And this hope for something better depends on one's already having had *an experience of partial salvation.* The negative contrast experience thus has a positive and a negative element: It involves the experience of positivity amidst negativity, salvation amidst suffering, liberation amidst oppression. And this reflects a reality which contains both good and bad, joy and sorrow, justice and injustice.

The negative and positive aspects of this experience are interdependent. We could not even experience the negative as negative, much less resist it, if we did not have something positive with which to contrast it. But there is also an asymmetry between the aspects of this experience. *We know and experience what is positive primarily as the negation of what is negative.* We experience peace primarily as the negation of whatever kind of war we have experienced or are threatened by; we experience salvation and liberation as release from our particular sufferings and oppressions.

The negative contrast has a productive force; it gives rise to criticism and practice, the practice of resistance to every threat to the humanum. In a number of places, Schillebeeckx says it is the element of meaning which makes possible the practical critical force of the negative contrast experience. In an important footnote,[24] he says it is the *dialectic* between the element of meaning and of meaninglessness which makes this possible. Finally, while the experience of the contrast between suffering and salvation propels us to right practice, right practice yields an experience of salvation and greater sensitivity to the negative contrast.

As well as giving rise to criticism and protest, the negative contrast experience also leads us to act in *positive* ways to produce meaning. This positive side of practice not only involves building things anew but also remembering and recontextualizing what is positive in the old. Without this, Christianity would be impossible.

Because the negative contrast involves the experience and practice of partial salvation, it leads to the quest for or at least the question of *ultimate salvation.* For some it *discloses* God and final salvation; the latter is understood primarily negatively.

Finally, our hope and our experience of meaning, the call of and to the humanum, *is sustained by a positive sphere of meaning*—indeed, has its source in God. God can be disclosed by the negative contrast experience as the source of our hope and of our resistance as well as through partial salvation's calling forth total salvation.

The Negative Contrast Experience Is Foundational for Ethics

Here I shall discuss how the combination of qualities which characterize the negative contrast experience provides excellent grounds for accepting it as foundational for ethics. This negative contrast experience captures the starting point and core of ethics and provides us with a first imperative for ethics.[25]

An Experience and an Anthropological Constant

The importance of seeing the negative contrast as an occurrent, concrete, and historical experience cannot be overstressed. Every other claim we make for it depends for its credibility on the negative contrast's being first an experience. It is an experience before it is a logical construct or a technical term or a tool for analysis. This is important to its foundational character because knowledge and belief are based first on experience.

Schillebeeckx stresses, in most of the passages we have read, the experiential character of the negative contrast and the authority this gives to it. We have heard how "ever since humankind has existed," the oppressed and those in solidarity with them have been weighed down by "calamity, pain, misery and alienation," but, encouraged by "fragmentary experiences of well-being," have held high a vision "given different colouring in accordance with particular . . . situations" but of "a kingdom of justice for oppressed peoples." This experience of suffering and striving against suffering has been told "in a story, stretching from generation to generation." It is those who experience the contrast most acutely who have the epistemological privilege over experts and established authorities, regarding what is wrong and what would count as getting it right. Today, it is peasant farmers, factory workers, refugees, political prisoners, union organizers, lay catechists . . . , women more than men, blacks and browns more than whites, who are the ethical 'authorities.'

Because the negative contrast is an experience, the ethic to which it gives rise is concrete, contentful, historically relevant, true or appropriate to reality, and effective. Because it is a fundamental and powerful experience, it motivates people to action and encourages the most urgent and most necessary action first. But the negative contrast is made doubly powerful as a foundation for ethics by its being, not only an occurrent, concrete, particular experience, but also a universal human tendency and, in its productive force, a universal value and imperative. It is an anthropological constant.[26]

We have seen that the negative contrast yields a value and imperative which is universal because it is negative. Everyone can agree that we should resist every threat to the humanum. But as well as its being a universal value and imperative, resistance to suffering is a human tendency. Again it is relevant to refer to the passages quoted from the *Jesus* books. The one speaks of "negative experiences *accumulated through centuries* of affliction, with here and there the fleeting promise of a happier lot" from which "there eventually emerges an *anthropological projection.*" The other begins: *"Ever since humankind has existed,* among the oppressed and their prophetic spokespersons a vision has arisen . . . ." We have a fundamental tendency toward, as well as value in, seeking what is good for the humanum. Schillebeeckx argues that just as there are limits to what we can do to our environment without undermining our quality of life and even survival, similarly there are limits to what we can do to ourselves or to each other which, if overstepped, will lead to spontaneous protest.[27] This means there are limits to the demands God can make on us. We will eventually rebel against a god who demands excessive praise of God at the expense of humans.[28] And this includes, not only the poor but the rich who are being manipulated by science, religion, and consumerism, as demonstrated by the hippie movement of the 1960s.[29]

What Schillebeeckx is saying here is important, and it is optimistic. He is suggesting that there is something in humans which will eventually rebel against what is bad for humans even when we are being manipulated to think that what is bad for us is good for us. He speaks of the call of and to the humanum. From a theistic perspective this must relate to God who is on the side of humanity. From a secular perspective, it may be thought of as a kind of survival mechanism. But even here the presupposition of a fundamental given directionality, meaning, and value to human life must be acknowledged.

As an anthropological constant, the productive force of the negative contrast is both a tendency and a goal, a fact and a value. It is both something that humans tend to do and what they ought to do in order to be fully human. This implies that we tend to be ethical, not only in the sense of being the kinds of beings who choose between right and wrong, but in the sense of tending toward the good, of tending to resist suffering at a level below consciousness and deliberation—*although this does not preclude the presence of conflicting tendencies.*[30] We see, however, that, at this fundamental level, there is not a complete break between what is the case in terms of our human tendencies and what, morally, ought to be the case.[31]

As involving a human tendency, the contrast experience yields an ethic which is possible. As universally giving rise to a practice and imperative, the contrast experience respects the demand that, at a fundamental level and in spite of cultural differences, a common humanity encounters a common external reality and should have a common ethical foundation. That it is both an occurrent experience and an anthropological constant, that it yields both a concrete, contentful, historically relevant and also a universally relevant ethical practice and imperative, provides very powerful grounds for affirming the negative contrast experience as foundational for ethics.

Negativity Is Epistemologically Prior; Positivity Is Ontologically Prior

Negativity has been in the foreground of our discussions of the negative contrast experience. We must experience a contrast between negativity and positivity in order to recognize negativity as negative, as something which should not continue. We experience positivity primarily as the negation of what is negative, peace as not war. We can know with much greater certainty, and so we can reach more common agreement about, the negativity that must be overcome than we can about our positive utopias. Indeed, negativity holds the key to universal agreement in ethics and what is good for the humanum. We can agree on the primacy of resistance to every threat to the humanum. The epistemological priority of negativity is built into the nature of experience itself. Given that all of our experience is interpreted, that we lay onto experience our models and frameworks, we can be certain we are in touch with an objective reality when it resists our interpretations, when we experience negativity.

It is oppressed groups and those in solidarity with them, groups who are suffering most, who experience most acutely and are pressed to respond first to the negative contrast. Through their trial-and-error practice of resisting negativity, they provide the groundwork for the revision of norms, thus showing the rest of us what we ought to do.

Those experiencing negativity most acutely have an epistemological privilege in ethics. If ethical authority does not root itself in the concrete experience of negativity, but if, on the other hand, it relies on abstract, purely positive utopias, "somewhere nearby a Jesus of Nazareth is being nailed to the cross." Positive total visions, whether they are this-worldly or not, tend to be "murderous visions."[32] Even Jesus did not act from a well-defined concept of final salvation and the view he had arose, at least in part, out of his negating negation:

> Rather, he saw a *distant* vision of final . . . salvation—the kingdom of God—in and through his own fragmentary actions, which were historical and thus limited or finite, 'going around doing good' *through healing, liberating from demonic powers, and reconciliation.*[33]

While we act, not in the name of already defined concepts and norms, "but in the name of human values still being sought, and revealed in a negative manner" and while these values are "veiled, positive, though not yet articulate," these values *are positive* and our efforts must be sustained by a positive sphere of meaning. *While negativity is epistemologically prior, positivity must be ontologically prior.*[34]

For Schillebeeckx, the positive sphere of meaning which sustains our ethical practice is God because God is the source and ground of our efforts and our hope. He recognizes, however, that nontheists are ethical and are sustained by the hope that goodness will prevail. In recent work he sees that, while nontheists cannot coherently deny the role of a positive sphere of meaning, they can coherently deny God.[35] But, independently of God as source and ground of ethics, why must negativity be sustained by a positive sphere of meaning?

Schillebeeckx is influenced, in the epistemological and ethical stress that he gives to negativity, by the critical theorists,[36] but he criticizes them for being purely critical. They do not acknowledge the positive aspects of tradition which should be retained or retrieved nor do they make any positive claims for the direction in which society should go. While he accepts their Enlightenment values of freedom and rationality, he thinks that, because of their flight from positivity, they have no grounds for valuing these values. They cannot situate freedom and say why freedom from this or that is valuable.

Presumably, what Schillebeeckx has in mind is that, while we understand positivity primarily in terms of the negation of negativity,

and while negativity should guide us in our positive aims, positivity cannot be reduced to the negation of negativity or our efforts will lead to a negation of both suffering and salvation, to a pure negation, to nothing at all. But life can be and almost always is worthwhile, whatever our suffering, and this presupposes the ontological priority of positivity. If there were not this basic experience of and commitment to positivity even if found primarily in the negation of negativity, and if we did not have positive visions however vague and incomplete, there would be nothing to value except an ultimate negation of negativity into nothingness. And there would be no point in struggling against negativity except by the short route of suicide.

It is by acknowledging the epistemological priority of negativity that the negative contrast experience can yield an ethic which is both concrete and historical and also universal in character. The awareness of positive values, although not concrete or articulate, but still vague, introduces an essential balance to the stress on negativity. *The positing of the ontological priority of a positive sphere of meaning saves our ethics from being reduced to a search merely for nonsuffering, for nothingness. Indeed, it affirms that life itself is valuable and to be nourished, that negating negation is for the end of positive salvation.* The combination of the epistemological priority of negativity and the ontological priority of positivity leads us to recognize, not that we should have no positive policies or visions at all, but that they must remain provisional, incomplete, and open to the future. We are called to innovativeness in their pursuit.

The Productive Force of the Negative Contrast Experience Is a Practice Before It Is Knowledge

From the various Schillebeeckx texts we have seen: Grassroots activists respond to the world's problems by their practice before theoreticians develop norms on the basis of these people's practice. It is the practical responses to the suffering of those who suffer and not the utopian dreams and theories of others that is ethically most relevant. The universal preunderstanding for every positive view of humanity, which is the productive force of the negative contrast experience, is a practice before it is knowledge.[37]

That the productive force of the negative contrast experience is a practice before it is articulated knowledge is connected with the negative contrast's being an experience before it is a technical term or an explanatory force. We come to reflectively understand what is ethical

and salvific, what our very ethicity is about, through experience and practice. In part, we come even to experience these things through right practice. That the negative contrast is an anthropological constant, a human tendency, helps us to appreciate how the experience of suffering-and-salvation can propel us to act even before we reflect. In times of crisis, such as war, people very often just do respond creatively, and in a trial-and-error sort of way, to overcome suffering. This priority of practice over explicit theorizing is natural to humans and is essential to being effective against suffering and every form of negativity. Because the experience of negativity is, by and large, reality's rejection of our interpretations and forms of practice,[38] we have to revise these, find new forms of interpretation and practice, in order to overcome negativity. In ethics, at the fundamental level, innovative, trial-and-error efforts to overcome negativity must come before norms and theories of right practice. Historical reality requires it. But also, because we are free, creative, responsible beings, our anthropology is appropriate to it.[39]

The Negative Contrast Experience and Our Deepest Unstructured Sense of What Is Important

The negative contrast experience is both a concrete occurrent experience and an anthropological constant. It recognizes an epistemological priority of negativity while maintaining an ontological priority of positivity, and its ethical productive force is a practice before it is articulated knowledge. These features contribute to making the contrast experience a fitting starting point and foundation for ethics. Because the contrast experience is an experience, the ethic it yields is concrete, contentful, respectful of our historical character and historically relevant. Because it is an anthropological constant, the ethic it yields is universally relevant, respecting that we belong to a common humanity encountering a common world. Because, for the contrast experience, negativity is epistemologically prior, and because the contrast experience aims at negating negation, this starting point for ethics has both a concrete particular and universal character. But because, for the negative contrast, positivity is ontologically prior, it affirms the worthwhileness of life and condemns seeking oblivion in nonsuffering. That the ethical productive force of this experience is a practice before it is reflective knowledge assures that this ethic will be truly historical and will truly seek to alleviate concrete suffering by the innova-

tive efforts of its practitioners. Because it is an ethic which is appropriate to our anthropology and to reality, it is possible and promises to be relevant and effective. But, having said all of this, having given all these reasons why the negative contrast experience provides an appropriate foundation for ethics, the question still remains whether the content of the ethic, the practice and value it promotes, is appropriate to our deepest unstructured sense of what is important.[40]

I have argued that, in the context of massive excessive suffering and oppression, if we do not bring resistance to these things into the center of our ethical concern, then we lose credibility as ethical beings. Resisting particular cases of concrete suffering for the sake of bringing about partial salvation morally must conform to our deepest sense of what matters. Of course, what we mean by "suffering" and "salvation" is crucial. Schillebeeckx's examples indicate that, for him, suffering centrally involves structurally caused poverty and oppression, and salvation means first, but not ultimately, negation of that suffering.[41] Here I wish merely to assert that whatever qualities the negative contrast experience has which make it fitting for an ethical foundation, ultimately it is no better than the fundamental practice and value, the "ethic" that it yields. And what ought to be our deepest sense of what is important cannot be proved. We can give grounds, appeal to evidence, discuss and argue, but if others do not see and agree, then there is a point beyond which there is nothing more that we can say. *If resisting suffering and oppression, if seeking even moments of salvation in history, do not conform to our deepest sense of what is important, then we cannot accept the negative contrast experience as foundational for ethics. If we judge these things to be most important, then, for all the reasons I have given, not just resistance to suffering, but resistance to suffering as emerging out of the negative contrast experience is a most appropriate foundation for ethics.*

THE NEGATIVE CONTRAST EXPERIENCE LENDS ITSELF TO RELIGIOUS AND CHRISTIAN DIMENSIONS

The discussion of the negative contrast experience and the criticism and practice to which it gives rise can go on, and for the most part in my analysis has gone on, independently of explicit mention of God or Christianity. But the negative contrast experience has a theological dimension. For some, it discloses God and final salvation, and it is fitting to Christianity. Jesus provides both a radical example and a para-

digm of one who lived out of the negative contrast. The Easter experience of his disciples provides the positive side of a negative contrast which discloses God and salvation in a particularly intense way.

The Negative Contrast Experience Discloses God and a Suprahistorical Salvation: a Human Ethic and a Theological Ethic

Schillebeeckx argues that the negative contrast experience discloses God as its "deeper basis and condition of possibility." Our fragmentary moments of joy and meaning, the basis for our hope and trust, are grounded in God. The call of and to the humanum is the call of and to the will of God. But, while God grounds the negative contrast experience and the ethic to which it gives rise, this experience and ethical practice disclose God to humans.[42] Indeed, theists and nontheists alike affirm by their ethical practice an "existential trust in life," a trust that the future has meaning and even that, against all odds, goodness will prevail. Schillebeeckx describes this as a decision in favor of God which can be explicitly recognized and articulated and, according to theists, is so.[43]

In a different way from that in which the contrast experience can disclose God as ground, it can disclose a suprahistorical salvation and God as necessary to this salvation. The contrast experience discloses a *full* salvation, not as something lying beneath it as it were, but as something *more*, lying beyond it but called forth by the *partial* salvation contained in it. It is intrinsic to the experience of salvation and part of the concept's meaning that its being fragmentary is not enough. The momentary experiences of joy give rise to the demand for more joy. Indeed, for Schillebeeckx, salvation is really salvation only when it is universal and complete. We cannot genuinely talk of having salvation when there is suffering or even the threat of suffering anywhere.[44] Partial salvation, then, is an invitation to final salvation. Conversely, hope for salvation, or even making any sense of final salvation, requires the experience of partial salvation. They are interdependent notions.

While *we* can alleviate physical, psychological, and social sufferings, we cannot overcome them completely. We cannot eradicate the sufferings of illness or death or grief at the loss of another; nor can we eradicate all forms of social oppression and deprivation.[45] Indeed, we cannot even articulate ultimate salvation in a complete and positive way. However much we may be participants in bringing about final salvation, but for the power of God it is not possible. In disclosing final

salvation, the negative contrast experience discloses something which is suprahistorical and which requires God. Finally, while the experience of partial salvation discloses final salvation for some, others conclude that historical partial salvation is all that we can hope for, and we must work at increasing and deepening that.

Because the negative contrast experience can disclose God as ground of our right practice and final salvation as the completion of our experience of partial salvation, the human ethic yielded by the negative contrast experience, while autonomous vis-à-vis religion, is not alien to it. This is a human ethic, but it lends itself to being also a religious ethic.

The Negative Contrast Experience Is Paradigmatic of Christian Experience

In order to show that Jesus provides a radical but paradigm example of one who lived out of the contrast experience, I shall discuss two central themes in Schillebeeckx's interpretation of the story of Jesus—Jesus' *Abba* experience and his rejection. Schillebeeckx identifies the latter as the "breakage point" in Jesus' story.

Jesus Is a Radical Example of One Who Lived Out of the Negative Contrast Experience: His Abba Experience and His Rejection

For Schillebeeckx, Jesus' Abba experience, his experience of God, is the positive side of a negative contrast experience. To understand his Abba experience we must look for what motivates him, what he identifies himself with—his raison d'être. But because we do not have the data to analyze Jesus' psychology, and because Jesus did not talk about himself, we must rely on Jesus' actions for this. While his Abba experience is source and ground of what Jesus said and did, access to his Abba experience is gained only by looking at what he said and did.[46] We shall look at a few of the most outstanding features of Jesus' life as portrayed in *Jesus*.

Schillebeeckx argues that John the Baptist's message that the baptism of repentance demands orthopractice must have been a disclosure experience for Jesus.[47] Jesus learned from John that, while we can hope for a future without suffering, what will be the content of that future is related to what we do now. But, by his Abba experience, he extended the notion of God as judge to include God as graciousness and love. Indeed, Jesus' central message was that God is always and radically on the side of humans and against everything which opposes human welfare. God's kingdom is near "despite every empirical experience to the contrary."[48] That Jesus believed this is made manifest by what he said and that this is true is indicated by what he did. By the parables he preached and by the parable he was, Jesus opened up a new experience and a new way of seeing experience, a new logic for living where enemies would be loved, hierarchies abandoned, and giving would be according to need but also gratuitously, and certainly not as reward.

Whatever we understand empirically by Jesus' miracles, their significance is that he acted to alleviate the suffering of those who asked him, however sinful they were. He never used his powers to legitimate or to benefit himself, to set himself above others. In healing on the Sabbath, in dining with "sinners and tax collectors," in assuring people that their sins were forgiven, and in doing all of this in the name of God and God's kingdom, Jesus demonstrated the force of his Abba experience as the experience of the God whose primary aim is to bring hope to those whose conditions are hopeless. Schillebeeckx describes people's attachment to Jesus as representing both the helpless cry of humankind's ongoing calamity but also as the hope which, with Jesus, entered into history. The contrast between the world in which Jesus walked and the vision he brought to life in people is striking.[49]

While we can gain access to Jesus' Abba experience and self-understanding only through what he said and did, and while what he said and did would have helped to bring about and deepen the experience, Jesus' Abba experience cannot be reduced to what he said and did.

> Jesus' *Abba* experience is an *immediate awareness of God as a power of cherishing people* and making them free. . . . To delete the *special* 'relation to God' from the life of Jesus at once destroys his message and the whole point of his way of living; it amounts to denying the historical reality, 'Jesus of Nazareth.'[50]

Indeed, we deny the basis of Jesus' and all specifically Christian hope if we deny that his Abba experience is authentic.[51]

Not only can we not reduce out Jesus' Abba experience and retain Christian hope, but the contrast between the suffering and evil that Jesus experienced, and what he said and did, can be explained only by reference to his Abba experience. This experience must be seen as one side of a negative contrast:

> In the calamitous and pain-ridden history within which Jesus stood it was impossible to find any grounds . . . which would serve to explain and make sense of the unqualified assurance of salvation that characterized his message. *Such a hope . . . is quite plainly rooted in a personal awareness of contrast: on the one hand the incorrigible, irremediable history of human suffering, a history of calamity, violence and injustice, of grinding, excruciating and oppressive enslavement; on the other hand Jesus' particular religious awareness of God, his Abba experience, his intercourse with God as the . . . 'one who is against evil', who will not admit the supremacy of evil and refuses to allow it the last word.* This religious experience of contrast is, after all, what informs his conviction and proclamation of God's liberating rule, which should and can prevail even in this history, as Jesus knows by experience in and from his own praxis.[52]

Jesus' Abba experience, then, is the positive element of his experience of negative contrast. It involves an "immediate" experience of God but "as a power of cherishing people." It is not a merely contemplative experience which, Schillebeeckx seems to allow, may be unmediated by negativity but which, for that reason, has no productive force. Rather, as "the soul, source and ground of Jesus' message, praxis and ministry as a whole,"[53] Jesus' Abba experience, in the context of his negative contrast experience, yields a productive force, indeed *the* productive force of Jesus' life. Jesus' Abba experience is a contrast to the profound suffering and evil that he experienced in the world around him; it is a promise of something better and it propels Jesus to act.

However, the contrast between Jesus' Abba experience and the suffering he saw around him was not the only or even the center of Jesus' experience of the negative contrast. The rejection of his message and his works, and his torture and violent death, formed the most radical contrast with his Abba experience. This was not just a matter of the difference between an experience of God's love and concern on the one hand and Jesus' personal destruction on the other. It was a matter of Jesus' proclaiming God's kingdom on the one hand and *its being rejected by God's people* on the other. It is significant that Schillebeeckx argues that the "breakage point" in the story of Jesus, the "rift," comes not between his life and death nor between his death and resurrection, but within his ministry, between his early acceptance and success and his later rejection and failure.[54] *By stressing the significance of Jesus' Abba experience and by placing the "breakage point" in Jesus' story between Jesus' acceptance and rejection, Schillebeeckx, in effect, emphasizes the story of Jesus as a story of one who radically experienced the negative contrast and who provides a paradigm for our right action.* By placing the "breakage point" where he does, Schillebeeckx raises, as urgent questions, the issues of *why* Jesus was rejected and, more importantly, *how he responded* to his rejection. Did he respond in a way which indicated that he continued to act out of the negative contrast? We must ask how, ultimately, in light of his Abba experience, he came to understand his own imminent death.

Schillebeeckx points out that whether Jesus is bringer of curse or salvation is not only a question for us but was raised most dramatically when he was alive. "The 'divine' in him, his coming 'from God,' is not something given apodictically, with a compelling absence of ambiguity; it calls for a vote of confidence." The people who met him had to decide whether they were for him or for the Jewish establishment. Schillebeeckx recounts how in Mark, very early on "the Pharisees . . . held counsel with the Herodians against him, how to destroy him" (Mark 3:6), how Luke and Matthew tell that he was rejected by whole cities (Luke 10:13–15; Matt. 11:20–24), how Jesus, when under siege, concentrated on training the twelve, and how he insisted, after his disciples had returned from missionary journeys and before the feeding of the multitudes, that they seek solitude and rest (Mark 6:30–31, 6:45; Matt. 14:22). According to the gospel accounts, after the feeding of the multitudes, Jesus considered his mission to have failed in Galilee and he turned toward Jerusalem. Because Jesus was not a fanatic but a rational and politically astute person, he must have been aware of the danger of going to Jerusalem. But not only must he have been aware, first, of the possibility, and, later, of the inevitability of his death, he must also have arrived at some view of what it would mean in the context of his mission. Could he be wrong about what was God's will? Could God have abandoned him? How could Jesus reconcile his Abba experience with his rejection and impending execution? *In asking this final question, we are seeking Jesus' answer to the question of God in the face of evil and innocent suffering.*[55]

Schillebeeckx argues that Jesus' response to his imminent death was one of radical surrender to God. This is demonstrated in his refusal to speak on his own behalf before the Sanhedrin, thus providing the Sanhedrin with the legal grounds for condemning him. It is demonstrated in his 'speaking' to his disciples by offering them his cup at the Last Supper (Mark 14:25). This shows that he "is not just passively allowing death to overcome him but has actively integrated it into his total mission," as a final service to God and to humans. And it shows his "unshaken assurance of salvation" even though he did not have a well-defined view of what this eschatological salvation could be. Finally, in spite of his having integrated his death into his total mission, Jesus really did experience failure. But he was neither abandoned by God nor did he believe that he was.[56]

Jesus' life, what he said and did, accorded perfectly with the will of God but was opposed to the interests of those who 'Lord' it over others, and for this he was killed. Jesus' death was thus the will of some humans and opposed to the will of God. Jesus died for us as he lived for us *by accepting suffering only in order to resist it, to overcome every threat to humanity*. It is only rational to understand Jesus' "radical dedication to both God and to humanity even to the point of death, [as] *despite* the fact that he was done away with by human beings."[57] Because Jesus, despite rejection, suffering, and impending death, continued to be guided by his Abba experience and to pursue God's will to the end, he makes the Easter experience of his disciples possible. And he provides us with a most graphic and radical example of one who experienced and lived in the way of the negative contrast.

Christians' Easter Experience
in the Context of the Negative Contrast Experience

Right up to his death, Jesus' Abba experience, as a contrast with suffering, propelled him to act against suffering and to hope for a final overcoming. However, when it became clear that Jesus was going to be killed, many of his closest disciples gave up hope, turned from him, and fled. After a short time, they were moved to proclaim Jesus as risen and to proclaim his message even at the risk of losing their lives. Schillebeeckx calls this profoundly moving event an Easter experience, a powerfully positive experience that the disciples could contrast with the despair of their immediate past. This experience was in radical contrast with their experience of the world and led to their rejection by many. A similar Easter experience, which forms part of a negative contrast but which gives especially strong grounds for the hope that goodness will prevail, moves Christians today.

Mary Magdalene was the first recipient of the Easter experience. Unlike most of Jesus' close disciples, Mary did not abandon Jesus but must have felt abandoned until she experienced a *"loving assurance"* that "this Jesus lives." We can hypothesize that, when added to what must have been her memories of Jesus' constant concern, this experience gave her reason for hope, and, as a contrast to her despair, provided her with the strength to act for others. She could, as it were, release her embrace of Jesus and go from him to inform the other disciples that he was risen (John 20:17–18).[58]

In the case of Peter and many of the other disciples, not only would they have felt abandoned, but guilty, because they had abandoned Jesus and scattered for protection. Their Easter experience was one of forgiveness, with the implication that Jesus must be alive to forgive them. Their despair and fear turned to hope and fearlessness. And they sought out one another, reassembled.[59]

Thus the stories of the first Easter experiences can be seen as striking examples of Schillebeeckx's negative contrast experience in operation. Despair gives way to hope against hope, a hope against the empirical evidence, which is born of the experience of loving assurance and forgiveness, that is, the experience of Jesus as alive. But the contrast between this and the suffering and sense of hopelessness that remains all around propels fearless and selfless action of resistance to suffering, as the stories in the *Acts of the Apostles* relate. This action leads to the disciples being rejected and made to suffer. Jesus' resurrection and the Easter experience of his disciples did not change the pattern of persecution dealt out to those who resisted persecution. They accepted suffering in order to resist suffering. The negative contrast remained and remains.

According to Schillebeeckx "there is not such a big difference" between our Christian faith today and that of the first disciples.[60] An Easter experience is both possible and necessary if we are to have Christian faith at all. Our belief cannot be based strictly on the authority of others' experience, of tradition. How do we describe a contemporary Easter experience when we have not experienced Jesus in history and cannot experience him as risen in the way Jesus' first disciples did?

It is clear that the modern Christian need not experience some dramatic shift from hopelessness to hope based on some kind of experience, such as forgiveness. But there has to be some sort of conversion experience, however gentle and perhaps unnoticed which, for the person raised as a Christian, constitutes a break with religious 'belief' based solely on authority and, for the person not raised as a Christian, moves beyond what reason can yield. And, however unarticulated, this experience must involve a reorientation, a radical change in the Christian's life. In order that this reorientation involve an Easter experience, it must include the confidence that suffering, evil, death, *can be* overcome based on the conviction that they *have been* overcome. The Easter experience can be understood to make sense of, to ground, and, in part, to be disclosed by our human experience of acting out of a hope against hope, out of a negative contrast experience. The Easter experience is not identical with an experience of hope. The gospel stories, together with the practice of some people living now, must disclose the risen Christ in order to yield an Easter experience.

Like Jesus' Abba experience and like secular experiences of meaning and joy, the Easter experience provides the *positive element* of a negative contrast experience. But, like these others, we speak of the Easter experience as an *experience*. Just like any secular experience of joy, and like Jesus' Abba experience, the Easter experience, phenomenologically speaking, must be understood as introducing a *contrast* and as being in contrast with and mediated by negativity. Just as Jesus' Abba experience was not, primarily, a contemplation of God which made Jesus feel happy independent of his rejection and the suffering that was going on around him, so the Easter experience is not, primarily, such a feeling. Both experiences produce opposition to suffering, and this is possible only because the experiences themselves involve the contrast between suffering and salvation.

THE NEGATIVE CONTRAST EXPERIENCE
YIELDS A LIBERATIONIST ETHIC

This section begins the task of shaping and defining an ethic of resistance to suffering. It indicates how the negative contrast experience and its ethic pervade liberationist thought, what is meant, in the context of this ethic, by suffering, and how the ethic which begins to emerge forms a striking contrast with classical ethics.

The Negative Contrast Experience Is Implicit in Liberation Theology

The phenomenon to which the notion of the negative contrast experience refers, and the ethic which it yields, pervades liberationist thought. All the liberation theologies begin with particular sorts of cases of concrete suffering that are given in experience. They insist that we respond by resisting that suffering. Latin American liberation theology arose in response to the suffering caused by acute poverty and political repression on that continent, that is, in response to the starvation of masses and the systematic torture of protestors. Black theology and feminist theology arose in response to the concrete sufferings and deprivations rising out of racism and sexism. Some African liberation theologies stemmed from concern about the effects of colonialism on African cultures. And some Asian liberation theologies emerged in response to religious intolerance.[61] Dorothee Soelle speaks to the dominant middle class in the North who suffer meaninglessness caused by isolation and consumerism.[62] Schillebeeckx, on the other hand, gives an outline for a "western" liberation theology which would resist the situation wherein the rich north controls the politico-economic structures which make for poverty in the south and ecological destruction everywhere.[63] Gregory Baum calls this unpreparedness to accept the world as it is because it should be different and can be changed, the "common faith" of the various liberation theologies.[64] This "common faith" reflects the fundamental human experience of suffering and striving against suffering captured by Schillebeeckx's negative contrast experience.[65] We can consider in a little more detail how the negative contrast experience is at work at least implicitly in liberation theology by looking at a few notions which pervade these theologies and which reflect and are illuminated by the contrast experience.

The liberation theologians of the poor take as central the view that God is especially in the poor, that God reveals Godself especially to and through the poor, that the good news is addressed especially to them and they are its preferred interpreters, even that the future of history lies in their hands.[66] Other liberationists say similar things about other oppressed groups. They locate God especially in blacks and women, groups who have been judged traditionally to be less human and less in God's image than whites and men.[67] All these claims are acutely paradoxical because they locate the symbol of salvation in the

place of greatest suffering and oppression. But part of what the liberationists are getting at is that God is revealing Godself by pointing to
the stark contrast between what is and what ought to be. God is pointing to the place of greatest suffering as where salvation must go on,
and God is promising that the very attempt to overcome suffering, to
negate negation, will itself involve an encounter with salvation. What
liberationists are saying, in effect, is that God calls us to act out of the
negative contrast experience.[68]

The notion of a hermeneutical circle is also central to liberationist
thought.[69] Schillebeeckx captures the bones of the hermeneutical circle
through his description of how recalcitrant reality presents us with a
new negative experience which forces us to change our concepts and
practices. While the exact causes and even the precise nature of the
negativity may not, without investigation, be evident, reality informs
us of a rift between the harmony we thought prevailed and the disharmony that does prevail. Reality demands that we change our established ways of thinking and practice in order to mend this rift. Finally,
when we bring our new ways of thought and practice to reality, reality
will respond anew. The past negativity will be overcome (although,
inevitably, new negativities will emerge, to which we will be called to
respond). On Schillebeeckx's description, at this most fundamental
level of experience, there is a juxtaposition of negativity and positivity,
at least in the sense of a juxtaposition of what is and what ought to be,
and there is the demand to negate the negation. At this level we are
also describing the fundamental way of learning both ethically and sci-
entifically by way of the hermeneutical circle.

The notion of hope against hope pervades liberationist thought,
and it reflects the negative contrast experience. Hope against hope is
hope in spite of the evidence. It involves people's striving for salvation
while weighed down by suffering in a context where the best ground
for their hope is found in their very efforts. Sobrino speaks in this way
and adds, in line with the notion of the negative contrast experience,
that, due to the limitations of our historical perspective, the content of
the hope can only be described *negatively*. He gives this hope against
hope the status of criterion for the authenticity of the church of the
poor.[70] Much like Schillebeeckx, Gutiérrez places this hope against
hope in epic dimensions. He defines the movement of human history
in terms of the dialectic which exists between the suffering that has
gone on for generations and the resistance and hope of the people:

For this downtrodden people, suffering and captivity are nothing new. These have always been here. But the will to rebellion and hope have always been here too. Long has this people been in exile in its own land. But long, too, has it been in exodus, on the road to its redemption.[71]

A Liberationist Understanding of Suffering

While the character of the suffering that we are especially called to resist will emerge more fully in the following chapters, in order to see an ethic of resistance to suffering as a liberationist ethic at all, it is important to say something here about what we mean by suffering.

Virtually all suffering is something we endure as something passive and imposed. It restricts, victimizes, oppresses, and deprives. Suffering is something we need to be liberated from. Not only humanly created poverty, racism, and sexism, and the social structures which support them, oppress us. But also the physical disabilities and psychological sufferings created by 'nature' or unavoidable circumstance are not neutral. They are unchosen negativities and they will oppress unless we resist them. *Thus suffering is virtually synonymous with oppression, and an ethic of resistance to suffering must be understood as an ethic of resistance to oppression.*

It may be objected, however, that some suffering humanizes, makes us more compassionate, and some suffering we can do nothing about: the suffering caused by illness, physical disability, or grief at the loss of a loved one. We cannot say that *all* suffering is negative, oppressive, or to be resisted. Some suffering is not negative, and some suffering we cannot overcome.

We can respond to both of these objections in the same way. It is true that suffering can serve to humanize as well as dehumanize. But in order that it do so it cannot remain completely passive, something we suffer, something that oppresses. We must make it productive of good. We must use it to help us to be more sensitive and compassionate. And, it is precisely suffering that we cannot overcome, objectively speaking, which we must make productive of good and not oppressive.

Soelle asks *who* is likely to resist suffering? She finds that it is not those who avoid suffering any more than those who have been destroyed by it, but rather those who have been sensitized by suffering and who have made it productive. She refers to the story of Jacques

Lusseyran who, when a child, was blinded but acted for others when he led a high school resistance group against the Nazis. He was sent to Buchenwald concentration camp where he threw himself into developing solidarity among the prisoners. He made productive the blindness that he could do nothing about by going out to others in need. And he resisted the Nazi oppression he could do something about.[72]

From a liberationist perspective, virtually all suffering is oppressive and should be resisted, either by attempting to overcome it or, when this is not possible, by making it productive. But an ethic of resistance to suffering which will capture the ethic implicit in the various liberation theologies must stress the primary importance of resistance to the excess of "unmerited and senseless" suffering wherein some, "without finding meaning for themselves, are simply made the crude victims of an evil cause which serves others."[73] We must be particularly concerned about the suffering of the poor, women, and people of color. Their oppression is caused by humanly created and humanly revisable social and conceptual structures. As we shall argue in the next chapter, if resistance to suffering means resistance to the worst suffering first, then the option for the poor will be our first concretization of this imperative.

Finally, the one sort of suffering which is not oppressive is suffering to resist suffering. This is the only suffering that God blesses. Ironically, the need for this kind of suffering is implicit in the imperative to resist suffering.

A Liberationist Ethic Compared to Classical Ethics

From a liberationist perspective, what we experience is an "already damaged humanum" and cosmos, a given disorder and disharmony in the world as we experience it.[74] This means that there is no given blueprint for right action which the individual ought to follow, but people must gear themselves outside themselves and creatively seek to mend the world. Because the disorder is expressed in our social structures, we must join in solidarity to transform them. This approach turns on its head classical ethics as traditionally lived and understood.

For Plato, the form of the good acts as a pre-given blueprint, a model for goodness, and the absolute standard of value judgments. The aim of ethics is to conform to the form of the good which demands withdrawal from the sensory world of human suffering. For Aristotle, the aim of ethics is not to conform to an ideal blueprint external to the self but to conform to the demands of an already given human nature. This human nature requires that we develop moral virtue in order to achieve a mean between extremes of desire for the end of happiness. Kant is like Aristotle in taking positive aspects of an abstract universal human nature as his starting point in ethics but unlike Aristotle in claiming that we ought to act morally out of duty to the law of our nature rather than for the sake of happiness. For Kant, in line with the Enlightenment, individual reason makes us free and independent of the laws which determine the natural world; it makes us ethical beings. Ethics becomes the requirement that reason be respected. This is captured by Kant's universalizability principle which is yielded by reason itself and provides the criterion for determining universal but practical norms for action such as the imperative to tell the truth.[75] Utilitarianism is normally concerned with maximizing pleasure but is occasionally formulated in terms of minimizing pain. It takes its universal utility principle as its starting point and determines, in a rather mechanical fashion, what we ought to do to produce the greatest quantity of pleasure (or the least quantity of pain). There is some similarity between utilitarianism, when defined negatively, and a liberationist approach in that both start out to overcome suffering. They mean different things by suffering, however, and take different items into account in moral decision-making. Also, they value the individual who suffers quite differently. Utilitarianism also presupposes a fundamentally given order and a capacity for universal reason to bring life into line with that order. Indeed, it relies so heavily on our capacity to manipulate a predictable reality for the sake of bringing about the best consequences that utilitarians have commonly been criticized as playing God.[76]

All of these ethics, as traditionally lived and understood, begin from a presupposition of an already given harmony in the universe. For the most part, they begin with what is positive, abstract, and universal in the world or in human nature. All are profoundly ahistorical. With the exception of utilitarianism, rather than aiming at serving the needs of the other, they concern themselves first with self-perfection. This contrasts dramatically with the liberationist perspective which, as we have seen, begins with an "already damaged humanum" and cosmos and is concerned first for the other. We shall argue in the next chapter for the worst-off other. From the liberationist perspective, neither in the external world nor in the abstract universal reason of an abstract universal human nature, is there a pre-given blueprint for creating or recreating the good and harmonious self in a good and harmonious world. An ethic that begins here begins with illusion. Human 'nature' must be seen first, not in terms of universal abstract characteristics of reason or freedom but in its concrete expressions of suffering, brokenness and need. Harmony and order have to be sought by first acknowledging, then working from and through, the disharmony and disorder that is given in experience toward a future which can neither be predicted nor completed. If there were no suffering, there would be no need for ethics. Suffering is what makes ethics necessary—and the negative contrast experience is what makes ethics possible.

CONCLUSION

We have argued that Schillebeeckx's negative contrast experience is foundational for ethics. It captures the experiential starting point for ethics, that which makes ethics possible. In its productive force, which involves the practice and value of resisting every threat to the humanum, it captures what is at the center and core of ethics and provides a first imperative for ethics. This ethic, while autonomous vis-à-vis religion, is appropriate to a religious and Christian ethic. The negative contrast experience and the ethic it yields is implicit in liberation theology and is appropriate to a liberationist ethic. But we can claim even more for the negative contrast experience. We have argued that the unitary experience of suffering and salvation which propels us to resist suffering and strive for salvation captures the rhythm and raison d'être of human history. We have pointed out that there is an analogue between the negative contrast experience and experience in general. It is the experience that negates our conceptual frameworks and our modes of practice, that also assures us that we are in touch with an objective reality. To respect this genuine experience, we must respond by negating the negation, the rift, which exists between the demands of reality and our ways of thinking and practicing. *And finally, the unitary experience of suffering and striving against suffering not only captures the rhythm of human history, but also, analogically speaking, captures the rhythm of the cosmos itself.* Not only are we called to negate negation in our science as well as our ethics, but everything in the cosmos tends to respond in an analogous way. In nature, we can think of this as the necessity to adapt and seek new equilibrium.

NOTES

1. For Schillebeeckx's extended discussion of experience see: Edward Schillebeeckx, *Christ: The Experience of Jesus as Lord*, trans. John Bowden (New York: The Crossroad Publishing Co., 1983), pp. 29–79.

2. Ibid., pp. 31–36.

3. Ibid. Quotations on pp. 34 and 35 respectively. (My italics.)

4. Ibid., pp. 37–38.

5. Edward Schillebeeckx, *Jesus: An Experiment in Christology*, trans. Hubert Hoskins (London: Wm. Collins Sons Co. Ltd., 1979; Fount Paperbacks, 1983), p. 74.

6. Edward Schillebeeckx, *God the Future of Man*, trans. N. D. Smith (London: Sheed and Ward, 1969), pp. 149–50.

The negative contrast experience is mentioned in three places in this book, all within the general context of the relationship between church and the secular world. See pp. 136, 149–64, 191.

7. Ibid., p. 153. (My italics.)

8. Ibid. Quotations at pp. 153–54, 154, 191, respectively. (My italics.)

9. Ibid., p. 164.

10. In this particular context, Schillebeeckx may have in mind those who are working at the grassroots and attempting to be in solidarity with the oppressed. In other contexts, he makes clear that he is speaking also and especially about oppressed groups themselves. (See second quotation on p. 8 of this chapter.) Liberation theologians of the poor stress the epistemological privilege of the poor not only as regards their suffering but their understanding of scripture. (See pp. 28–29 of this chapter.) I accept and stress these views throughout the book. They are based on the epistemological authority of experience itself, that knowledge is fundamentally based on experience. However, it is also true that oppressed groups are often, for a time, blinded by ideologies which attempt to justify their oppression. In the Philippines, for example, many people still believe that suffering is God's will. And some associate hope, not with the outcome of struggle, but with luck. However, whether the unmasking of false ideologies goes on with or without the help of educated sympathizers is not really relevant to the epistemological privilege of the oppressed. Once in touch with their oppression, they know best what it involves and what constitutes authentic liberation from it.

11. Edward Schillebeeckx, *The Understanding of Faith: Interpretation and Criticism*, trans. N. D. Smith (New York: The Seabury Press, 1974), p. 91.

12. Ibid., p. 92. (My italics.)

13. Ibid., p. 91.

14. Ibid., p. 98. Schillebeeckx is suggesting that friendship and love may disclose God as gratuitous. He acknowledges that humans do experience gratuitous meaning without affirming God.

15. Ibid., pp. 91–92, 98.

16. *Jesus*, p. 19.

17. *Christ*, p. 648. (Exclusive language replaced.)

18. *Jesus*, p. 20. Quotations at p. 20.

19. Ibid., p. 24. (My italics.)
20. *Christ*, p. 48. (My italics.)
21. As well as *Christ*, p. 48, see, for example, p. 642.
22. See diagrams on pages 10 and 11.
23. *Jesus*, pp. 621, 622.
24. See *Jesus*, p. 622; *Christ*, pp. 48 and 819, ft. 158. Schillebeeckx admits there can be a contemplative experience of meaning which is not mediated by negativity but, for this very reason, it does not have a productive force.
25. I discuss what I mean by "foundation" on p. 2 of this chapter.
26. While Schillebeeckx does not include the negative contrast experience among the seven anthropological constants he discusses in *Christ*, pp. 734–43, he confirmed in private discussion in Nijmegan in July of 1986 that the negative contrast experience is far more central to his thought than he ever indicated and that it can be understood as an anthropological constant. I discuss his anthropological constants in chapter 3. They include both universal tendencies and values.
27. Ibid., p. 734.
28. Ibid., p. 22.
29. *Interim Report on the Books of Jesus and Christ*, trans. John Bowden (New York: The Seabury Press, 1981), pp. 56–57.
30. We have a tendency toward self-interest at other's expense, and we also take the course of least resistance. We accept the way things are rather than make the effort to change them.
31. Much of early twentieth-century Anglo-American moral philosophy was hindered by the entrenched belief accepted from G. E. Moore and long before him from David Hume, that "one cannot derive an 'ought' from an 'is.'" This made moral reasoning impossible and ethics groundless. The Naturalistic Fallacy fallacy is now widely acknowledged. Schillebeeckx's very description of anthropological constants as "permanent human impulses and orientations, values and spheres of value" would seem to reject, at the fundamental anthropological level, a radical distinction between fact and value.
32. *Christ*, p. 649.
33. *Christ*, p. 791.
34. See, for example, *God the Future of Man*, p. 136; *The Understanding of Faith*, p. 92.
35. *Jesus in Our Western Culture: Mysticism, Ethics and Politics*, trans. John Bowden (London: SCM Press Ltd., 1987), pp. 5–6, 58–63.
36. Critical theory developed between the World Wars with a view to reviving the emancipatory aims of the Enlightenment. One of this theory's central concerns has been to show how the once-liberating science and technology have come to quench critical thought through their positivistic pretense to be value-free and representative of the only true nature of reality. From its own perspective, critical theory is not based on a theoretical view of the ends of humans or of society nor, indeed, on any positive images or norms at all. Rather, it is based on the insight that humans are responsible for history and are the causes, and can be the transformers, of what is exploitative in history. According to Schillebeeckx, in order to avoid the masked self-interest of theo-

ries and ideologies, the critical theorists restrict their comment to criticism and do not realize that their very capacity to criticize presupposes some positive ground. See *The Understanding of Faith*, Chapter Six, "The New Critical Theory," pp. 102–23. See also: Edward Schillebeeckx, "Critical Theories and Christian Political Commitment," trans. N. D. Smith, *Political Commitment and Christian Community*, *Concilium* 84, eds. Alois Muller and Norbert Greinacher (1973), pp. 48–61; William L. Portier, "Edward Schillebeeckx as Critical Theorist: The Impact of Neo-Marxist Social Thought on His Recent Theology," *Thomist* 48 (1984), pp. 341–67.

37. By "knowledge" I mean here "conscious reflective knowledge" which we associate with propositional and linguistic knowledge.

38. This, of course, is not the case as regards the suffering caused by natural disasters. We must object most strongly to interpretations of earthquakes and volcanoes as God's punishment, test, or instruction. In response to the most devastating volcanic eruption in our century, that of Mount Pinatubo in the Philippines, such celebrities as Imelda Marcos, President Cory Aquino, and Cardinal Sin offered these three explanations respectively. The Book of Job ascribed these explanations/justifications to Job's "friends" and Job's God rejected them as explanations/justifications for any kind of suffering.

39. I shall not say more on this topic here because chapter 4 is devoted to it.

40. Charles Taylor talks about our deepest unstructured sense of what is important in his article, "What Is Human Action?," *The Self: Psychological and Philosophical Issues*, ed. Theodore Mischel (Oxford: Basil Blackwell, 1977), pp. 103–35. Further reference will be made to this article in chapter 5.

41. How I understand suffering will be discussed further in this chapter and chapter 2. See pp. 30–31 (of this chapter) and pp. 55–59 (of chapter 2).

42. Quotation at *God the Future of Man*, p. 74. See also *The Understanding of Faith*, pp. 96–101; *Christ*, p. 791.

43. *God the Future of Man*, p. 74.

44. *Christ*, p. 726; *The Understanding of Faith*, p. 95.

45. Schillebeeckx does not sympathize with the attitude of Stoics and others that suffering and evil cannot affect the wise who are protected by their possession of the true and the good. To treat suffering as illusory and ignore it rather than resist it is not satisfactory. See *Christ*, pp. 683–84.

46. *Jesus*, pp. 257–58.

47. Ibid., p. 115.

48. Ibid., p. 143.

49. Ibid., pp. 186, 193.

50. Ibid., p. 268. (My italics.)

51. Ibid., p. 270. Although Schillebeeckx describes Jesus' Abba experience as an immediate experience, it must also be understood as a *disclosure* experience, mediated by secular experience, such as Jesus' experience of John's preaching. It is immediate in the sense that it is genuinely an occurrent experience, not merely a knowledge which is the product of an inference from occurrent experience, such as the experience of John. Christians need not accept that

Jesus' experience of God is, strictly speaking, qualitatively different from our experience but only that it has an authentic referent and cause.

52. Ibid., p. 267. (My italics. Exclusive language replaced.)

53. Ibid., p. 266.

54. Ibid., pp. 294, 642.

55. Ibid., pp. 295, 299. Quotation at p. 295.

56. Ibid., p. 309. The explanation for Jesus' cry from the cross, "My God, my God, why hast thou forsaken me?" (Mark 15:34), is that it is the first line of a psalm which, when quoted in Jesus' culture, evoked the theme of the whole. The psalm to which Jesus refers involves God's nearness even when God seems to have abandoned us. See *Christ*, pp. 824–25.

57. *Interim Report*, p. 134. (My italics.)

58. *Jesus*, p. 344. Quotation at p. 344. (My italics.)

59. Ibid. pp. 388–89, 345.

60. Ibid., p. 346.

61. Deane William Ferm, *Third World Liberation Theologies: An Introductory Survey* (Maryknoll, New York: Orbis Books, 1986). This is indicated in the "Introduction," pp. 1–2, and demonstrated throughout the text.

62. Dorothee Soelle, "'Thou Shalt Have No Other Jeans Before Me' (Levi's advertisement, early seventies): The Need for Liberation in a Consumerist Society," Brian Mahan and Dale Richeson, eds., *The Challenge of Liberation Theology: A First World Response* (Maryknoll, New York: Orbis Books, 1981), pp. 7–16.

63. Edward Schillebeeckx, "Theologie als bevrijdingskunde: Enkele noodzakelijke beschouwingen vooraf," *Tijdschrift voor Theologie*, 24 (1984): 388. This article was privately translated by J. H. Kuikman.

64. Gregory Baum, "The Christian Left at Detroit," *Theology in the Americas*, ed. Sergio Torres and John Eagleson (Maryknoll, New York: Orbis Books, 1976), p. 401.

65. This common faith embraces something more specific for our time than that strictly captured by the contrast experience. It embraces the paradigm shift operative in the call to the option for the poor which will be discussed in the next chapter. But more universally, and at the root of that notion, lies the negative contrast.

66. See, for example, Gustavo Gutiérrez, *The Power of the Poor in History*, trans. Robert R. Barr (Maryknoll, New York: Orbis Books, 1983), pp. 4, 15, 18, 27, 53, 65, 103, 197; Jon Sobrino, *The True Church and the Poor*, trans. Matthew J. O'Connell (Maryknoll, New York: Orbis Books, 1984), pp. 40, 49, 56, 91, 93, 140, 141, 291–96.

67. See, for example, James H. Cone, *A Black Theology of Liberation* (Philadelphia: J. B. Lippincott Co., 1970), pp. 108, 192, 213.

68. Until a visit to Basic Christian Communities in Negros, I thought liberationists' claims (that the future of history and the salvation of us all lies in the hands of the poor) to be hyperbole. But what I found was very poor people, landless peasants and squatters without permanent jobs, who were articulate about the causes of their poverty and oppression, both verbally and in dance

and song. But also, through their courage, sharing, and responsibility, they were making small gains in improving their living conditions against profoundly unjust social structures which landowners, with the aid of politicians and military, persist in maintaining. When I marveled at their struggle and the dignity it had given them, they would simply point to their God "but for whom they could not . . . ." Through their radical yet paradigmatic form of kingdom building, not only were they living out the salvation of all of us but also, my sense was that they, much more than the politicians in Manila, were making history. They seemed neither to be seeking election into a political system that would not work for them nor to be seeking to overthrow it with violence. Rather, in a limited way, they were creating new structures simply by living a new way and encouraging others to join. (The transforming power of BCCs applies, of course, not only to society but also to church. *Some* comparison could be made with women-church.)

69. To take but one example, Juan Luis Segundo discusses the hermeneutical circle in Cone's black theology of liberation in *The Liberation of Theology*, trans. John Drury (Maryknoll, New York: Orbis Books, 1976), pp. 25–34.

70. *The True Church and the Poor*, pp. 155–56.

71. *The Power of the Poor in History*, p. 206.

72. Dorothee Soelle, *Suffering*, trans. Everett R. Kalin (London: Darton, Longman and Todd, 1975), pp. 88–91.

73. *Christ*, p. 725.

74. See *The Understanding of Faith*, pp. 91 ff. See also *Christ*, p. 659. Schillebeeckx explicitly contrasts his view of the starting point for ethics with earlier views which presuppose a given order in *Jesus in Our Western Culture*, pp. 49–50. He adds to his concern for the humanum concern for the cosmos on pp. 29–30 but expresses this as for the sake of the humanum. I shall argue in chapter 3 that other species and the environment are valuable in their own right. But I build this perspective into my statement of a liberationist approach from the beginning.

75. One formulation of Kant's universalizability principle is as follows: Act only on that maxim through which you can at the same time will that it should become a universal law. We cannot rationally will that lying, for example, should become a universal law.

76. To some extent the thought of this paragraph is supported by: Alasdair MacIntyre, *A Short History of Ethics*, Fields of Philosophy Series (New York: The Macmillan Co., 1966); *The Encyclopedia of Philosophy*, 1967 ed., s.v., "Ethics, History of," by Raziel Abelson and Kai Nielsen, p. 87.

2

The Option for the Poor
Is Foundational for Ethics

INTRODUCTION

Chapter 1 attempted to articulate some universal features of our experience that are also relevant to ethics. It argued that the very movement of human history is captured in terms of suffering and striving for salvation. Ethics is primarily located in this striving against suffering and for salvation. However, because we all suffer, if we do not say something more about our ethical imperative to resist suffering, we may interpret it to be concern merely for our own suffering and that of our friends. *This chapter moves from the more universal discussion of chapter 1 concerning suffering and salvation, captured in the negative contrast experience, to a contemporary, more narrowly liberationist approach. It concretizes and completes the imperative of resistance to suffering for our time.* This imperative remains abstract and incomplete as it stands.

Some of the most urgent, serious and massive social sufferings of our day are poverty, racism, sexism, colonialism, speciesism, and destruction of the environment. The various liberation movements and theologies reflect this. This chapter will argue that the *first concretization of the imperative to resist suffering for our time is captured in the notion of the option for the poor.* In its generic sense, this notion embraces a paradigm shift from an ethic which stresses personal perfection to one that stresses the need for joining in solidarity with oppressed groups for structural change. In its specific sense, it names the worst-off group of all, the materially destitute. Together with the negative contrast experience, the option for the poor can be said to be foundational for ethics in the sense of its being the first concretization of the imperative to resist suffering. It is at, and concretely must be brought to, the center of ethics.

This chapter begins with a discussion of what we mean by option for the poor and oppressed and what is the paradigm shift involved.

The chapter goes on to argue that the option for the materially destitute should provide the first concretization of the imperative to resist
suffering. It concludes with a defense of the partisanship involved in
taking up the option for the poor.

THE OPTION FOR THE POOR:
MEANING AND SIGNIFICANCE

This section will investigate what the option for the poor means by
looking at the history of the notion in the responses of Latin American
liberation theologians to key church documents after Vatican II. Then it
will explore the significance of the option for the poor as an option of
the poor, of the rich, and as God's option.

Liberation Theologians' Understanding of "The Option for the Poor" in the Context of Key Church Documents

The option for the poor has been described as the most controversial
religious term since the Reformers' cry, "Salvation through faith
alone."[1] It has been described as a "Copernican revolution" for the
church[2] and as forcing on us the new theological paradigm which is
liberation theology.[3] Yet at the same time it has been described as a
trademark of the Latin American church and an option of the universal
church[4] and as having "made its way from a suspect periphery to the
established center of church language."[5] In significant ways, it turns
classical ethics on its head. What then is the message captured by this
phrase which is so revolutionary, so different from what Christianity
has always taught and attempted to live in relation to the poor? Is the
term being co-opted and the message neutralized by its coming into
general acceptance in the church, if indeed it is coming into general
acceptance? What is at stake here, and is it important that the 'revolution' continue?

    I shall begin by looking at the Latin American context that gave
expression to the notion and commitment captured in the phrase. In
particular, I shall look at theologians' responses to key church documents, to those of Medellín and Puebla, and to the 1984 Vatican
Instruction on the theology of liberation. The reason for referring to
church documents is that they provide a context for exploring the
notion of the option for the poor. The reason for explicitly considering,

not the documents themselves, but theologians' responses to them is that liberation theologians pick out and articulate what is new in the documents and contrast this with the traditional view. The documents oscillate between the views. It is the contrast, the paradigm shift, that is important for my argument.

From Vatican Council II to Medellín, 1965–1968

The Second Vatican Council did not precede liberation theology but strongly encouraged its development by rejecting a radical separation of the sacred and the secular both in its theology of grace, and, more concretely, in its stress on the church's dialogue with and to the world. The Council emphasized that human history, including the political, economic, and social conditions in which humans live now, really matters to God and must be of central concern to the church and to Christians. When he announced the Council in 1962, John XXIII gave it this direction: "The church is and wishes to be the church of all, but principally the church of the poor."[6] The Council recognized structural causes of poverty and the relevance of the social sciences, including those of a Marxian orientation. And it called on local churches to consider their context, their relationship to their own world in light of human need.[7] The Synod of Latin American bishops at Medellín in 1968 was Latin America's response to this call.

When, following Vatican II's directive, the Latin American bishops looked at the situation in which their own people were living, they found that not only did the vast majority not have their cultural and spiritual needs met, but they did not have political and legal rights. Moreover, they were in the direst of poverty, without the bare necessities for material survival. Knowledge of this situation was not new, but that it should be central to the concern of a church which now saw its mission as in the world was new. *When Vatican II's rejection of a radical separation between the sacred and the secular was translated into the Latin American context, the outcome was the call to take up the option for the poor.* While the term was not yet used in the Medellín document,[8] liberation theologians agree that "the option for the poor" was this document's guiding hermeneutical and ethical principle. The document interpreted Latin American history and society from the point of view of the poor. This included both how the poor experience reality and what is in their best interest. It placed a moral imperative on church, Christians, and all people of good will to take up the option for the poor in their concrete practice. Indeed, it indicated that interpretation and practice are interdependent: Understanding guides practice but practice illuminates understanding.[9]

Medellín rejected the view implicit in Vatican II that poverty is caused by underdevelopment; rather, it maintained that poverty is caused by dependence and domination. The peoples of the Third World did not need development but liberation. Gutiérrez argues at length that underdevelopment in the Latin American context must be understood as the by-product of development in the industrialized countries. Local elites in poor countries share the wealth that is being exported in return for shaping political and legal structures to facilitate exploitation by rich nations. Thus, to try to overcome poverty by 'development' of the politico-economic structures which cause poverty will not work. Radical structural changes are required to alleviate the acutely unjust situation. But because it is in the interest of the rich, who are powerful, to leave the structures as they are, they will not permit real structural change without a struggle. For Gutiérrez,

> an option for the poor is *an option for one social class against another.* An option for the poor means a new awareness of class confrontation. It means *taking sides with the dispossessed.* It means *entering into the world of the exploited social class, with its values, its cultural categories.* It means *entering into solidarity with its interests and its struggles.*[10]

This captures both the hermeneutical and ethical aspects of the option. And it expresses that partisanship, taking sides with the poor against the rich, is involved in the liberation of the poor.

Liberation theologians point out that the Medellín document not only recognized the need for structural change and the conflict this would involve but, in this context, acknowledged social sin, the sin involved in participating in unjust structures. And it recognized structural violence, the violence done to people, not by bombs and bullets, but by the social organization which makes them landless, jobless, without shelter, food, or medical attention, and without a vote or any means of changing their situation—which makes them suffer hunger, sickness, degradation, despair, and early death. While Medellín spoke against using violence to change the social 'order,' it recognized the inevitability of eruptions of violence in self-defense against the structural violence the poor suffered. Finally, Medellín insisted that the church side with the poor in an inevitably conflictual and violent situation.[11]

Baum helps to clarify this paradigm shift by distinguishing "soft" and "hard" meanings of liberation, both of which are found in the Medellín document. He argues that the soft or liberal view does not "name the plague" from which people suffer, does not state the causes of injustice, but suggests that individual holiness without structural change will lead to more just societies. It is nonconflictual. The hard liberationist view, on the other hand, analyzes and names the unjust situation of exploitation by rich nations aided by local elites. It points out a "rupture" within the social order that requires not only personal conversion but solidarity of and with the oppressed to overcome their oppression. It offends.[12]

Puebla, 1979

In the 11 years between the meetings of the Latin American bishops at Medellín and Puebla, poverty on that continent grew worse and, in response to protests for structural change, political oppression became more brutal. Hope for 'development' should have been exposed as an illusion and the cost of struggle for liberation made clear. However, the oscillation between hard and soft views of liberation expressed in Medellín had not been resolved before Puebla. Indeed, the conservative elements in the church, both within Latin America and in Rome, had become more militant. Liberationists feared that Puebla would come down hard on their project.

The preparatory document for the Puebla meeting supported liberationists' worst fears. Gutiérrez protests that it made no mention of Medellín and, in contrast with the earlier document, confused material poverty, which kills, with spiritual poverty, which involves an attitude of openness to God. He charges that it concerned itself with secularization, the industrial process, and the history of the episcopate but not with poverty, the working class, or those who had been killed for their solidarity with the poor. It mentioned inequalities in general without naming them; it talked about the evangelization of all in such a way as to neutralize the option for the poor, and it used abstract 'academic' language.[13]

After much lobbying by liberationists, the final document that emerged was quite different. It expressed continuity with Medellín. It distinguished material from spiritual poverty, condemning the former which it defined as deprivation of the most elementary material goods and denial of full participation in sociopolitical life. It named the poor as including indigenous peoples, peasants, manual laborers, marginalized urban dwellers, and particularly the women in those groups. And it named the cause of poverty as the accumulation of wealth by a small and powerful minority, made possible by social structures. Consistent with Medellín, Puebla repeatedly spoke of institutionalized injustice, structural poverty, and a situation of sin. And like Medellín, it demanded that the church take sides with the poor.[14]

The 1984 Vatican Document on Liberation Theology

Segundo sees the 1984 *Instruction on Certain Aspects of the "Theology of Liberation,"* published by the Vatican's Congregation for the Doctrine of the Faith, to be a condemnation not only of liberation theology but of the whole anthropocentric thrust of Vatican II.[15] Theologically, the doctrine of grace is at stake, whether God lifts 'mere' nature to supernature or whether the human world is graced from the beginning, making what happens in history of utter importance. Practically, the nature of the church's and the Christian's mission in the world is at stake, whether directly to draw individuals to eternal salvation on the basis of prescribed rules, which have little or nothing to do with the welfare of humans in history, or whether to serve God indirectly through serving humans, thus to aim at the salvation of history.[16]

Segundo argues that, while the document accuses liberation theology of reducing the good news to an earthly gospel, in fact, due to the dualism with which it operates, it is the document that reduces the good news to an other-worldly gospel. The document argues that it is the overcoming of personal sin and not changing social structures that is necessary for salvation and social justice. Connected with this, the document associates ethics with the "transcendence" of the person. Apparently, ethics and salvation revolve around what transcends history and escapes matter and determinism—a soul's intentions. In this same vein, Segundo accuses the document of spiritualizing poverty. It suggests that God is present in the poor, not as a protest against poverty, but because there is something to be valued in it. And our response to poverty should be first to contemplate God's mysterious presence in the poor and, only second, seek to alleviate that suffering. Finally, the document interprets scripture accordingly: The significance of the Exodus is not to deliver Israel from slavery and into the liberation of the Promised Land but to found the people of God and the Covenant cult celebrated on Mount Sinai. Furthermore, the church's understanding of Scripture is seen to be impartial, made possible by a "special knowledge" it has called the "light of the gospel." The document thus rejects the need for hermeneutics in understanding scripture, which it connects with partisanship to which it strongly objects.[17]

By thus restricting meaning and value to a sacred realm separated from secular history and by rejecting the means and motivation for overcoming poverty, the document operates against any meaningful option for the poor. The document argues strongly against a Marxian analysis of society in terms of class struggle, on the grounds that the latter presupposes a deterministic law of history and advocates hatred and violence. The document takes these to be inconsistent with a Christian perception of the goodness of creation, of human free choice, and of the commitment to love all and to reject violence. "The commandment of brotherly and sisterly love extended to all humankind (thus) provides the *supreme rule* of social life." To practice universal love, to include all, involves "transcending" the historical conflicts which divide people. But, Segundo argues, this is to ignore the suffering that historical conflicts cause. It is to ignore the need for partisanship.[18]

> To opt (or to choose sides) in a conflict means to enter into it and to accept the inherent partisanship of one of the two sides—in this case, that of the poor. Every option limits. . . . But at the same time the strength and efficacy of the option comes precisely from its partiality.[19]

The Option for the Poor Involves a 'Copernican Revolution' for Ethics and Theology: a Summary

The option for the poor embraces a 'Copernican revolution' or a paradigm shift in our ontology, anthropology, theology, and ethics. The breakdown of the radical distinction between the sacred and the secular is connected with a breakdown between the mental and physical, freedom and determinism, the personal and social, the individual and the structural. It recognizes that this world and our mental/physical existence in this world really matter. It recognizes that we are free to transform this world but that our freedom is historically situated, embodied, and limited. It recognizes that, as we are fundamentally mental/physical so too are we fundamentally social and we must unite for structural change as well as seek personal conversion.

The 'revolution' involves a hermeneutic which demands that we understand scripture, history, and the contemporary situation from the point of view of and in the interest of the poor rather than 'neutrally,' which in effect is from the point of view of the rich. We must reject any interpretation of scripture which harmonizes "the poor" with "the poor in spirit" because then its condemnation of material destitution gets lost. We must rewrite history from the side of the losers, that is, the poor, the colonized, and women, in order to reveal the causes of their and our oppression and struggle against it. We must look at contemporary issues, issues of land and tax reform, for example, from the point of view of the worst off.

Clearly we must adjust our practice to our new interpretation. However, practice does not simply follow upon interpretation. The two are interdependent. To a large extent, genuinely seeing from the point of view of the poor comes from already having taken a risk in acting for change. Demonstrating against a demolition of a squatter area helps both poor and rich to awaken to the situation of the poor and to perceive and feel the injustice of homelessness.

If we interpret society from the perspective of the poor, we will reject the view that the rich are called to give to the poor as a matter of charity in favor of the view that, for justice' sake, we all must change the humanly created structures which cause the enormous gap between rich and poor. And while individuals can share their possessions in the way of "dole outs," only the effort of a group can change the structures which are participated in by the group. So, rather than ethics being about having the necessary knowledge, power, and freedom to attain the personal perfection for which the individual will be rewarded with heaven, ethics becomes a group's joining in solidarity with limited knowledge, power, freedom, and responsibility in order to bring about social historical change which Christians hope will have eschatological significance. Implicit in the need for structural change is the need for social analysis in order to unmask hidden structures of oppression. While Medellín and Puebla mentioned politico-economic causes of poverty and oppression, we must think much more broadly and deeply in seeking social justice. Legal, educational, religious, linguistic, conceptual, attitudinal, value, and many other structures which inform our cultures as well as our social organization are all relevant.

Connected with the notion of solidarity is that of social sin. Social sin is something in which we are all immersed. It makes us its agents and victims. It includes conscious and unconscious participation in oppressive structures that we sometimes create but more often inherit and which we cannot escape even when we try. Rich or poor, we cannot, for example, avoid buying products from all companies which exploit their workers, other nations, and the environment. But while the phenomenon of social sin acknowledges that we cannot be "pure," we can, of course, resist these structures of oppression—even while we are forced to participate in them.

Solidarity with the poor involves taking sides with the poor[20] against the structures of their oppression and against the rich insofar as they persist in supporting the unjust structures from which they benefit. This is different from a classical approach for which partiality is seen as unfair. The option for the poor takes concrete inequality as its given, equalization as its aim, and partisanship as its means. Thus, for example, it supports giving preference to women and minority groups in jobs.

From a liberationist perspective, taking sides and even being prepared for conflict is the only way to universal love and the salvation of all. If society does not reshape itself so as, especially, to include the excluded, the poor, and the marginalized, they will remain left out of the benefits of society. The rich are not excluded from the imperative to take up the option for the poor, but many of them exclude themselves.

Implicit in what we have said but not explicitly mentioned in the theologians' discussions of the church documents is that we must revise our understanding of personal sin. Traditionally, we have assumed that greed, an aggressive taking from others what belongs to them, to be a paradigm of sin. But, for the poor, it is a self-erasing self-sacrifice and passivity that are the central flaws. The poor must be the first agents of their liberation.

Significance of Taking Up the Option for the Poor as Related to God, the Poor, and the Rich

The Option for the Poor Is an Option of the Poor

Liberation theologians seem to say contradictory things about the poor. On the one hand they describe the poor as radically dehumanized, as nonpersons or not yet persons of whom God demands nothing. God has a special love for the poor because they are poor and not because they are good. The kingdom is theirs and they do not have to do anything in order to 'deserve' it. On the other hand, theologians argue that the poor are the privileged interpreters of the good news and that it is through them that God will save history and us all.[21] But there is an implicit connection between the two. *It is through the project by which they become persons that the poor become the forgers of history and the salvation of us all.*

When theologians talk about the poor as nonpersons, a part of what they mean is that the masses of the destitute, before they begin to reflect on the causes of their poverty and organize for change, often do not have a sense of their own dignity and worth. They do not see themselves as subjects who ought to have the power to shape their own lives and participate in shaping their society. They do not see themselves as having rights to share in the benefits of society—rights to food, shelter, clothing, medical care, education, jobs, and legal protection. They are not treated as persons with dignity, as is made manifest by their situation.

Certainly the destitute in large cities of the Third World, the squatters, pushcart people, street children, "Smoky Mountain" foragers, see others as seeing them as eyesores, garbage, something to be swept out of sight. But we can question whether most of the poor ever see themselves, and their own children, quite like this. The important point that the theologians are making is not that the poor are nonpersons, not free and responsible, from which, according to a traditional line of reasoning, we can conclude that God and society cannot expect anything from them. Rather, *the kingdom is for them and the structures of society must be changed to include them unconditionally, whether in their personal lives they are good or very, very bad.*

The kingdom belongs to the poor just because they are poor. And those of us who are rich are obliged to do what we can to alleviate poverty without consideration of people's moral worth. *But if the materially poor and all oppressed groups are to experience liberation in history, then it is most essential that they take up their own cause.* As we have already argued, the poor are epistemologically privileged with regard to their poverty.[22] They know what they are suffering and, at a concrete level, they know what would alleviate their suffering. Squatters in poor countries know that they suffer constant threat of demolition with or without warning, as well as unhealthy living conditions. They know also that relocation which does not take into account their sense of community, workplace, schools, medical facilities, and water, may be a solution for those wanting to build a shopping mall in their area, but it is no solution for them. Because the poor can identify with the stories of oppression, struggle, and promise which fill the Judaeo-Christian scriptures, they can articulate and show those of us who are not poor what the scriptures are about. They know best what would count as good news—food, shelter, a job, freedom from harassment by the authorities—because they know best what is the bad news—hunger, homelessness, joblessness, and abuse.

Not only do the poor have an epistemological privilege as regards their poverty and oppression. Because they are the ones who are suffering from these conditions, they have the strongest motive for changing them. Indeed, the subjective side of liberation cannot succeed if the oppressed do not overcome the sins[23] of passivity and self-erasure. They must participate in their own liberation.[24] This, in the context of oppression, is just what it is to have a sense of dignity, to express integrity, to take responsibility for one's life and share in the responsibility of society. And this is what the poor and all oppressed groups are doing. A revolution in terms of a reshaping of attitudes, values, and relationships is going on within communities of the poor and other oppressed groups—women, blacks, and gays.

Segundo expresses skepticism that the masses can be or even ought to be conscientized in a way which is truly liberating. He argues that becoming the subject of one's own history involves the expenditure of high-cost energy because it involves understanding and making decisions about very complicated issues in the context of strong resistance from those who do not want change. But the law of conservation of energy demands that, in most of our engagements, we conform to the way things are, using high-cost energy only in restricted spheres such as in family or professional life. With respect to Paul's call to Christians to be liberated from the Law for the sake of creative love and to be critical of rather than to passively submit to societal structures and norms, Segundo argues that "if *per impossible* . . . (this) attitude were to become a general one, that would not be a miracle but rather a disaster."[25] In other words, for everyone to pay the high price in energy for being truly moral and truly Christian is neither possible nor desirable.

Segundo concludes that this does not mean the masses will be damned. The few are leaven; they provide the leverage for raising the many. But, we must ask, on his view, how is liberation of the masses possible in history? Not only liberation *from* debilitating material poverty must be sought, but also liberation *to* taking their lives, their history, into their own hands. Truly, struggling for liberation takes enormous energy. But it is also life-giving. Muteness, isolation, alienation, suppression, self-deception, meaninglessness, and conformity are also very energy-consuming—and not life-giving.

Segundo suggests that much of what goes by the name of consciousness-raising is manipulative and involves brainwashing. This may be a danger, but is it always or even generally true? Is the relatively egalitarian sharing and assuming responsibility in Basic Christian Communities manipulation? Is it brainwashing when squatters organize to demand their rights; youths depict their struggle in story, song, and dance; workers and peasants join to form unions to better their lot; street children counsel one another?[26] In a one-and-a-half-year period between 1986 and 1988, in a single diocese in North Cotabato, Mindanao, at least 64 people were killed, mostly BCC leaders and their children, for their nonviolent involvement in taking up the option for the poor.[27] Is Segundo wrong in thinking genuine conscientizing is not going on but right in suggesting that if it were occurring on a large scale, it would be too costly? Clearly, that must be decided by the people who are paying the cost and by those who, by their example, are energized and moved to join the effort.

The Option for the Poor Is an Option of the Rich[28]

Segundo argues that: *"The kingdom of God is not announced to everyone"* because it cannot be preached as good news for everyone. It is joy for the poor but it is woe for the rich.[29] For Gutiérrez, the gospel message is not anyone's private property; it is for all. If it were exclusively directed to the poor, then it would not make the difficult demands on the rich that it does. Those of us who are nonpoor would be 'off the hook,' as it were, simply by being ignored.[30] Segundo and Gutiérrez are not contradicting one another. *The prerequisite for having the kingdom announced to us as gospel or good news is that we have the values of the kingdom. And, to have these values, the rich today must take up the option for the poor.*

While both rich and poor are conditioned by structures of oppression, the rich benefit from them and the poor suffer under them. Rich individuals and nations create and maintain both the politico-economic structures which determine the distribution of wealth and power and the cultural attitudes and values which hold these structures in place. We who are rich, then, are centrally involved in the oppression of the poor. We are not completely ignorant of our role and, with some effort, can become very clear indeed about the effects of our decisions on the poor. Also, rich individuals, nations, and corporations have significantly more power than the poor to change the structures of the poor's oppression. Thus, the option for the poor should be a strong moral imperative for the rich. We cause poverty and can alleviate it. But we benefit from the way things are so we normally resist change. But as long as we do this the kingdom is not for us, because it is not good news for us.

While those of us who are rich must "give up" power, status, and possessions, our taking up the option for the poor is not purely negative. If and only if we take up the option will ours be the kingdom, not only in heaven *but also on earth*.[31] But what does this mean? It is necessary to shift perspective, to take seriously the phenomenon of social sin, and realize that the rich are also oppressed by the radical gap that exists between rich and poor. Our responsibility for the structures that oppress the poor is limited. And our very greed and powerseeking are socially conditioned, in part inherited. Boesak argues that whites in South Africa will not be free until blacks are free. Whites are dehumanized, oppressed, put into bondage, by a system which forces whites to be blatantly exploitative and dehumanizing of blacks. The phenomenon of consumerism provides a more complex example. It involves a value and practice of the rich which is made possible by and reinforces an economic system that makes others poor, wastes nonrenewable resources needed for future generations, and exploits the earth. By and large, we who are consumers do not want to give up our benefits and the status it brings. However, consumerism dehumanizes, offering us a momentary illusion of power over the object which we waste and destroy, and a sense of superiority to those we deprive. But consumerism is addictive, compulsive, and unsatisfying.

It is important that we not collapse the distinction between oppressor and oppressed. There is no class of people oppressing those of us who are rich qua rich and, generally speaking, we experience ourselves as benefiting and not suffering. The poor struggle to be released from their oppression while we fight to maintain the status quo and the power lies with us. But it is also necessary that we see the oppressor as also oppressed so as to appreciate the option for the poor as a common project of rich and poor. I do not wish to suggest that those of us who are rich ought to take up the option primarily for our own sakes; we ought to take up the option for the sake of the poor. But only by going out to the poor will the rich be liberated from the depravity of dominance and obsessiveness with possessions and power, or simply from isolation, alienation, and meaninglessness. Only by going out to the poor will we be liberated into dignity, integrity, meaning, commitment, and connectedness with the vast majority of the human race. In order that we see this, experience it, structures more subtle than politico-economic ones must change. Some of our deepest attitudes and values must change.

While the option for the poor is a common project of poor and rich, the two groups have somewhat different contributions to make. We have said that the poor have an epistemological privilege as regards their oppression and what would count as its alleviation. So it is important that the rich listen to the poor, be guided by the negative criterion and not be tempted to draw up abstract positive utopias. And this involves a shift in the perceptions of power on the part of poor and rich. The rich have power over the poor and we have some power to remove that. We have more power to change social structures than do the poor; we have the power of formal education and articulateness and often a breadth of experience which can serve the needs of the poor. But the poor have the power of truth; they provide the criterion for effectiveness. The primary role of the rich will be one of creative response to the poor.

In spite of their epistemological privilege, because the poor are deprived of education and access to a variety of experience, a minority of the nonpoor have a crucial role in facilitating the poor's exploration and articulation of the causes of their poverty, and their organization for change. But this is only really successful when the poor come to take over their own conscientization and organizing. Otherwise, taking up the option by the nonpoor involves, first, participating as a citizen and church person (if we are one), to bring the organization of our societies and churches more in line with the needs of the poor. We must see that these institutions direct the greater part of their human and material resources toward the poor. This involves making personal choices which both meet our personal interests and talents and which serve the move to a just society. It involves "giving up" both power and wealth. For a few this will mean living with the poor and more or less like the poor. However, not competition over how much we "give up," but, rather, effectiveness, is what is relevant. Finally, though, *being in direct contact with the poor, at least sometimes, is the single most enabling factor in shifting the understanding, feelings, and, inevitably, practice of the nonpoor.*

God's option for the poor

There are some theologians who object strongly to the notion of God's taking sides with one group and against another. They see this as a group's co-opting God for their side and as inconsistent with both the demands of justice and the sovereignty of God.[32] It is true that, when an organized group says, "God is on our side," there is the danger of this group's thinking it is certain to win and of its committing atrocities in God's name to ensure that it does. But when blacks in South Africa and the destitute everywhere say God is on their side it is hard to deny that the God of justice and love is on their side in their struggle against oppression, whether or not God would bless everything they do.

As we have already said, God is especially in the poor as a protest against their poverty, as a call, the call of the negative contrast to both poor and rich to rebel against the acute deprivation and oppression of the vast majority of humans. God is in the especially powerful resistance the poor can make against their oppression, especially powerful because the poor are especially suffering and understand their suffering best. God reveals Godself especially to the poor. As we have discussed, the poor understand the promise of good news best, most realistically, because it is they who experience the bad news most concretely. It is through the poor, in their need and in their own protest and practice for justice that God draws the rich to join in solidarity with the poor in order that we all will find God and our own salvation.

God's revelation in Jesus was biased in favor of the poor. Jesus' preaching and practice of good news was directed especially toward the poor, the oppressed, the outcast. Through his parables, he displayed a vision of a world where action was guided by human need and, in his proclamation of the beatitude, he promised such a world, such a kingdom. Through his healing the blind, the crippled, and the possessed, and through his feeding of multitudes and celebrating meals with tax collectors and other social outcasts, Jesus actively brought about liberation to the poor and oppressed. Furthermore, Schillebeeckx points out, the "unmistakable *bias* in Jesus' exercise of love with a view to God's universal rule" only reflects God's bias in choosing a Jew, one of the most persecuted of peoples, to reveal God's universal love.[33] We have seen Segundo speak even more strongly of Jesus' bias or, more precisely, of the bias of the kingdom. He refers us to the story of Lazarus and the rich man to justify his claim that, not only is the kingdom for the poor even if they are bad, but it is not for the rich even if we are good.[34]

Finally, picking up on Schillebeeckx's point, Haight points out that God's option for the poor can be both partial and for all. Haight argues that the God of Jesus loves

> each one as if there were no others . . . [thus establishing] all human beings in a radical equality of absolute worth in God's eyes. . . . Precisely because of this egalitarian love, God is concerned in a special way for those whom we human beings disvalue, demean, injure, and dehumanize by prejudice, hatred, sin, and injustice. . . .

He adds that God's option is not against anyone in the sense that it is a call to everyone to take up the option for the poor.[35]

THE FIRST OPTION IS FOR THE MATERIALLY POOR

We have argued that the ethical imperative rising out of the negative contrast experience, the imperative of resistance to every threat to the humanum, must be concretized and completed. I suggested in a preliminary way that the call to take up the option for the poor should provide this concretization for our time. The last section explored what is meant by the option for the poor, the paradigm shift involved in it. Because we concentrated on the Latin American context out of which the term arose, we stressed that, in terms of content, "the poor" means "the materially destitute," not "the poor in spirit." But the option has a generic as well as specific sense. It is a call to respond to the various forms of social oppression that people suffer today.[36] This section will argue that the option for the materially destitute should be the first concretization of the imperative to resist suffering.

A Growing Number of Groups Are Seeking Liberation

In 1974, Peter Singer warned:

> If we wish to avoid being numbered amongst the oppressors, we must be prepared to re-think even our most fundamental attitudes. We need to consider them from the point of view of those most disadvantaged by our attitudes, and the practices that follow from these attitudes. If we can make this unaccustomed mental switch we may discover a pattern in our attitudes and

practices that consistently operates so as to benefit one group—usually the one to which we ourselves belong—at the expense of another. In this way we may come to see that there is a case for a new liberation movement.[37]

Singer went on to make a case for animal liberation.

Our sensitivity to oppression has continued to expand to include not only the poor, women, people of color, religious and cultural minorities, but also homosexuals, the aged, other species, and the environment. . . . This growing awareness has led us to see that virtually everyone is oppressed according to some classification or other, and virtually everyone benefits at the expense of some others according to some classification or other. So we cannot divide the *individuals* in the world into oppressors and oppressed. Very poor white men are oppressed and also belong to classes which oppress. Partisanship, then, must involve taking sides with the poor, with blacks, with women—with individual people, yes—but with individuals under specific descriptions, so that partisanship does not involve taking sides with some individuals against other individuals as such. It involves taking sides with one person as a landless peasant and with another as a woman banned from a particular position of service in her church.

The expansion of our sensitivity to the various forms of oppression is positive. But it leads to the need for some sort of prioritizing regarding the forms of oppression or again we will be justified in having concern only for ourselves and our friends.[38]

The Option for the Materially Poor Is the First Concretization of the Imperative to Resist Suffering

It is not completely self-evident that an ethic which attempts to reduce suffering should be an ethic which goes out to the worst off first. A utilitarian ethic may aim at minimizing the overall quantity of suffering, but may also let the worst off go to the wall, as it were. However, an ethic of *resistance* to suffering, based on the universal experience of suffering and *struggling* for salvation, which aims at both liberating humankind in history and following Jesus in participating in the kingdom, does demand that we should go out to the worst off first. But, then, in the context of the multiplicity of forms of oppression which make claims on us today, who are the worst off? What should be the first concretization of the imperative to resist suffering?

It is sometimes argued, particularly by middle class people, that those whose sensitivities and skills have been most developed can suffer most deeply and intensely. The psychological torment of a Vincent van Gogh is quoted. In response, we must insist that, while a liberationist ethic does not exclude any suffering from its moral concern, the suggestion that those who have more can suffer more cannot be accepted. The stories of the poor from Ethiopia to Romania to the Philippines give the lie to this. However, I shall not attempt to measure the intensity and depth of people's psychological experience of suffering. *For the purpose of concretizing the ethical imperative to resist suffering, we may 'measure' suffering in terms of the degree of deprivation of what makes for full humanity, that is, in terms of that which poses the deepest threat to the humanum, but also, which human action can alleviate.*[39]

But what counts as a threat to the humanum? What is it that makes for participation in a full humanity? In the general context of our attempting to define what is good for the humanum primarily in terms of the negation of what is bad for it, Bernard Lonergan's integral scale of values as developed by Robert Doran may be used as a measure of deprivation of full humanity.[40] The scale is as follows:

5. Religious value involves the grace which enables the subject to be authentic.
4. Personal value involves an authentic subject who is an originator of values.
3. Cultural values constitute the meanings and values that inform the community.
2. Social values involve the social institutions which should guarantee vital values for all. Legal and political rights are found at this level.
1. Vital values are material needs necessary for health.

Looked at from below, the scale may be seen in a sort of evolutionary way, as moving from more basic levels which set problems that only development at higher levels can solve. Seen from above, the scale is therapeutic, each level conditioning the satisfactory operation of the levels below it. The higher levels are characterized by greater creativity and differentiation.

I find this scale useful in a number of ways. In the first place it articulates the obvious, that *if vital material needs are not fulfilled no other.*

needs can be fulfilled. The destitute are furthest removed from full humanity, having not even the means for survival much less the social, cultural, personal, and religious expression of humanity. This is not strictly placing the poor before women or people of color. There is an ambiguity in these classifications of oppressed groups. To classify a group as poor is to name the suffering, whereas to classify a group in terms of sex or color is to name the rationalization for any number of sufferings but is not to name the forms they take. However, a central form that racial and sexual discrimination takes is that of preventing some groups from sharing equitably in the material benefits of society. The poorest people also tend to be women and people of color. By naming concrete values of a flourishing humanity which, if denied, constitute profound deprivation and oppression, the scale captures the fact that poverty is not a parallel category to racism or sexism. According to this scale, first priority must be given to the poor, but racism and sexism are not spoken to as such. The scale captures what we know, that some members of each group of women, indigenous peoples, and the aged, will be much worse off than others, but the worst off of all will be the destitute in every group, including white middle-aged heterosexual men.

Once vital needs are fulfilled, things become less clearcut in terms of degrees of deprivation. But, due to the dependence of higher levels on lower levels we could say that, after material deprivation, those denied legal and political rights are the next worse off because, without these, they will not be able to attain social status and the power to shape their society. One could argue that women had status and power to shape society long before they had political or many legal rights. Without the latter, however, women had the former only at the whim of men. We could influence only to the extent that we were 'allowed.' So we can argue that, after the materially destitute, those who are denied legal and political rights are next worse off, while those who are socially and culturally devalued, denied good education and fulfilling careers, are not quite so bad off. Also, we cannot wait for society to give equal social status to women or blacks before it gives us protection under the law and the vote. It is quite right that the law should force justice in those spheres where the law can reasonably do so. And genuine status and participatory power will emerge. Those in solidarity with the oppressed can form an exception, however. Soviet dissidents, for example, who were denied political and legal rights and were incarcerated for their views represent a sort of Christ-figure, not at all deprived in their capacity to express their humanity. Such people are made to suffer precisely because they are authentic subjects who introduce values which conflict with cultural norms. They are not on the bottom rung, having their material needs met, and awaiting legal and political rights before the meanings and values of the culture are opened to them.

According to the scale, problems at a more basic level must be resolved higher up. This captures the liberationist view that social structures must be changed to overcome poverty, and values must be changed in order to change social structures. The personal authenticity of some, but not all, must be motivated toward this change. This also shows that poverty, political unfreedom, racial and sexual discrimination, are, in a fundamental sense, everybody's problem. Something is wrong with the personal authenticity and cultural values of those not suffering at the more basic levels if they are not geared toward changing things at these higher levels for the end of correcting things lower down. This illuminates how the oppressing class is also oppressed. Finally, while the scale supports the view that the materially deprived are the worst off, it demonstrates that full humanity requires social, cultural, personal, and spiritual development as well. There is no danger of this view's being reductionist in the direction of material welfare.[41]

Not everyone agrees that it is the materially destitute who are most deprived of their humanity. Clarke, for example, argues that poverty should be measured in terms of loss of human dignity, where this involves a group's being treated as *and accepting for itself* that it has little or no worth. And this need not be associated with material deprivation.[42] We must respond that, in our world, material destitution is caused by social structures held in place by groups who benefit from them. Being thus submitted to severe material deprivation, poverty of the sort which makes for physical and mental disability and an early death, is the worst way in which a group can be told that it has no worth. To accept debilitating poverty and devaluing is much worse than not to do so, but this verges on being an abstract distinction for those who have no forum for expressing themselves, who see no avenues for improving their situation, and who have no grounds for hope.

Finally, a secondary but important consideration in determining what should be the first concretization of the imperative to resist suffering is the numbers involved, the quantity as well as the quality of deprivation of the humanum.[43] It is important when we consider that taking up the option centrally involves a reshaping of society. And the materially very poor make up the vast majority of the human race. They are mostly people of color and women more than men. Their numbers are growing, and their poverty is growing, and the gap between the very poor and the nonpoor is getting wider. The global situation today particularly cries out for making the materially destitute our first option.

The Forms of Oppression Are Connected

The materially destitute are the worst off in the obvious sense that they lack the bare necessities of life. This means that society and its political, economic, legal, and educational structures must be reshaped so as to include *especially* the materially very poor. Institutions such as government and church should distribute their human and material resources *especially* to these. It is up to us, the participators in society and its institutions, to see that they do. Personally, in our work, however, given the interests, abilities, and needs of our context, we may explicitly gear ourselves toward alleviating poverty, sexism, human rights abuses . . . or none of these. But whether we are doctor or factory worker, artist or engineer, we can contextualize our work in a way which is liberating or oppressive, and which more directly responds to one oppressed group or another. And this is appropriate. The worst-off members of all oppressed groups are the poorest, and, whatever our personal contribution, we should address that concern. *The overcoming of different forms of oppression does not, fundamentally, involve a competition for resources but the cooperation of groups with a fundamentally common faith and common cause.*

The various features involved in the paradigm shift for ethics that we discussed in the last section characterize not only the option for the materially poor but for all oppressed groups. That is why we can speak of a generic as well as a specific sense of the option for the poor. Some kind of social structures and institutions, whether they be economic, conceptual, or value structures, play a central role in poverty, racism, and sexism, and also in discrimination against the aged or homosexuals. Solidarity, taking sides, finding new ways of seeing as well as practicing are important in all these cases. The need to overcome passivity and self-effacement is the same for the various oppressed groups. Also, Lonergan's scale of values is useful in helping us to articulate common contents of the various forms of oppression: poverty, denial of legal and political rights, denial of a respected place in society, and of the power to shape one's own life and participate in shaping that of one's society. In connection with this, as we have already noted, the worst-off women and people of color are the poorest ones and relatively more of the poor are women than men, blacks than whites. But why women and blacks are more likely to be poor and powerless is because the forms of oppression reinforce one another. For example, the economies of the north are organized so as to require full-time and part-time employment. This benefits the rich. Women have the major responsibilities in the home, particularly in the rearing of children. This benefits men. Due to responsibilities in the home, women are often only available for part-time employment. And almost all part-time work is of low status, low pay, and minimum benefits. Working hours could be redefined, women and men could share child rearing, and part-time employment could be opened to high-status, high-paying forms of work. Sexism makes women poor—and women's poverty makes men and some women sexist.

There are similar forms of power and powerlessness involved in the various forms of oppression. The dominant group has exploitative power, power over the oppressed group, power to use the oppressed for its own ends. Where the goals of exploiter and exploited coincide, this power can give the appearance of paternalistic benevolence. Consider the husband who regularly wines and dines his wife but who will not 'allow' her to pursue her career. He enjoys the first and would be inconvenienced by the second. And this very combination of 'give and take' reinforces his dominance. Often, exploitative power is not held in place directly by the threat of physical force but by an ideology. Men, whites, the rich, and the colonizers are seen as superior in some way, more intelligent, knowledgeable, or virtuous. This justifies their and our being the agents and guardians of right order. Right order involves, for example, working for profit, Christianizing the heathen, things to which both employer and employee, colonizer and colonized, must submit, but which benefits the one group at the expense of the other. Exploitative power thus joins forces with manipulative power, which distorts reality and leads the oppressed to accept their situation. When this happens, any resistance to oppression is punished, not only by the dominant group but by the majority of the victims themselves. Finally, the alienation resulting from accepting oppression often leads to an eventual lashing out in what may appear to be irrational ways. The woman denied her career may become unable to focus and so become incompetent in her household duties, which further reinforces the ideology that keeps her in the home.[44]

Given that various forms of oppression are both structurally similar and interdependent, we would expect that the attempt to overcome one form of oppression would contribute to the overcoming of other forms of oppression, but this does not automatically happen. Although structurally similar in broad terms and at a fundamental level, different social analyses are required at a less general level to unmask sometimes different oppressive networks of social structures and institutions. Using inclusive language in liturgy will not, in itself, operate against racism, although the connections between taking male and white to be normative ought to be apparent. We have an enormous capacity to compartmentalize and deceive ourselves, to condemn one form of oppression, often the one which we ourselves experience. We refuse to see, even when they are pointed out to us, other forms of oppression which consistency demands that we condemn as well. How many of us who are opposed to classism, sexism, and racism are also opposed to speciesism?

PARTISANSHIP IS JUSTIFIED IN TAKING UP THE OPTION FOR THE POOR

We have argued that we should bring the option for the poor into the center of ethics. And this involves partisanship in favor of the poor and oppressed, primarily against the structures which oppress them, but also against those groups and individuals who resist changing these structures, insofar as they do resist. However, it has been assumed throughout the classical tradition, and by many today, that *partisanship is bad by definition. It is not objective, therefore it biases truth, and it shows favoritism, so it is unfair and thus unjust.* It strikes at the heart of both epistemology and ethics.

It is essential that we respond to this objection if we are going to justify the centrality to ethics of taking up the option for the poor. Partisanship cannot be avoided. It mediates truth and justice.[45]

Why Ethics Must Be Partisan

Our Historicity Demands Partisanship

The very fact of our being historical, of being spatially and temporally located and limited, means that we constantly have to choose between alternatives—between relating to one group, pursuing one career, acting out of one value and for one goal or another. But because our world is unharmonious, disordered, radically unjust, reflecting conflicting values and goals and represented by conflicting groups, to choose one value or goal or group is not merely to exclude another but is often to take sides with the one against the other.

Jesus was as limited by his historicity as anyone. He could not respond to the needs of all but had to make choices from among groups and had to make choices between opposing groups. Segundo argues that the point of Jesus' parable of the Good Samaritan is not to show that everyone can be our neighbor but that there is not anyone who cannot be our neighbor. We cannot be personally concerned about everyone with whom we relate, with the grocer and the librarian, for example; we have to treat most people in terms of their roles. Jesus broke dialogue with the Pharisees, and he abandoned John the Baptist in his time of greatest need. He probably thought his energies were better spent relating directly to the poor than to the Pharisees. And if Jesus had gone to John when he was imprisoned he, too, might have been arrested and prevented from serving the needy.[46]

Our very awareness of our historicity must lead us to recognize that we are limited in terms of our capacity to give and to relate to others. We must choose between needs, and ought to choose those of the most needy.

Illusoriness Involved in Choosing Neutrality, Objectivity, and Universality

In spite of the fact that our very historicity implies that we have to take sides, there are situations which create the illusion that: (1) we are being neutral, we are not choosing when, in fact, we do and must choose, or (2) we are being objective in the sense of supporting a value-free situation when the situation we support is but an option which is value-loaded, or (3) we are choosing a universal such as universal love, when we are being partial, choosing to side with some who are in conflict with others. In all these cases, it is when we choose the established order, the structures that are in place, the powers that be, the status quo, that our choice may give the appearance of being objective or universal or simply a neutral nonchoice. *We can give the impression of neutrality, of not choosing at all, because to support the established order is to engage in routine, to move with the flow, to refrain from deliberation and perhaps even to disattend from the situation.* At most, it appears that, along with nearly everybody else, we are allowing things to remain the same but are not actively doing anything, certainly not taking sides in a conflict. But this is not correct. While social structures may take on a life of their own in the sense that they may extend into spheres for which they were not intended and outlive anyone's conscious decisions about them, structures do not remain in place without people actively supporting them, however unconsciously. This or that transnational simply would not survive if people did not buy its products.

For example, Segundo discusses a document produced by the Chilean bishops during the Allende government.[47] The document argued that the church could not take sides in the political sphere because it aims at the eternal salvation of all and to take sides would exclude from the church those Christians who had opted for the other side. However, it also said that socialism was not an acceptable alternative to the existing capitalist system. It was under the illusion that it had not taken sides because it saw the existing economic structure as reflecting the natural order of things. Christians for capitalism did not have to go by that name in order to support the existing structures, whereas those advocating change did have to unite under a banner for socialism. Christians for socialism but not Christians for capitalism were seen as creating conflict, division, in society and church.

This example embraces all three illusions, that of neutrality in claiming not to take sides, objectivity in supporting the status quo, and universality in terms of church's claim that its status quo position assured that both sides were included in church. But let us pursue this last point a little further. The Chilean bishops saw the role of church as mediating salvation to all to be incompatible with its taking sides in the politico-economic sphere. They thought that everyone must be included in church, that internal church unity, a common faith, must be maintained, not in terms of the universal call to the option for the poor, but by evading problems of poverty, sexism, racism, etc. We are forced to ask, What is the common faith that constitutes church unity? The concrete historical situation is reduced out, so that faith becomes a ritual which it is difficult to see as other than meaningless and magical, aimed at manipulating God into assurances about an afterlife. This is not all. *To take an ahistorical approach is, in effect, to support the historical situation which exists and to resist change. And to do it in the name of God is to sacralize resistance to change or partisanship in favor of the established 'dis-order.'*[48]

Classical Ethics: Ahistorical and Illusory

Classical ethics of both Aristotelian and Kantian sorts begins with positive abstract views of a universal human nature that is individual, not essentially in relation. Their anthropologies and ethics are ahistorical; they present themselves as timeless when they are biased in favor of the established order of their time. Virtues, such as greatness of soul, which Aristotle recommended as essential to human happiness, represented the upper-class values of his time. While Kant's categorical imperative, because it is formal, seems to escape historical relativity, it tends to be applied so as to conform to whatever are the norms of a given society. Alasdair MacIntyre argues that, although nothing was further from Kant's intention, "Anyone educated into the Kantian notion of duty will, so far, have been educated into easy conformism with authority."[49]

Starting in ethics from the viewpoint of an abstract, positive, and universal human nature presupposes an abstract sameness and equality in our humanity. Kant's view that humans are of equal worth and so deserve equal treatment, to be treated as ends and not only as means, is utterly important as an ideal. It served to undermine the feudal view that a profoundly inegalitarian class structure was both natural and divinely ordained. It provides grounds for arguing that the poor, women, and people of color, are as worthy as the rich, men, and whites. Today, with our recognition of social conditioning, we see that treating people as equals is not treating them impartially and without favoritism. *Equality is an abstract ideal; inequality is the concrete, historical reality. In order that equalizing go on, we have to take sides, be partisan.* We must counter the histories of inequality by, for example, giving "less qualified" women and ethnic minorities preference in high-profile and high-status jobs; otherwise the context, the reconditioning, will not be developed where women and minorities can become "more qualified."

The Universal Is Sought through the Particular: Love through Partisanship

Seeking universal justice or love through 'impartial' treatment of everybody does not succeed because people are not starting out from a position of equality. If the powerful do not make a special effort to seek out the powerless, to find the neighbor, to walk a different path, then they will relate only to their peers, and the power and benefits of society will remain with them. Jesus' love was biased, favoring the poor and deprived, outcasts and sinners, so that all would be included in the kingdom. We might ask, however, just how are we to achieve universal justice and love by taking sides with one group against another?

All are invited to take up the option for the poor and, if everyone accepted, then everyone would be united in the project of building a just and loving society. Taking sides with the poor would not be taking sides against anybody. But given that many will not take up the option, and thereby will take sides against the poor how, practically speaking, can this partisanship lead to universal love? How can using the means of conflict, confrontation, and perhaps violence, lead to harmonious community?

Our whole human history bears witness to the fact that when, over a long time and on a large scale, means contradict ends, when the means of injustice and manipulation are used to achieve a just and free society, the end is not achieved. A utopian society cannot be brought about by means which destroy the dignity, integrity, trust, and affectivity of a people. The 'material' for the utopian society is destroyed because the people is destroyed. And the oppressive and manipulative means in effect become the end. Why? Structures set up to facilitate the means cannot easily be dislodged, making the means *difficult* to give up; the cost of the means in terms of energy and commitment for those engaging in it accumulates, making them *less and less likely* to give it up; the depravity resulting from engaging in the means makes them *less able* to change.

The partisanship involved in the option for the poor does not embrace this kind of contradiction. The class struggle objected to by the 1984 Vatican document on liberation theology is rejected. The poor class is not destined to rise violently against the rich oppressor class and, fed by hatred and vengeance, to turn the tables on the rich. The Vatican document rightly sees this as opposed to the Christian view of freedom and the commandment to love all. This is not, however, what is meant by serious liberation theologians who use the language of class struggle. The idea that class struggle is historically determined contradicts the entire program of liberation theology to mobilize people to act for change, and it undermines a liberationist ethic. *To take up the option for the poor is an ethical imperative and must be chosen.* The liberationist program does not seek a reversal of situations but justice for all and is motivated by love and not hate. It does not see physical violence as inevitable and certainly not the central means to change. But it points out that the eruption of violence by the poor is a sort of self-defense against institutionalized violence, which is itself always held in place by the threat of direct violence.[50] Indeed, the liberationist program demands that liberationists attempt to bring more and more groups and individuals into concrete connectedness with them. They can do this in a variety of ways: They can show that to oppress is to be oppressed; they can show that human solidarity demands that no human is truly liberated until all are; they can appeal to stories and examples (for Christians particularly the story of Jesus) in order to move people.[51]

Looking from a different angle at the issue of taking sides with an aim to including all, we must note that *taking sides with and of the materially very poor is taking sides with and of the vast majority of the human race. Disorder, disharmony, and the already damaged humanum are not exceptions to the rule; they represent the rule.* Indeed, as we have seen, virtually everyone is oppressed in some way, and in need of liberation. This does not justify replacing partisanship on behalf of the worst off with self-interest on everybody's part. But this does show that the starting point in attempting to alleviate the suffering of the worst off is but the starting point of the attempt to mend the whole. The scale of values demonstrates that, where there is massive poverty, there is something wrong with the structures and values guiding the order of society. This is to say that there is something wrong in the lives of those not suffering poverty. The call to the liberation of the poor must open out to a call for an integrated liberation of society.[52]

CONCLUSION

The last chapter argued that Schillebeeckx's negative contrast experience is foundational for ethics. It yields a first imperative of resistance to suffering. But this imperative is too abstract. We all suffer, and we do not intend that we should be ethically concerned only with ourselves and our friends. This chapter argued that an articulation and concretization of the universal imperative, appropriate for our time, is captured in the call to take up the option for the poor. This should be brought to the center of ethics.

In its generic sense, the option for the poor refers, not only to the materially poor but to various oppressed groups, including women, people of color, colonized peoples, and many more. While there are significant differences in the causes of and solutions to the various forms of oppression, there are also fundamental structural similarities captured in the paradigm shift in ethics that the option demands. Centrally, this involves the need to interpret as well as act from the point of view of, and in the interest of, the oppressed; recognize the structural causes of oppression, and join in solidarity with the oppressed in order that those structures may be changed; recognize the partisanship involved in this and also the importance of the oppressed's taking up their own cause.

In its specific sense, the option refers to the materially poor. Our first option and the first concretization of the imperative to resist suffering should be for the materially destitute. They are the worst off because they do not have the means of survival without which nothing else matters. Society, and that means institutions such as state and church, must be reshaped to include the excluded and the materially destitute first of all. And all of us, rich and poor, must participate in reshaping the social order and shaping the kingdom. In our occupations, we will take account of our own abilities, interests, opportunities, and contexts in determining how directly and in what ways we might serve the ends of liberation.

Because traditionally ethics has seen partisanship as grievously unethical, and because it is also central to taking up the option for the poor, we defended partisanship. We argued that if there is to be justice, and the love which includes everyone in the benefits of society, we cannot merely treat everyone as though she or he were equal. We must engage in equalizing by favoring the worst off. This is the only means by which we can even approach universal justice and love. Besides, we cannot avoid taking sides. To attempt to be neutral, to do nothing, is to support the structures that are in place; if we do not explicitly side with the oppressed, including those groups of which we are oppressed members, we will at least implicitly side with oppression.

Finally, while the option for the poor concretizes and so completes the imperative to resist suffering and so follows from an ethic based on the negative contrast, because the option responds so clearly to the needs of our time,[53] because it is compelled by our experience of the world, it, in turn, lends support to an ethic based on the negative contrast. We could have begun with the demand of experience that we bring the option to the center of ethics and gone on to analyze this and give it a universal experiential ground, by appeal to the negative contrast.

NOTES

1. Donal Dorr, *Option for the Poor: A Hundred Years of Vatican Social Teaching* (Maryknoll, New York: Orbis Books, 1983), p. 1.
I use "option for the poor" coined after Medellín, and not "preferential option for the poor," as used at Puebla. The latter is intended to weaken the partisanship involved in the former, so that it merely means having "special concern for the poor," the term used in the 1984 Vatican instruction on liberation theology. I therefore reject it.

2. Virgil Elizondo and Leonardo Boff, "Editorial: Theology from the Viewpoint of the Poor," *Option for the Poor: Challenge to the Rich Countries*, trans. Francis McDonagh, *Concilium* 187 (1986): ix

3. Rebecca S. Chopp, *The Praxis of Suffering: An Interpretation of Liberation and Political Theologies* (Maryknoll, New York: Orbis Books, 1986), p. 62.

4. Elizondo and Boff, "Editorial: Theology from the Viewpoint of the Poor," p. ix.

5. Thomas E. Clarke, "Option for the Poor: A Reflection," *America* (January 30, 1988): 95.

6. Elizondo and Boff, "Editorial: Theology from the Viewpoint of the Poor," p. ix.

7. See Roger Haight, "The Origins and Relevance of Liberation Theology: From Vatican Council II to Liberation Theology," and "The Origins and Relevance of Liberation Theology: Liberation Theology in the Language of Vatican II," *PACE/Professional Approaches for Christian Educators* 17, ed. Mary Perkins Ryan, 1987. Haight explicitly states that he is stressing the points of continuity between the Vatican Council and liberation theology.

8. Gustavo Gutiérrez speaks of Jesus taking a radical option for the poor in *A Theology of Liberation: History, Politics and Salvation*, trans. and ed. Sister Caridad Inda and John Eagleson (London: SCM Press Ltd., 1974), p. 228. This book was first published in 1971, shortly after Medellín.

9. See Gutiérrez, *A Theology of Liberation*, p. 35; Gutiérrez, *The Power of the Poor in History*, p. 112; Gregory Baum, "Class Struggle and the Magisterium: A New Note," *Theological Studies* 45 (1984): 690–92.

10. *The Power of the Poor in History*, p. 45. (My italics.) See also *A Theology of Liberation*, pp. 26–27 on class struggle and pp. 81–99 for justification of the theory of dependence.

11. This perspective pervades the liberationist literature. See, for example, Gutiérrez, *The Power of the Poor in History*, pp. 25–35. See also Juan Luis Segundo, *Theology of the Church: A Response to Cardinal Ratzinger and a Warning*

to the Whole Church, trans. John W. Diercksmeier (Minneapolis: Winston Press, 1985), pp. 61–65, 110, 124–28.

12. Gregory Baum, "Faith and Liberation: Development Since Vatican II," *Theology and Society* (New York: Paulist Press, 1987), pp. 8–12.

13. *The Power of the Poor in History*, pp. 111–24.

14. Ibid., pp. 127–37.

15. Whenever I speak of the 1984 Vatican document in this chapter I am referring to Segundo's interpretation of it. Most liberation theologians have been less critical of it. See, for example, the Epilogue to Roger Haight's *An Alternative Vision* (New York: Paulist Press, 1985), pp. 257–68.

16. *Theology and the Church*, pp. 73–77.

17. Ibid., pp. 12, 25–27, 56–65, 43–45, 39.

18. Ibid., p. 108. Quotation from *Instruction on Certain Aspects of the 'Theology of Liberation"* (IV, 8), p. 173 of *Theology and the Church*. (Segundo's italics. Exclusive language replaced.)

19. Ibid., p. 41. (My italics.)

20. Throughout, when I speak of solidarity and taking sides with the poor I include the solidarity of the poor with the poor, the taking of sides of the members of every oppressed group with their group against the causes of their oppression.

21. See for example: Gutiérrez, *The Power of the Poor in History*, pp. 4, 53, 65, 92–93, 197; Juan Luis Segundo, *Jesus of Nazareth Yesterday and Today, Vol. II, The Historical Jesus of the Synoptics*, trans. John Drury, 5 vols. (Maryknoll, New York: 1985), p. 140.

22. This is nuanced in chapter 1, footnote 10.

23. *To speak here of sin is not to blame the poor for their situation but it is to liberate the poor to their right and obligation to take up their own cause.*

24. Soelle adds to Schillebeeckx's claim that suffering must be responded to by criticism and practice of resistance, the need to lament as a first step, the step of really getting in touch with suffering. See *Suffering*, p. 70.

25. *Liberation of Theology*, Chapter Eight, "Mass Man—Minority Elite—Gospel Message," pp. 208–48. Quotation at p. 230.

26. In the context of a drop-in center to which they belong, I have seen skits written and acted out by Manila street children in which they describe passersby as seeing them as garbage, eyesores, something to be swept off the streets. Their stories tell of being thrown out of their homes by drunken fathers, falling into drugs, losing their money in gambling and to syndicates, falling prey to pedophiles, turning to prostitution to buy medicine, being picked up and abused by the police, and just being hungry, lonely, and afraid. These children are articulate and, by their very performing, they are taking their lives into their own hands and trying to reshape society.

27. This includes 1 priest, 17 lay BCC and other church leaders, their children, farmers, teachers, and local politicians who stood with them. It does not include the attempted murders, tortures, rapes, etc. Most were killed by government-funded paramilitary and by vigilante groups unofficially associated with them. While the persecution of the church in North Cotabato is very strong, it is representative of what is going on in many other places in the Philippines. For the 64 documented cases see Peter Geremia, PIME (ed.), *Church Persecution: A Test Case: Kidapawan Diocese, Nagliliyab* Series, no. 13 (Quezon City: Claretian Publications, 1988), pp. 17–21, 31–32.

28. By the rich I include all of those who are not poor and who, when they take up the cause of the poor, are taking up the cause of the other and stand to lose in terms of materials and status however much they may gain in terms of integrity, joy and the things that make for being human.

29. *The Historical Jesus of the Synoptics,* p. 90. (Segundo's italics.)

30. *The Power of the Poor in History,* p. 128.

31. Whatever Segundo might mean, I do not wish to suggest that those of us who are rich and powerful will be excluded from the kingdom of heaven. That is not for us to decide. As I shall argue in the final chapter, I am inclined to think that humans are in one boat, affecting, by our choices now, the shape and richness for all of us of a life to come. But we may and often do exclude ourselves from building and enjoying the kingdom on earth.

32. James Gustafson criticizes, on these grounds, the view that God has an option for the poor. He calls it a unitarian view of God. See James M. Gustafson, *Ethics from a Theocentric Perspective,* Vol. 1, *Theology and Ethics* (Chicago: The University of Chicago Press, 1981), p. 25. I shall respond to objections to the partisanship involved in the option for the poor in the last section of this chapter and again in chapter 5.

33. *Jesus,* p. 593. (My italics.)

34. *The Historical Jesus of the Synoptics,* pp. 113–14. Segundo points out that while we assume the rich man was not good nothing in the story tells us that he was not. But, of course, genuinely to 'be good' is to take up the kingdom value by which we are included in it. See footnote 31.

35. Haight, "God and Jesus Christ," *PACE/Professional Approaches for Christian Educators* 17: 95.

36. Ferm, *Third World Liberation Theologies: An Introductory Survey,* p. 118; Dorr, *Option for the Poor,* p. 3.

37. Peter Singer, "All Animals Are Equal," *Animal Rights and Moral Obligations,* eds., Tom Regan and Peter Singer (New Jersey: Prentice-Hall, Inc., 1976), p. 149.

38. When I speak of our concern for ourselves and our friends I am thinking of something personal and very likely unjustified, and not of oppressed people's taking up the cause of their group. The latter, as I have argued, is crucially important.

39. In our world, most deprivation is humanly caused and oppressive. And, of course, that deprivation which is imposed is much more destructive of what makes for full humanity than that which is not. Also, suffering that we and our structures cause is suffering we can do something about. We are looking here for what is the worst-off oppressed group.

40. The integral scale of values is discussed in Bernard Lonergan's *Method in Theology* (New York: The Seabury Press, 1972), chapter two, "The Human Good," pp. 27–55. It is developed by Robert Doran in a way particularly appropriate to liberation theology and to supporting the option for the poor. See Robert M. Doran, *Theology and the Dialectics of History* (Toronto: University of Toronto Press, 1990): chapters four, twelve, thirteen, and fifteen. I select from and develop his views for my purposes in this essay. I agree with Lonergan that the scale represents an ascending order of value but argue that vital values must come first. Using the integral scale of values to develop a criterion for prioritizing human deprivation was suggested to me in 1989 by Thomas Esselman, then a doctoral student at the Toronto School of Theology.

41. Doran claims a universal status for the scale of values and describes it as being an element of 'transcendental anthropology.' I shall not pursue this important issue here whose justification seems to depend on the scale's isomorphism with Lonergan's levels of consciousness. I do not know how to improve on the ambiguous position of the liberationists who, on the one hand, shy away from claims for a positive universal human nature based on transcendental arguments, but who, on the other hand, describe factors of reality which articulate boundaries of possibilities for humans.

42. "Option for the Poor," p. 96.

43. Sobrino points out the relevance of the massiveness of poverty to bringing the option for the poor to the center of ethics. See "Jesus' Relationship with the Poor and Outcasts: Its Importance for Fundamental Moral Theology," trans. Paul Burns in *The Dignity of the Despised of the Earth*, ed. Jacques Pohier and Dietmar Mieth, *Concilium* 130 (1979): 13.

44. Joan Chittister has a useful discussion of Rollo May's five senses of power in *Job's Daughters: Women and Power* (New York: Paulist Press, 1990), pp. 9–51. Interestingly, as well as warning us against exploitative, competitive, and manipulative power, she warns us of how nurturant power, identified as women's power, has been used against women who need to be nurtured as well as to nurture. We could add that this power is used against other oppressed groups such as the colonized and uncolonized people of color. We can conclude that what she describes as integrative power, involving mutual concern, is what all oppressed groups must see come to the fore.

45. Here I am concerned to defend partisanship in *ethics*. In chapter 5 I shall defend partisanship in *theology*. The argument in chapter 5 will show that at a most fundamental level, in all our disciplines and endeavors, humans cannot avoid partisanship. And that argument will serve to underpin the arguments offered here.

46. See *The Liberation of Theology*, pp. 158–65. While I agree with the general thrust of what Segundo is saying regarding Jesus' and humans' limitedness, he applies the law of conservation of energy, a principle which is important to Segundo's thought, too strictly to the psychological and emotional realms. Some people have a capacity, which the rest of us should develop, to show personal caring to those we tend to treat simply in terms of roles. This is possible because love can energize; it can produce the energy to love more.

47. Ibid., pp. 131–33.

48. Ibid., pp. 40–45. The established order is always, inevitably, oppressive to some. It is by definition oppressive to the very poor within it. And, today, as well as being acutely oppressive to the very poor who make up at least 70% of humans, the global order is oppressive to women and people of color who, too, make up most of the human population. . . . But, of course, not every aspect of the established order is oppressive, and not every movement for change is a liberation movement.

49. *A Short History of Ethics*, pp. 68–78, 190–98. Quotation at p. 198. See also MacIntyre's *After Virtue: A Study in Moral Theology,* 2nd edition (Notre Dame, Indiana: University of Notre Dame Press, 1984), for his defense of a basically Aristotelian ethic as appropriate to a historical consciousness.

50. See Baum, "Class Struggle and the Magisterium," pp. 690–701, for a clear discussion of the difference between the sense of class struggle to which Catholic theology traditionally has objected and what he calls the "partial solidarity" which liberationists promote.

See chapter 4 for a more detailed discussion of ends and means and violence.

51. This point is not merely abstract. In the Third World, there is certainly conflict between the powerful and powerless. In Philippine street theater, I have seen the military and politicians portrayed as evil incarnate. But, in the context of some Basic Christian Communities at least, I have had the sense that there is a tendency to want to preach the good news, to include more and more people in the people's struggle. Recently, in a tense situation involving the much feared paramilitary CAFGUs, BCC, and union organizers, a torture victim and myself, my BCC guide, as well as offering cigarettes to the CAFGUs, started singing, "We Shall Overcome" and encouraged all to join!

52. While there are large numbers of poor in many inner cities in the north, it is, of course, in the south where we are struck by the fact that the vast majority of the human race is poor. In a rural area, such as sugar-producing Negros, where BCCs among the poor are very strong, and the rich are very few, one senses that it is the rich who are isolated and excluded from their once-feudal community, from Christianity, and from humanity. It is the poor, although still hungry and dying before their time, who have commitment and direction in their lives. Many of the rich retreat behind private armies and very few move over with the poor.

53. The option for the poor is more than a concretization *for our time,* of the negative contrast experience. Both material poverty and the demands of the paradigm shift have a kind of universality about them. Considering the option in its specific sense, the materially destitute will always be worse off in theory even in the unlikely event that severe material poverty should be eradicated. How massive is their number relates to whether the materially very poor should, concretely, have first priority in reshaping society. As long as there are oppressed people, material poverty is likely to be the first manifestation of their oppression. Considering the option in its generic sense, while no doubt the structure of the paradigm shift that I have described will not prove 'timeless,' now that we see the significance of social conditioning we must see

the central ethical significance of structural change and the need to take sides. Because structures are in constant need of revision in our changing history, but also because they are hard to change, structurally caused oppression will always be a tendency.

3

A Liberationist Ethic Is an Ethic of Social Solidarity

INTRODUCTION

An ethic which emerges out of the negative contrast experience, and which takes as its first concrete imperative the option for the poor, must also be an ethic of social solidarity.

Because the negative contrast experience demands an ethic of resistance to suffering, it demands an ethic which compels us to move outside ourselves and gear ourselves to responding to actual situations of need in the world. Without denying the relevance of intentions and motives, personal integrity and integratedness, this ethic directs intentions and motives toward, and partly defines integrity and integratedness in terms of, action against suffering, deprivation, and oppression in the world. While I may include myself among the suffering, I am but one among many. An ethic of resistance to suffering is fundamentally social in the sense that it primarily involves concern for and responding to the needs of others.

But the negative contrast gives rise to a social ethic in another sense. Schillebeeckx describes it as a social experience emerging out of a social context, an experience had by peoples and historical groups responding to historical situations. He describes how, down through the ages, oppressed groups and their spokespersons have kept alive the struggle for justice and the vision of a concrete salvation defined in terms of the negation of their immediate suffering. Also, in acknowledgment of what today is recognized to be the structural character of social suffering, Schillebeeckx argues explicitly that the productive force of the contrast experience must involve two stages, an immediate even if vague response of resistance followed by a scientific analysis necessary to produce a concrete plan for social action.[1] Basically, the negative contrast experience gives rise to a social response to social suffering in the context of a social hope for social salvation.

Taking up the option for the poor involves responding to the suffering of social groups who are oppressed by unjust social structures. It involves these groups joining together and others joining in solidarity with them in order to transform social structures of oppression. The option for the poor with its Copernican demand for partisanship already presupposes a social ethic with its prior Copernican demand that we acknowledge that structural change cannot come about simply by a summation of personal conversions, that the whole is not merely the sum of parts. Rather, personal conversion is conditioned by the social structural context, and personal ethics must be located within social structural ethics, an ethic which seeks structural change.

But liberationists do not support an ethic of social solidarity just because it is implicit in their fundamental commitment to resist suffering and take up the option for the poor. The empirical situation urgently demands that we respond to poverty, racism, sexism . . . and the situation reveals that this requires changes in economic, political, educational, religious, and other structures, together with culturally inherited attitudes, values, and concepts.

This chapter will explore a liberationist ethic as an ethic of social solidarity. It will begin by investigating liberationists' social interpretation of the kingdom of God. This will bring to the fore material for the social anthropology which liberationists largely presuppose and the social ethic which they do not systematically develop. The chapter will go on to develop an anthropology and ethic of the social individual who is a subject in relation to others and to social structures. Also, it will discuss how personal ethics must be reinterpreted and relocated within a context of an ethic aimed at transforming oppressive structures. Finally, it will argue that an ethic which seeks right relations and liberating structures must be extended to include other species and the environment in their own right.

A SOCIAL INTERPRETATION OF THE KINGDOM OF GOD

To some extent I shall treat the liberationists' interpretation of scripture in this chapter and chapter 4, analogously to the way I treated their discussion of church documents in chapter 2, as a means of bringing out a liberationist ethic and anthropology. But the Christian scripture has an authority for liberationist theologians and for the argument of these chapters. Generally speaking, a liberationist interpretation of scripture is justified.[2]

Appropriate to this chapter's concern with social solidarity, I will concentrate on the kingdom of God,[3] a central symbol for Christian liberationist theologians as, they argue, it was a central symbol for Jesus.

The Kingdom of God Is Central to Liberationist Theology and Is Interpreted as Fundamentally Ethical

Walter Rauschenbusch, whose theology of the social gospel foreshadows the liberation theology of the poor in an uncanny way, stresses perhaps more than anyone else that *the* ethical task is to build the kingdom on earth. Speaking in the early part of the century, out of the context of the dire effects of the industrial revolution in the United States, he describes the need to Christianize the social order, to bring economic, political, and religious structures under God's rule of justice and equality for all.[4] While contemporary liberation theologians reject Rauschenbusch's optimism that social structures can systematically and in a quasi-evolutionary way be Christianized, and while, aware of religious pluralism, they would not speak of Christianizing structures, the kingdom of God has a central place in their theology as well, and the transformation of social structures is at the center of their ethics. But neither Rauschenbusch nor contemporary liberationists make the kingdom of God central to their theology solely because this suits their social concerns. Rather, they argue, the kingdom of God was what was central to Jesus. Jesus was not concerned to legitimate himself, to point to himself as divine; he was concerned to point beyond himself in order to reveal the will of a God of pure positivity who is categorically on the side of humans and against all evil and suffering. And God's will for us is the kingdom of God, a kingdom of justice, peace, freedom, and love where the blind will have sight; the hungry, food; the prisoners, freedom.[5] But Jesus revealed the kingdom as an ethical task as well as an eschatological gift. According to Schillebeeckx: "That this kingdom comes means that God looks to us men and women to make God's 'ruling' operational in our world." Orthopractice is the right conduct of the kingdom.[6] Participating in 'building' the kingdom is really all ethics is about, although ethics is not all the kingdom is about.

From a liberationist perspective, the ethics of the kingdom is central to Christology. The first concern is not with Jesus' ontology, with questions of his divinity *insofar as these are separate from ethical issues*, but with Jesus as revelation of the ethical, as showing us a more humane way of life, as speaking to our experience of unmeaning and suffering, and particularly to the social injustice that weighs down our world. For Segundo, Jesus must be seen first as witness, as one who offers us his life and death to show that the well-being of others, especially those most in need, should be our ultimate value. Exploration of Jesus' divinity must rise out of this and should be considered in terms of the moral norm he lived by and how he lived by it.[7]

The Earthly and Historical Side of the Kingdom of God Is (Re)discovered and Stressed, But the Eschatological Side Is Affirmed

To understand Jesus' preaching of the kingdom as presenting us with an ethical task does not in itself necessitate that the kingdom be seen as genuinely having an earthly and historical side. Jesus' preaching of the kingdom has sometimes been understood as our personal call to perfection so that we may be united with God in heaven. While it was acknowledged that we could not literally merit this union, it was believed that God's graciousness would fall on us if we obeyed certain rules thought to be of God, which often had little to do with improving human lives in history.

This, of course, is diametrically opposed to a liberationist perspective. Schillebeeckx argues that the parables show that a fundamental element of the kingdom message is that our action should reflect God's generosity without any 'right of payment.'[8] For Segundo too, the kingdom is not a reward for morality but, rather, it brings about the fulfillment of basic needs.[9] Liberationists operate from the perspective that the person is mental/physical and historical, so the concrete conditions under which life is lived in this world really matter, and any promise of a kingdom to come is only credible or even meaningful within a context of some glimmering of it in history. Jesus' preaching and practice involves the healing of those suffering physical and mental torment, the befriending of society's 'untouchables,' and the unmasking of a profoundly oppressive religiosity. Jesus' revelation is a call, an imperative, for humans to act so that God's kingdom may come by God's will being done on earth. *The* basic moral question becomes what can we do to bring about the kingdom of God *in history*.[10] This involves, by God's power, our bringing the social order under God's reign. And, finally, there is an intrinsic connection between what we do in history and what the character of the eschaton will be.[11] Liberationists are not reductionist.[12] The relationship between history and eschatology, between historical liberation and final salvation, is central to their discussion.

The Kingdom of God Is Fundamentally Social and Political; Our Contribution Requires Both Personal Conversion and Structural Change

The very notion of a kingdom is social and structural. When we reflect on the words and actions of Jesus, however—that the kingdom involves making the hungry to be fed, the prisoners to be set free, sinners and all forms of outcasts to be befriended, religiously sanctioned oppression to be unmasked, and all forms of lording it over another to be abolished—we see that they embody a fundamentally social imperative to resist suffering and to change our personal relationships and the structures in which they are embedded toward the end of community based on equality.

No one would deny that Jesus preached personal conversion. But the personal conversion that he preached was to social concern. Gutiérrez points out that, in teaching us to "leave father and mother," Jesus was encouraging us to break out of our cultural milieu in order to go out to those in need.[13] Segundo argues that examples such as Jesus' dialogue with the rich aristocrat (Luke 18:18–23) and his parable of the rich man and Lazarus (Luke 16:19–31) show that the kingdom cannot be good news for the rich; they cannot be included in the kingdom, until and unless they are converted to the communal values of the kingdom.[14]

But Jesus' preaching and practice of the kingdom involved not only his 'going around doing good,' but also his explicitly challenging the evil within his own Jewish community, particularly the oppressive politico-religious structures and those who held them in place. Jesus objected to the religious leaders' interpretation and use of the Mosaic Law. Rather than treat the law for the sake of human flourishment, they used it to give themselves power and status and to marginalize the people. They did this by stressing the intricacies of the law, which the common people did not know and so did not abide by. Thus the poor were seen as 'sinners'—and this justified their being poor.[15]

The Kingdom Requires Agape or Altruism

Liberation theologians, in common with the whole Christian tradition, understand Jesus' revelation of the practice of the kingdom as involving selfless love, acting for others. Jesus' entire life shows that God's rule for God's kingdom is essentially about "compassionate dedication" to others. For Schillebeeckx, this constitutes the sign of the breaking through of the kingdom. And because Jesus "set no limits to his sacrifice for the suffering of others" but died for having gone around doing good, "the heart of the New Testament message" centers around "suffering through and for others as an expression of the unconditional validity of a pattern of doing good and resisting evil and suffering." If resisting suffering and doing good for others are the kingdom's values, then suffering for the sake of others will be an inevitable consequence of helping to bring it about.[16] For Segundo too, Jesus' ultimate moral and religious criterion was to remedy human suffering, to respond to the needs of others. And Jesus' death is the logical conclusion of his life of 'doing good' for others.[17]

The Kingdom of God Is for All But It Is Shaped to Respond to the Needs of the Poor and Oppressed, the Outcasts

The kingdom Jesus lived rejects every form of domination of one human over another. Jesus "de-classed" himself by eating with sinners and tax collectors. He attempted to communicate with society's outcasts in order to remove their isolation. But more than this, he tried to alleviate the suffering of and bring into community the poor, the sick, and those who were publicly classified as sinners, "all who in the society of Judaism at the time were shut off from fellowship with their Jewish kin, barred from the table of Pharisee or Essene."[18] We begin to see that while Jesus engaged in selfless giving as a means, the goal of his self-sacrifice was community based on reciprocal giving and receiving, mutuality.

For liberationists the Beatitudes are key to showing who the kingdom is especially for: the poor, the hungry, the sorrowful. And Jesus' practice shows that this must be taken literally, not spiritualized to, for example, the poor in spirit. The kingdom is shaped especially to include the excluded. Thus, we can see the social character of the kingdom in a new way. It is defined by who it is especially for, and who it is especially for are the poor, the oppressed, the outcast. But what about the nonpoor? Segundo distinguishes the disciples, who are committed to the liberation of the poor, from the rich, the dominant ones, who have not been converted to the cause of the poor. For the latter, the kingdom of God is bad news and can be made to be good news only if they change their values to those of the kingdom.[19] This is not to deny that the kingdom is for all. The unconverted simply exclude themselves; the kingdom is not what they want. They are dis-connected from, not appropriately related to, others in community.

The Symbol of the Kingdom of God Is Utopian

Gutiérrez argues that Jesus' announcement of the kingdom "reveals to society itself the aspiration for a just society and leads it to discover unsuspected dimensions and unexplored paths."[20] In other words, as Jesus reveals our humanity to ourselves, as he, in his person, brings to some determinateness what most of us have barely and only vaguely sought, so too he reveals the glimmering of a just, loving, and egalitarian society which we recognize as what we have always really wanted.[21] Also, Jesus' announcement of the kingdom, as an articulation of what we have always aspired to and of what is possible for us and of what is beyond what is possible for us, that is, as a goal and a vision, draws and even jolts us into discovering "unsuspected dimensions," such as the dimensions of reciprocal and selfless relationship and of our being subjects of history, dimensions which are hidden by the sense we have of the naturalness of hierarchy, competitiveness, and greed in human relationships. And Jesus' announcement of the kingdom leads us to discover "unexplored paths," new ways of living which are more in keeping with the vision of the kingdom. The kingdom as utopian captures the hope and promise that it brings; it captures our power to contribute to its coming and also the limitation on our power.

This view of the kingdom as utopian, as visionary, as what we can understand and so aspire to but cannot achieve, yet as guiding what we value and how we live our value, is challenged by the view that Jesus' preaching and practice of the kingdom must be reinterpreted in light of the fact that the parousia that he was expecting imminently did not arrive. It has been argued that because, for Jesus, the parousia was imminent, he was not concerned with social change in this world but only with personal conversion in order that we may merit admittance to another, heavenly, world. And this view has been used to soften the radicalness of Jesus' message, demonstrated both by the way he lived, going around doing good without concern for society's norms and securities, and by the advice he gave to others, such as to the young rich man, to give up all he owned and follow Jesus.[22]

Segundo responds that the logic of Jesus' life is inconsistent with the view that Jesus believed the end was near. An urgent situation leads to radical but also simple behavior which does not look to long-term results or consequences. But Jesus' preaching and practice were remarkably complex. He sought not only to change people's deeds but their hearts and values, their concepts, and their ways of perceiving their world. Jesus sought to unmask the most subtle kind of lie against humanity, the claim that humans are not equal before God, and, with this, he sought the most fundamental kind of structural change in the politico-religious Jewish law. And he engaged in a complex conflict with the religious authorities toward this end.[23]

A Social Interpretation of the Kingdom of God Involves a Social Anthropology and Ethic: A Summary

By giving the kingdom of God a social interpretation, liberationists stress its connection with the social order in history and with social ethics. Central to Jesus' practice of the kingdom was a very personal attempt to mend and reshape personal relations. He sought to break down hierarchy and privilege, by including the excluded, the outcasts such as the poor, sick, disabled, possessed, women, foreigners. . . . He did so by curing, socializing over meals, talking theology with them, in short, by befriending them. Jesus' ethic was thus fundamentally outward looking; it valued compassion and building relations of justice, solidarity, equality, and mutuality among all humans, especially the most marginalized. But Jesus also directly challenged the politico-religious structures of his Jewish community which gave the religious leaders power, prestige, and wealth and which oppressed the common people. It was for this that Jesus was executed.

The social interpretation of the kingdom reveals a social anthropology, an anthropology for which we are essentially in relation to other humans and to social structures and institutions. But it also stresses the need for personal conversion to social concern. We are social individuals. Because the social interpretation of the kingdom is both an ethical task to change our personal relations and the structures in which they are embedded, to change the world, and also an eschatological gift whereby our very performing of the ethical task gives us grounds for hope, not only for our future in history, but also for the future of all humans beyond history, the social interpretation of the kingdom reveals that we are fundamentally not mere minds or bodies, but mental/physical.

AN ANTHROPOLOGY OF THE SOCIAL INDIVIDUAL

Liberation theologians, together with most other twentieth-century thinkers, reject the notion of a human nature as a fixed essence which is independent of historical context and from which we can read off the limits of knowledge and goals of morality. While some sort of anthropology is necessary for and implicit in every ethic and theology, we must ask how is any anthropology possible for a perspective within which historical consciousness and a certain degree of relativity must be respected? This section will argue that our historicity demands a historical anthropology, one which seeks the permanent features of our historicity while, at the same time, accounting for change in our concrete anthropology. Happily, we shall find that features of our historical connectedness coincide with features of our social connectedness. Indeed, from a liberationist perspective we must see ourselves as social individuals. The section will go on to consider central features of the social individual: humans as mental/physical, in relation to others, and in relation to social structures and institutions.

Aspects of a Structure for a Historically Conscious Anthropology

Humans are fundamentally social, historical, and situated freedoms, who are conditioned by and who condition our world. But recognition of this is a recent phenomenon. Because we are fundamentally reflectively conscious, and interpret, evaluate, and act out of this reflectiveness, new awareness does not simply mean coming to know what we did not know but what was always true. It involves the emergence of a new consciousness, the possibility of new choices, in part, of a new humanity. But because this new awareness is also the acknowledgment of an opportunity newly offered by reality for a human capacity newly discovered but experienced as already there, it has the character of our becoming ourselves and not merely something different from what we were before.[24]

In line with this, Schillebeeckx argues that critical reason has only recently come to recognize that it must be self-critical and must take its own historical circumstances into account, that critical reason itself is influenced by its context. And, for this reason, we can only have what he calls anthropological constants, and not a fixed notion of a human nature, to guide reason's critical ethical task.[25]

Schillebeeckx articulates seven constants which include our relationship to our body and nature, to other humans, to social structures and institutions, and to our spatio-temporal context, and which involve the interplay between theory and practice, a commitment to the basic goodness of life, and, finally, the synthesis of all of these. He describes these as a system of co-ordinates necessary for *personal identity within social culture*.[26] While this fits perfectly the needs of an anthropology of the social individual, it is equally important that, although Schillebeeckx does not point this out, his constants capture conditions of our historicity that are necessary for the guidance of reason's critical ethical task in the context of our not having a fixed human nature. *Our very strategy for resolving how there can be an anthropology in the context of historical consciousness—by articulating permanent features of our historicity—also yields an anthropology of the social individual.* Looking at permanent features of our historicity is, in large part, looking at permanent features of our relationality and sociability. This is so because historicity involves a connectedness of interdependence while ahistoricity involves an isolated independence.

In ethics, we must always take anthropological constants into account. They provide outer boundaries, constitutive conditions, possibilities of and limitations on human living. They point to "permanent human impulses" and "spheres of value." To ignore these constants is to undermine what is necessary for our flourishment and our very survival. But while they must guide our ethical decision-making, precisely because they are permanent, and our historical context is changing, they cannot provide us directly with concrete norms for action.[27]

Turning to the actual constants that Schillebeeckx articulates, we see immediately that our relationship to our bodies and to nature provides both possibilities and limitations on what we can do to live and to live a truly human life. It is because we are fundamentally related to our body, that is, that we are mental/physical, that we are also essentially in this world, in matter, and require other humans, social structures and institutions, and a spatio-temporal context. We need these things in order to develop as human subjects who have a political and economic and cultural history, who are in history. All of these necessary conditions of our humanity can, in their concrete expressions, oppress as well as liberate, but because we can change them we can make them liberate. The interplay between our practicing and theorizing is our means of genuinely developing as a society, changing what is oppressive while retaining what is liberative; it is our means of learning both from our tradition and from our new experience; it is our means of making meaning and making history. Faith in the goodness of human life, that we can make it better but that it is not all up to us, involves a faith in history and often in something beyond history; this faith is necessary to provide the hope that we need in order to struggle to make all the other relationships liberative. And, finally, the importance of seeing the synthesis of all of these constants as itself a constant is to show that a truly human existence, human wholeness, requires that we recognize the interdependence of all of these in our ethical decision-making; none can systematically override the others and none can be reduced out.[28]

Until fairly recently, we would not have thought that most of Schillebeeckx's constants were fundamental to our anthropology. So it is appropriate to ask how Schillebeeckx arrives at and justifies his constants. His method is eclectic. Within a context of endnotes which refer, in effect, to the intellectual preunderstanding of our age, his text appeals both to experience and to reason by combining phenomenological description and conceptual argument into a systematized whole. Ultimately he encourages us to 'see' the social conditions necessary to our flourishment and to our very survival as a disclosure of our everyday experience in the world.

Also, he clearly makes use of the negative criterion in drawing up his list. While Schillebeeckx does not include the negative contrast experience among his anthropological constants, we have seen that he treats it as a central permanent human impulse and value. However, it belongs to a different category from the constants just discussed. It guides critical reason in identifying other anthropological constants. The environmental crisis has forced us to see the moral relevance of our relationship to nature. World poverty and other forms of social injustice have made us see the moral relevance of our relationship to social structures and institutions, and so on. We do not arrive at and justify the negative contrast experience itself as an anthropological constant by abstract argument. Rather, we come to see it, and, with it, the hope that goodness will prevail, as a permanent "anthropological projection," through the stories of the experience of suffering and salvation that are passed down from one generation to another.[29] The history of human experience can give us knowledge of anthropological constants. And given our historicity and the rather ad hoc manner in which we arrive at anthropological constants, we must remain open to their expansion.[30] While we can validly articulate constant features of our historicity, different features will be in focus at different times and our articulation of them may change.[31]

But is Schillebeeckx's eclectic, partly inductively based method of gathering a list of anthropological constants acceptable? Can an appeal to transient experience justify a claim to anthropological constants with permanent validity? Segundo comments, perhaps surprisingly, that to establish necessary conditions of our experience requires a transcendental deduction, something which Schillebeeckx suggests does not convince us because it does not move us.[32] In fact, however, philosophers have used transcendental arguments, moving from the given in experience such as that we are self-conscious, to a necessary condition for this, that we are language-users or conscious of others, in order to demonstrate the necessity of Schillebeeckx's second and third constants, our essential relatedness to other persons and to institutions.[33] And these arguments provide some of the background of contemporary thought on which Schillebeeckx partly relies.[34] Transcendental arguments draw clear logical or conceptual connections between what we know with certainty and what this presupposes. And it is appropriate that they should *support* Schillebeeckx's looser, broader, more phenomenological and empirically based approach, by which he collects a number of connected constants. But because even our concepts and their relationships with other concepts change through time and on the basis of new experience, and because new problems require revised focusing, transcendental arguments cannot *replace* the Schillebeeckxian type of approach which explicitly makes room for expansion and revision.

The Human Is a Social Individual

The Enlightenment encouraged a view of the human as strictly individual, a unique and independent center of consciousness who is unfettered by essential bodily attachment, whose rationality is histori- cally unbiased, who is self-legislating, unrestrictedly free and responsi- ble, and who has absolute value. Twentieth-century awareness of cultural relativity, of how, across space and time, groups express radi- cally different beliefs, values, and conceptual frameworks, has led some thinkers to conclude that, excluding a hereditary biology, humans are only social and socially changing constructions, and psy- chological life is but a conditioned response to stimuli. For this view, humans are not genuinely free and responsible. Liberationists reject both of these extreme positions. For them, humans are fundamentally social individuals. We are not reducible to mind or body as for the other two views but are genuinely mental/physical, essentially related to one another and conditioned by, yet able to transform, social struc- tures. From this perspective human power, freedom, and responsibility are limited but real.

Thus, for the atomistic agent of the Enlightenment, liberation is not necessary; this person is already liberated. For the social construct of the twentieth century, liberation is not possible; this person cannot be freed. Only for the social individual who is restrictedly free and can transform oppressive conditions into liberating ones is liberation rele- vant.

Retaining Schillebeeckx's order, we shall look in more detail at three elements of the anthropology of the social individual: our relat- edness to our bodies, to other humans, and to social structures and institutions. All three have emerged from our discussion of the king- dom of God. And all three are deeply relevant to ethics.

The Social Individual Is Fundamentally Mental / Physical

Feminist theologians object to mind/body dualism on grounds of its oppressing women, who have been identified with the "inferior" side of the dualism, body, while men have been identified with mind. But also, feminists argue, to understand our anthropology in terms of this dualism falsifies what we are. Indeed, we can argue, that we are mental/physical is actually presupposed in our being social individu- als. It is also presupposed in the theology of grace and the concern for what happens in this world which Vatican II encouraged. And it is defended by philosophers who, in our century, have attempted to put to rest Cartesian dualism and the skepticism that goes with it. Because this issue is so fundamental to ethics and theology, and because theologians, like Schillebeeckx himself in his discussion of anthropological constants, normally rely on and do not draw out the arguments of philosophers, it is worth reviewing some of what they say here.

Descartes argued that, because he could know directly and infallibly that he exists as a thinking thing and because he could know, only through an argument for a nondeceiving God, that bodies and, through them, other minds exist, he, as a thinking thing, must exist independently of every body and of other minds. What he could know in separation could exist in separation. The private, personal, internal self is different from and ontologically independent of the public, social, external world including the human body. Speech is but the outward physical expression of an inner mental thought which is transmitted to another and, hopefully, stimulates that other to have a similar thought.[35]

The overwhelming twentieth-century retort has been that while Descartes may have reflected on the contents and even the operations of his mind independently of reference to matter, he could not have had the thoughts he did, for example, "I am a thinking thing," independent of his intersubjective context. Why? Because language is required for the sort of thinking Descartes was engaged in and language is essentially public, dialogical, and interactive. To take the now classic example of Wittgenstein's private language argument, in order for words to mean something they must retain a consistent meaning. Otherwise words can mean anything, which is nothing. But then, due to fallible memory, I cannot simply decide what words will mean for me. Language cannot be merely an outward expression of an inner thought because meaning must be public. So neither Cartesian dualism nor the skepticism with respect to other minds that it yields can get off the ground.[36]

While Wittgenstein's private language argument is regularly relied upon to support the view that our subjectivity depends upon our intersubjectivity, some have interpreted him as a behaviorist, reducing mental states to bodily processes. P. F. Strawson offers a somewhat parallel argument to that of Wittgenstein but it is designed to show that we are 'logically primitively' mental/physical. He argues that to be self-conscious I must be able to ascribe states of consciousness to myself. But to be able to ascribe states to myself I must be able to ascribe them to others. Why? If all psychological states available to me were mine, then I would have no need to and would, in fact, be unable to distinguish them as mine. But, if the availability of others is necessary to my becoming self-conscious, then others as subjects and not merely as bodies must be identifiable to me, must be publicly identifiable. This requires that psychological states and physical characteristics be ascribed to the very same identifiable, therefore mental/physical self, not the former to a mind and the latter to a body. And the relationship between private states and public behavior cannot simply be causal and contingent, as for Descartes, but must be one of much closer interdependence.[37]

But while these arguments attempt to show that we are essentially mental/physical, we can still ask what does this really mean? One thing it means, coming out of Strawson's discussion, is that we start out in life feeling/thinking/intending // behaving, and only later do we learn to separate private feelings, thoughts, and intentions from public behavior, so that we can behave differently from the way we think or feel. But our power even to do this is limited. I can learn not to cry when I am in pain. There is a real gap between pain feeling and pain behavior. But this is not so with some of our more subtle psychological states such as depression and jealousy. While I may know that I am depressed or jealous by how I feel, another can know I am in these states by how I behave. Behavior as well as feeling is constitutive of what depression and jealousy are so others can correct my interpretation.[38]

If we are to reject a radical distinction between the sacred and the secular, if we are to recognize that our historical life, what we do and what we suffer, really matter, then we must understand ourselves as mental/physical. And the implications of this for ethics are enormous. Our knowledge, intentionality, freedom, power, responsibility are all embodied and therefore limited or restricted. But for this very reason, as I shall discuss later, the sphere in which they operate, and so the scope of our moral concern, is greatly extended.

The Social Individual Is a Subject in Relation to Others

Gutiérrez and other liberation theologians speak of the poor as nonpersons. But Gutiérrez goes on to say that he does not mean this ontologically but rather that the poor are not treated as persons, and are made to feel that they are not persons.[39] While philosophers are concerned about logically necessary conditions for being a person, a reflective subject, liberationists are most concerned about empirical conditions for concretely flourishing as a subject. But the distinction is not a completely sharp one. Language use is necessary for personhood in the philosophical sense; articulateness and the opportunity to express oneself are necessary for one's concretely affirming oneself as a person. The discussion of our relatedness to others will move between these two levels.

Soelle tells of two German women, a city woman who has possessions but who is isolated and so is "reduced to" her individuality and to immanence, and a country woman who enjoys self-transcendence and meaningfulness due to her connectedness with family, church, and, through these, with the world and its problems. Soelle moves us from the discussion of the need to be language users in order to be self-conscious subjects, to the need to be genuinely communicative in order to flourish and be in right relation with others. She identifies isolation with muteness and an inability to focus on, understand, and express our situation, with apathy, an inability to act for change, and, simply, with being oppressed. She identifies connectedness or right relations with the ability to attend to and express, if necessary to lament then protest, our situation, and with political action, solidarity, and liberation.[40] Also, Soelle and other feminists move discussion beyond connecting our fundamental relatedness with one another to language, with its implicit emphasis on cognition, to connecting our relatedness to love. Beverly Harrison speaks of our creating one another by touching and seeing and hearing each other into life.[41] And, of course, how we touch one another will determine the quality of our lives. We experience how our productivity in our work, our capacity to respond sensitively to others, our sense of our own worth, and many other things, shift, sometimes dramatically, as we move from context to context, from one set of personal and institutional and perhaps cultural relationships to another. Not only are we created by our relationships but we are recreated by our changing relationships.

We can deepen both our understanding of our relatedness with other humans and also our understanding of suffering and the negative contrast experience if we consider the connection between them. While the experiences of suffering and salvation are profoundly personal, they are also social. *Oppressive suffering involves a break in, or failure to make, right relations*, the relations which characterize the kingdom of God. This affects not only those who are ostensibly suffering, but it affects all of us whether we recognize it or not. So, while we may respond to another's suffering just because that other is suffering, we are also responding to the need of the community and our own need.

We are bound by a fundamental solidarity with one another. We can compare the human community to a net knotted at each intersection; if one knot breaks, all that the net contains, the good life we have created, begins to fall away.[42] The community is called to direct its energies in an intensified way to those who are suffering, to mend the break in right relation for the sake of the suffering but also for the sake of the community of which each member is a part. Those who respond to others' suffering, who give, even if they do it solely for the sake of the other, will also, as a consequence, receive, both in the very act of giving and from those with whom they are making connection. Thus our relationality involves us in an ongoing process of giving and receiving. It involves mutuality as well as altruism. And this giving and receiving in mutuality, together with our being bound by solidarity, presuppose a fundamental equality which we ought to respect. Relationships of hierarchy and dominance are profoundly wrong relationships.[43]

The Social Individual Is a Subject of History: Social Structures and the Human Subject

The view that we are conditioned by social structures and institutions but can, within limits, change them, is central to the various liberation movements and to a liberationist ethic. A central aim of these movements and this ethic is to transform oppressive structures into liberating ones. We may begin to understand our essential relatedness to social structures and institutions by considering where did culture and tradition, where did our political and economic structures, where did the values and attitudes which support these structures, where did our language and conceptual framework all come from?

There is something of a 'chicken and egg' situation here. While the human individual is, partially, but essentially, constituted by culture, the various cultures, together with their structures and institutions, are clearly humanly produced. However, we may begin by imagining a desert island situation[44] where two individuals from radically different cultures learn to predict each other's actions, to acquire habits, and play roles vis-à-vis one another. They thus create a stable context of everyday life which frees them to attend to new and more complex issues. They pass on to their children what they have habitualized, that the man hunts and the woman cooks, for example. But because the children do not know the origins of these habitualized actions, they experience them as involving the natural, objective, unalterable, way of things for men and women. An institution has been formed which conditions the younger generation.

Because social structures become self-legitimating and take on a life of their own, they very often outlive their usefulness. Women may remain in the role of 'cook' after men have moved from hunter to politician or businessman. Also, these structures may extend, automatically, into spheres for which they were not intended. Women may be associated not only with cooking but with all the needs of the home and may be discouraged or even prevented from seeking work outside. Thus, liberating structures can become oppressive. And because they will be secured by theories to justify them, such as that men are hunters and politicians because they are aggressive and women cook because they are passive, the oppression is internalized.

Once in place, it is difficult to get rid of oppressive structures for at least four reasons: Their oppressive quality is hidden; it is easier to go along with them than to make the enormous effort it would take to change them; it is in the interest of those who have the most power to change them, to support them instead, so as to keep their privilege intact; and, even if a group is prepared to make the effort for change, it is often not clear how to go about it. But humans produce, and maintain, and so with the help of the social sciences, can change their social conditions.

However, while there is a tendency for liberating structures to become oppressive, we cannot live as humans outside of a context of social structures and institutions, society and tradition. Our very capacity to transcend our immediate situation so that we can see its relativity, think critically about it, and become active subjects of an ever-changing history, depends on our being conditioned by institutions, shaped by a tradition. But tradition does not simply pass down what it has learned, that is, its own solutions to problems; through social example, we learn how to learn, how to solve new problems in new contexts, how to criticize and improve on what society has taught us.[45]

Because our social conditions can serve to oppress or to liberate and because we bring them about, sustain them, inherit them, and pass them on to future generations, and because we can transform them, the implications for ethics are enormous. Indeed, because every aspect of our lives is contextualized by social structures, personal ethics must be understood within the context of structural ethics.[46]

Conclusion

It is crucial for the liberationist that we hold together our sociability and our individuality, our conditionedness and freedom, our relatedness and autonomy, and our public and private sides. Liberation only makes sense in the context of our being social individuals. And it is not mere individuals but social individuals, individuals for whom a context of embodiment, relations with other individuals, and social structures, are constitutive, who are in need of liberation. But anthropology cannot be separated from ethics because our being ethical is central to what we are. As social individuals, we are committed to respecting the embodied subject, forming right relations with others, and transforming oppressive structures into liberative ones.

AN ETHIC OF SOCIAL SOLIDARITY

This section will explore implications for ethics of our being social individuals, particularly of our being individuals in personal relations with others and in relation to social structures and institutions. It will consider how structural ethics, an ethic demanded by our relationship to social structures and institutions, is related to the ethics of personal relations, what we have always taken ethics to be about. Finally, it will look at the ethical implications of our relatedness to other species and the environment. We shall see that all ethics, including personal ethics, is social ethics and all, including the environment, should be included as objects of ethical concern.

Right Human Relations: Altruism and Mutuality

The Significance of Altruism

In our Western tradition there has been a broad tendency to associate evil or unethical behavior with greed, with taking for ourselves at the expense of others. And there has been a tendency to associate good or ethical behavior with love, with giving to others even and especially when it is at our own expense. In the context of this culturally inherited intuition, it is surprising how, while the great Western philosophical ethical theories oppose greed, important ones do not stress altruism. For Aristotle, respect for the mean ensures against greed; for

Kant, treating others as we wish to be treated does the same. But stressing the good of others at our expense would involve self-harm for Aristotle and unfairness to ourselves for Kant. Yet the events and stories which move us to experience goodness tell of selfless love. Seeking true happiness or to fulfill duty may be difficult, may force us to transcend our immediate desire, but these seem disappointing in the face of selfless giving. They seem to be self-interested or, at least, self-involved. The transcendence ethics requires is that of moving beyond the wants, needs, and duties of self in order to serve the other for her or his sake. All traditional understandings of the story of Jesus take this to be central. He went out to those who were most in need and who, in terms of the goods and securities and prestiges of this world, had the least to offer and, for this, for demonstrating agape, he suffered rejection, torture, and death.

It would seem that a liberationist ethic, because it is committed to responding to suffering, especially that of the worst off, must be based on altruism.[47] The world situation and the liberationist commitment demand it. Also, our social anthropology supports it. As put by H. Richard Niebuhr, moral value is not to be found strictly within ourselves; not, for example, in the relationship between our actuality and potential as it is for Aristotle, but in how we relate to others. My physical, intellectual, psychological, and moral development is of value primarily for others and only secondarily for myself.[48] So we are morally obliged to respond to the need of the other, not only in our action but in the very ways in which we develop our person. Somewhat like Niebuhr, but responding to Kant rather than Aristotle, Segundo argues that value is not to be found in things or persons in themselves but in their usefulness or "fruit." Therefore, we ought to understand ourselves, not as ends but as means in the service of humanity's full humanization.[49] Schillebeeckx connects altruism with our anthropology when he says "'Being a human for the other' is a task as it were sketched into the structure of our 'human constitution.'"[50]

Altruism and Mutuality

In line particularly with feminist thought we must be critical of a number of tendencies in the traditional Christian view of agape. We must be critical of a tendency to draw a sharp distinction between agape and Eros, the former involving a radically disinterested love, a practice of charity toward the unlovable because they are valued by

God, and the latter involving felt love for one's family, nation, race. . . . This distinction has been held to be ethically important because only disinterested practice, and not feeling and the practice that arises out of feeling, can be commanded, freely given. Eros, felt love, has been associated with sexual and maternal instincts, compulsion not freedom, unjust favoritism toward those one identifies as one's own, not a love which can be universally offered. But a radical distinction between Eros and agape reflects a radical distinction between body and mind, a genuine ability to detach ourselves from feeling and an inability to extend feeling to "the unlovable."

One manifestation of an agapeic love radically separated from Eros is captured in the 'Lone Ranger' image, the solitary and invincible hero who, often in dramatic and daring ways, saves others, but never needs saving 'him'-self. Theologians do not always distinguish between two views of the solitary hero: the hero who acts primarily for his own sake, in order to be virtuous or dutiful or Christ-like, and the hero who genuinely acts for the sake of the other. While the former is a distortion of what anyone could genuinely mean by agape, some feminists caution against the latter as well, on grounds that it involves the love of the strong for the weak and is patronizing.[51]

But even more, we are cautioned about the love of the weak, a view of Christian love as self-sacrifice which has been preached by men, who have seen selfishness as the arch-sin, and which has been practiced by women, not only at enormous cost but at utter harm to ourselves and to our very development as subjects. The point here is that *a universal ethic of self-sacrifice in a context of radical inequality will legitimate, indeed sacralize, oppression.* Clearly, however, this also completely distorts what could plausibly be advocated by an ethic based on altruism. Again, we must make a distinction, which may be captured by that between self-sacrifice and self-transcendence. The former involves the forfeiting of a free, responsible, self-determined self; the latter involves moving out from and beyond that self to serve the genuine needs of others. The former invites a master-slave relationship; the latter rejects it. Here is where it becomes important to insist that the sin of passivity, self-erasure, and masochism be placed alongside aggression, greed, and sadism, as central to ethics. And, as we have mentioned before, this is not to blame but to empower the oppressed to seek and demand a world in which all can flourish and contribute.

Some feminist theologians want to replace selfless giving in its best sense with mutuality, as our central understanding of agape and our ethical goal. Mutual love involves both giving and receiving on the part of both parties, based on recognition of an equality which is not complementary, not subject to stereotypical role-play. This is the love that builds community, and it is community and neither heroic nor self-destructive self-sacrifice which should be the Christian aim. Why? Because this is appropriate to what we are, embodied subjects, who "touch and see and hear each other into life" and so are fundamentally in relation and are not detached egos or anti-egos.[52] Also, it is appropriate to our understanding of Jesus, who aimed at building community and developing right relations when he reached out to the marginalized, denounced privilege, and insisted that the Law be interpreted according to the criterion of human welfare. He did not die for the sake of self-sacrifice but he accepted death for the sake of community.

To justify decentering altruism in favor of mutuality it is sometimes argued that the occasions of sacrifice are but "symptoms of disruptions in primordial harmony,"[53] the exception to the rule. Contrary to this, I have argued in line with Soelle and liberation theologians of the poor that we are starting from a position of disharmony, of an already damaged humanum and cosmos, so that ethics must begin by responding to negativity and must put those who are worst off first. In my view, this is correct. Poverty, racism, and sexism, which involve acute denial of material resources, power, and dignity, demand our first ethical response, a response which must be one of equalizing in order that truly mutual relationships can become possible. But only a few will respond. So the demand for sacrifice on the part of those few will be enormous. But the call to altruism in order to overcome oppression is not elitist; saints and heroes emerge from among the oppressed as well as from the dominant groups. Neither is it individualistic; it involves solidarity. In fact, *through consideration of what is involved in solidarity, we can begin to understand the connection between altruism and mutuality and between agape and Eros.*

In order to overcome the need for the radical distinction between Eros and agape we must show that we can extend felt love to those the tradition called "unlovable" or, more relevant to us, to the outcast, the marginalized. In fact, we can do so by engaging in the kind of solidarity that brings us into direct contact with the oppressed. This kind of solidarity with, say, the poor on the part of the nonpoor involves a being-with the poor, listening, learning, living with, joining in their suffering and oppression and struggle. The felt love that cannot help but emerge will form the affective base which is necessary for genuinely seeing from the point of view of the poor, and will form the passion for deep and lasting commitment to act for their upliftment. Also, when right practice and understanding are rooted in felt love, our ethicity is integrated. Something similar can be said of men in relation to women. It simply is not true that men have had "direct contact" with and have loved women all along; to be in touch with women and to love us is to join us in our struggle toward our own flourishing and the possibility of truly mutual relationships with men. Members of oppressed groups also, through an opening up of feeling, can love themselves and one another in a new solidarity to overcome oppression. And oppressed groups can extend their felt love to "the enemy," especially, of course, to those who, from the "enemy" ranks, wish to join in solidarity with them.[54] In the fullest sense, solidarity involves friendship, each party coming to truly experience the other as a subject with dignity and deserving of respect, as one for whom not only concern but liking is felt, and where the quality of giving and receiving, making community, is based on individual gifts and not on socially conditioned roles. Solidarity demands altruism as a means to equalization, but it aims at and may become a relationship of mutuality.

Altruism, Mutuality, and the Social Individual

In contexts of acute inequality between groups, altruism is required in order for equalizing to go on and mutuality to become possible. The need for altruism is accentuated by the fact that, inevitably, in these contexts only a few will make the effort for change and many, including most of those with the power to effect change, will resist this effort. But is altruism essentially involved in mutuality? How are we to understand mutuality?

When we think of a relationship of give and take, perhaps what first comes to mind is a selfish and manipulative arrangement where each party attempts to give less and take more. Or, perhaps we think of a measured, contractual arrangement of giving and receiving in equal portions for the sake of self-protection or even for the sake of justice. These perspectives are related to a view of the human as basically self-contained, atomic, the view for which the solitary cowboy is hero. These do not capture mutuality, but neither does the reduction of the individual to a mere means to the end of relationality or a mere part of a greater whole, reminiscent of the image of the self-sacrificing woman. In seeking to understand mutuality we must respect the human as a social individual for whom both relationality and autonomy are fundamental. And to do this, it seems, we must start not with my autonomous self nor with the goal of relationality but with the other whom I recognize as independent of me and yet in relation to me. Mutuality requires someone's taking an initiative, taking a risk, giving of self, not for one's own sake or for the sake of the relationship as such but for the sake of the other, with mutuality as a hoped-for further consequence. This is the only way in which we can hold together our sociability and our individuality. To place myself first is to lose relationality; to place relationship first is to lose the autonomy of the individual. But to place the other first is to acknowledge the other as an individual in relation to me.

But, while selfless giving is unconditional in the sense of its not demanding reward, if it is misused by the recipient, used to dominate, then obviously it must be retracted. Even when a mutuality of receiving and giving simply fails to develop, often we should move on, not because we are not getting an equal measure for what we are giving—often within a relationship there are periods where one party must give much more than the other—but if a relationship of reciprocity fails to develop at all, it is likely that our giving is inefficacious, not, in fact, responding to need any more than it is building right relation. Also, however, in very many cases my action is not directed primarily toward building right relations between myself and another but among others, so I will look for the efficaciousness of my actions in the relationships among others.

Mutuality, then, involves mutual self-giving, altruism on the part of all of those attempting to build relationship. It involves receiving as well, but even this involves a form of giving, an appreciation of and joy in the other. Altruism is a means to serve the other and the end of mutuality or a community of equals. And this is important. It is not something I seek as an end in itself. But altruism does have a certain ultimacy about it.

An extreme example, described by Schillebeeckx, indicates this. He tells of a soldier who refuses an order to kill a hostage condemned to die for his religious beliefs, although the soldier knows that this will mean not only the hostage but he too will be killed. Recognizing its gratuitousness, Schillebeeckx argues that the soldier's act expresses a fundamental respect for the other, a faith in the humanum, a conviction of the rightness of justice, a conviction that good is good and will prevail.[55]

We can add that an act of altruism, which is also an act of solidarity, itself can provide grounds for the hope that goodness will prevail. Why? It seems that selfless giving so conflicts with the way of the world as we experience it, becomes so impossible when we try to purify our motives in its direction, that it always comes as a surprise, as something gratuitous and free, whether we are its recipients, observers, or even its agents. When we find ourselves the agents of selfless giving, we still experience it as gift, as "this is not me acting but another acting in me." *In a world crushed by oppression, to be the agent, recipient, or observer to selflessness—surprisingly, it matters little which— takes us beyond ourselves and explodes the logic of drawing conclusions on the basis of the quantity of good and evil we experience. It can, in a moment, erase a lifetime of pain or emptiness or terror and shift our perception and commitment. Selfless giving is necessary if there is to be any ground for hope in a world where evil and the suffering it causes overwhelmingly prevail from a quantitative point of view.* Altruism/agape must be fundamentally involved in mystical experience and as central to the Christian Easter experience as it is to the story of what Jesus said and did.[56]

Humans in Relation to Social Structures and Institutions: Structural Ethics and Personal Ethics

For traditional ethics of a Kantian flavor, the moral agent is not only autonomous but radically free and responsible. This is so because ultimately what counts morally is good intentions, not performing right actions or bringing about good consequences, issues over which the agent does not have complete control. Also, the ethical demand is, due to Kant's universalizability principle, in theory at least, unambiguous and doable. Ethics is engaged in by individuals, and its subject matter is personal. The objects of ethical concern extend only to ethical subjects whose task it is to treat rational and free agents in a way befitting rational and free agents. All of this presupposes that humans are not restricted by body or history in their ethicity. It implies that personal perfection is attainable—and to be attained.[57]

For liberationist ethics, our knowledge, power, freedom, and responsibility are limited. This is because what counts morally is building right interpersonal relations and liberating structures. And we are affected in our attempts by our social conditions, by other humans and the structures and institutions our societies and cultures have produced. Only in a derivative sense can intentions be separated from actions and, in any case, what we actually do and effect also count ethically. The ethical task is both personal and corporate. And the objects of moral concern extend to everything which the moral subject can harm or help. All of this presupposes that humans are essentially embodied and historical. Personal perfection is not even meaningful.

Liberationist ethics is concerned with both personal ethics, basically, the ethics of personal relations, and what I will call structural ethics, the ethics of transforming oppressive structures into liberating ones. Structural ethics is something of which the tradition was more or less unaware. While there have always been exceptions, such as Jesus, generally speaking, social structures and institutions, even when they clearly caused suffering, were thought to reflect the natural, unchangeable, divinely ordained hierarchical order of things. But while virtually no one agrees with this now and virtually everyone thinks structures can oppress and can be changed, still, we have not internalized it. Neither in our ways of acting nor in our ways of thinking have we taken structural ethics to be of vital importance. We still see it as, at best, an appendage to personal ethics, which we still understand in a fairly traditional way, as though our social conditioning did not affect our personal ways of relating. And there are good reasons for this. *We are punished by society for breaking its code of personal ethics and we are most often ostracized for raising structural issues.* Cheating and stealing can destroy a career; slandering and adultery can wreck friendship and family. And our careers, friendships, and families tend to be what we value most, what we see life as about. Also, because questioning, protesting, and trying to change oppressive structures inevitably involve us in conflict with those who benefit from these structures, when we try we fail and are made to suffer.

But it is essential to come to appreciate what is involved in structural ethics. Structural causes of oppression are embracive and deep-running, affecting not only the social organization of society but the very language and concepts we use to criticize and evaluate. So structural ethics must involve an ethical attitude of active inquiry, even of suspicion of the structures that are in place. Consciousness-raising and mobilizing people to join in solidarity for change are required not only to unmask hidden causes of oppression but even to demonstrate that some groups, such as women, are oppressed. But the negative criterion, the experience of negativity, is our most powerful guide. This ethic requires social analysis to help us understand the causes of, and outline solutions for, oppression. But it also requires innovative practice, the use of trial and error, to find what will be effective in a changing historical context in order to bring about conditions which are fitting to the liberative value. It is an ethic which engages in conflict and partisanship, siding with the poor and powerless not only against the structures of their oppression but, inevitably, against the powerful in whose interest it is to maintain the status quo. This is an ethic for which our knowledge, power, freedom, and responsibility are recognized as more limited, but only because its domain is not so narrow and safe as that of traditional ethics. It enables us to free our freedom, extend our knowledge, exercise our power of connectedness, take responsibility for our shared responsibility; in short, liberate our ethicity. It calls us to create new conditions so that we may create new humans. And its task lasts as long as does any oppression or deprivation that we can do anything about anywhere.

We might begin to ask ourselves how personal ethics fits at all into this perspective. But surely, we may insist, that we relate to others at a personal level in a way which is respectful of their dignity is important, and that we not lie and cheat and steal and slander and commit adultery seem to be essential to this. Yet our traditional understanding of personal ethics and of an anthropology of the individual seems to have nothing in common with the social structural view.

Because social structures condition every aspect of our lives, including the way we think and feel and behave, *our personal lives and personal ethics must be understood to lie within and to be influenced by a context of changeable social structures and conditionings.* And personal ethics must be understood to be personal social ethics. All ethics is social ethics because all ethics concerns our relations with other humans and our world. Cheating, lying, slandering, and adultery, insofar as they are evils at all, are social evils.

Also, personal ethics must no longer be understood on a traditional model but must be seen to have many of the same features as structural ethics. All ethics, whether personal or structural, have the same ultimate value and criterion for right practice: resistance to every threat to the humanum and cosmos. And this is to say that all ethics, personal as well as structural ethics, must be outgoing, seeking the welfare of the other more than personal worthiness and virtuousness. Personal ethics is no more a mere ethic of good intentions than is structural ethics. And if human welfare is the final criterion in determining what counts as honesty or what will be our sexual ethics, what we ought to do within the personal sphere will be less clear-cut and more subject to change than on a traditional model. Due to the limitlessness of the quest of resistance to suffering, our power to accomplish what we attempt will be limited in the personal sphere as well as the structural sphere. And due to our limited knowledge and power, our moral responsibility will be limited. In short, *we are the same mental/physical social subjects whose freedom is restricted in the context of our personal ethics as in that of our structural ethics. And the same negative contrast experience compels us.*

What counts as alleviating suffering and forming right relations at the personal level will, in part, involve things like truth-telling, honesty, and sexual morality. What counts as truth-telling, honesty, and sexual morality, however, is highly culturally conditioned. But for this very reason they are given cultural definition. And, within the context of their cultural definition, there will be greater certainty about what to do, greater power and freedom to do it, and greater responsibility for doing it than when we are engaging in structural ethics. However, the interconnectedness between personal and structural ethics may lead to short-term instability with regard to some of these aspects of our personal ethics. Our personal ethics may inform us that it is dishonest to take what another legally owns unless our need is dire. But our structural ethical inquiry may bring into question the justice of the social organization which allows the other to possess so much more than we do. Or—some people's actual rebelling against the norms society has set for personal ethics, such as looting when the opportunity arises, may lead to asking structural questions. The academic would begin with the more theoretical structural questions; the destitute person would begin by changing her or his personal practice. If questions begin to be asked about a society's economic structures in the context of the poor's stealing from the rich, there may be a period of time when people find themselves engaging in civil disobedience of a sort which does not respect everyone's legal right to possessions. But when the crisis is over and economic structures are (or are not) changed, some sort of equilibrium will be reached and common agreement attained, regarding what will count as stealing and honesty in our personal social relations. It is convenient that personal ethics has a certain stability so that we do not have to wrestle with a moral crisis at every turn. It is also important that we can by and large predict the moral position of those around us. To act morally vis-à-vis truth-telling, honesty, and sexuality is, in part, dependent on mutual agreement, on all parties meaning the same thing by what they do, having the same sense of what is right in these spheres.

But understanding the relationship between personal and structural ethics is not just a matter of relocating a traditional content of personal ethics within a context of a revised anthropology with its ethical implications. Sexual ethics can no longer omit issues of social justice from its sphere, issues connected with the oppression of women and homosexual people. *Quite a new and important content is added to personal ethics—the struggling for right relations between women and men, poor and rich, characterized by egalitarianism and mutuality. This aspect of personal ethics parallels and largely provides the raison d'être, the "cash value," of the struggle for structural change.*[58] Indeed, our day-to-day struggle with personal relations supports or undermines some social structure or other, and social structures condition what will be our personal relations. In our time, the interplay between conceptual and linguistic, legal and economic structures, on the one hand, and personal ethical relations between women and men struggling for truer forms of connectedness, on the other, make this obvious. Margaret Atwood tells of the effects on a married couple of a male fascist takeover of their egalitarian society. In a world where plastic cards have replaced money, the first thing the fascists do is to cancel all women's cards, making women, at a stroke, dependent on men for survival. The first response of the couple is to join in closer solidarity, vowing not to allow the external threat to affect their relationship. But soon, subtly, *he* becomes paternalistic, assuring her that he will buy her whatever she wants, but enjoying the situation, and *she* becomes cold, brittle, rebellious at her dependency. Atwood's development of these characters brilliantly demonstrates how dependent are personal relationships on societal structures even for the most highly conscientized and caring people.[59]

Solidarity Extends to All: Right Relations With Other Species and the Environment

Because we share a common anthropology we ought to respect a basic equality and solidarity among humans. Because we depend on one another for our biological survival, for our very development as persons and subjects and for our human flourishment, we are morally compelled to act for the good of one another. Although we do not share a common nature or form of life with other species or the natural environment, we are connected with them and can affect their very survival. The current ecological crisis is also a human crisis; it demonstrates that we must stop exploiting the environment for our sakes. But how ought we to relate to the environment? Should we respect it for its sake? And are we morally obliged to stop harming other species? Are they proper objects of moral concern?

Other Species

Animal liberationists argue that we should express moral concern for other species as an extension of our moral concern for humans and based on the needs, interests, and capacities of the various species.

To support this we can show that the structure of a liberationist ethic can be extended to include other species. The animal liberation movement has arisen in response to enormous suffering, oppression, and deprivation of animals. It points to social structural causes of this suffering, including factory farming methods and the use of other species in cruel and wasteful experiments. And it does not avoid conflict with those who resist change. It engages in consciousness-raising and the unmasking of false perceptions. In this case, however, it is not so much the human structures that have to be shown to be the causes of suffering as that other species *are* suffering profoundly and that this is not all right. Just as false anthropologies vis-à-vis women, people of color, and even the poor have had to be brought to light together with and to some extent before the unmasking of unjust political and economic structures, animal liberationists point out that false views of animal natures have to be overcome.

Given the similarities in logical structure of movements for animal liberation and the liberation of the poor, *the only question remaining is whether there is something about the fact that other species are not human that should justify excluding them, and not the poor or women, from our ethical concern.* Here, however, I can but touch on some of the qualities of other species which make them objects of moral concern.

While the various species are radically different from one another and should be treated differently, many species show that they have their own long-term interests, purposes, and goals; they have their own complex forms of life of which they can be deprived. Wolves, for example, teach their young to hunt deer in a context where they do not expect to catch anything. Many species demonstrate complex emotions and can suffer psychologically as well as physically. Rhesus monkeys will starve themselves to the death rather than press a lever for food which also gives a severe shock to other monkeys, thus demonstrating the compassion which, in humans, we associate with altruism. A number of species show significant insight and creativity in the means they use to attain their ends. We see this, not only in chimps who will use boxes and sticks to reach bananas, but also in rats who, after one run through a maze, have insight into shortcuts. Chimps' use of American Sign Language demonstrates that they grasp linguistic meaning and have the rudiments of self-consciousness.[60]

Clearly, other species can suffer profound deprivation, exploitation, physical and psychological torment, in short, oppression, at the hands of humans and their institutions. We are familiar with experiments such as blinding, deafening, and removing the sense of smell of rats in order to show that, without senses, they have little ability to learn.[61] And we ought to be familiar with how white and tender veal is brought to our table—by force-feeding calves in dark cramped quarters for their short life span, so that they cannot even walk to the truck that will take them for slaughter.

In spite of all this, it has been objected along Kantian lines that, in order that other species be objects of our moral concern they must be moral subjects; in order that they have something like rights they must be able to take on something like moral obligations. For animals to have only rights against humans and humans only obligations to animals would be unfair.

A liberationist may reply that other species do not have our intellectual, emotional, and moral capacities but different ones, and we cannot enter into the same sorts of relationships with them that we do with other humans. However, we would do well to recall Bentham's reply to the question whether we are wronging animals, and not just ourselves, in torturing them: "The question is not, Can they reason? nor, Can they talk? but, Can they suffer?"[62] For us the question is not whether other species have obligations to us but whether they have their own interests and purposes, feelings, desires, and values of which they are being systematically deprived by us.

A liberationist ethic will understand our having obligations to other species in something of the way that adults have nonreciprocal obligations to children, not because other species should be seen as like children but, because we inevitably have power over both, we are forced to choose between an attitude of stewardship or exploitation.[63]

However, finally, while other species have their own intrinsic value based on their capacities, interests, and purposes, and are not mere means to our ends, and while sometimes we must put their needs and interests before our own, we would not be responsible if we did not acknowledge a hierarchy of values so that we may judge it wrong to kill an animal for food but we may not choose to save a drowning dog before a drowning boy.

The Environment

We would expect that the ethics of animal liberation and of environmental concern would support and complement one another. But there is a tension between the former, which expresses concern for individuals of species on the basis of their capacities, and the latter, insofar as it gives first concern to the health of the biosphere and, with this, to species survival. Indeed, the tension between anthropocentric and biocentric tendencies runs through the liberation theologies today: The theology of the poor, black theology, and animal liberation tend toward the former; environmental ethics, eco-feminism, and creation spirituality tend toward the latter. Clearly, it is important that the various liberation movements support and not serve to undermine one another, so it is important that they listen to and learn from one another. In this place, however, I wish only to warn against extreme biocentrism and to argue a position consistent with the line I have been developing and which may be too anthropocentric for some. But it is my view that, while the option for the poor must be the first concretization of the imperative to resist suffering, responding to the ecological crisis is clearly an urgent means. And it is more than a means; to explore our interdependency with our world must be for its sake as well as for our own.

With many others today, James Gustafson criticizes liberation theology on grounds of its being anthropocentric and thus partisan, treating humans and not God as the measures and measurers of all things, thus favoring humans over everything else. He thinks that because it is anthropocentric it is partisan, favoring some humans over others. He would not be impressed by the ease with which a liberationist approach can extend concern to other species because it measures its concern by the extent to which other species are like humans. It merely extends anthropocentrism. By contrast, he argues that everything is included as an object of moral concern, not as an extension from the human, but because everything is related to and in God. And we ought to relate to all things in a way which is appropriate to their relationship to God. How do we know what this is? From our experience of everything that is, of nature as well as society, we can discern what God is requiring and enabling us to do. But, then, who or what is God? God is Nature which is neither personal nor benevolent but which, in effect, seems to be the whole-empirical-world-in-connection and which, ultimately, seems only to have the power to respond in negative and positive ways to actions on it. While Gustafson claims that his position is theocentric, we may ask how, if God is Nature in the way he describes, this differs from biocentrism. And while Gustafson claims a special dignity of self-determination for humans and denies that humans are merely for the sake of the whole, it appears that this is what he is, in effect, promoting. He at least implies that there may come a time when we ought to choose against human survival for the good of the integrated whole.[64]

Aldo Leopold, the "father" of land ethics, explicitly argues that only the biotic whole has independent value; the parts or individuals that make it up have only relative value. He takes as his first ethical principle: "A thing is right when it tends to preserve the integrity, stability, and beauty of the biotic community. It is wrong when it tends otherwise."[65] Because this view associates integratedness with simplicity, it puts the less complex life forms before the more complex; because it associates stability with variety, it puts species before their individual members; because it puts the biotic whole before the things which make it up, it puts the strong individuals before the weak.[66]

But then, the balance between our sociability and individuality gets lost. The value of the individual human is purely relative, becomes less when there are deemed to be too many for the health of the biosphere, and becomes greater when there are deemed to be too few. *The view lends itself, especially in times of real, perceived, or manufactured scarcity of resources, to a lifeboat ethic where the weak must be sacrificed for the sake of the strong.* This is not a mere theoretical point. Garrett Hardin, for example, argues that rich nations should not give to poor nations but should save their extra resources for their own future generations. Joseph Fletcher argues that nations which have exceeded their carrying capacity should not be helped.[67]

While Segundo does not express concern for the environment as such, he develops an evolutionary theory which can be of use here. He argues that our experience is of a world which moves toward greater order, meaning, complexity, integratedness, and richness. And in humans, complexity and integratedness have reached a stage where we can understand and freely participate in this ordering activity; we can be co-creators in the evolutionary project. But we must do this by imitating the evolutionary project itself. At every level of evolution there is 'mind'[68] at work, acting purposively to order information so as to produce greater differentiation, thence greater integration and complexity. Mind not only acts purposively, however, but respects chance; it waits on the introduction of new and unexpected elements needed for new integration, and it allows the time necessary for truly integrating adjustments to take place. Only this combination of purposiveness and chance, which we may relate to acting and allowing, provides the flexibility that is necessary for greater integration and maximum survival. *In humans, mind's action for integratedness involves including the excluded, the marginalized, and the poor; it can be identified with ethics and with love.*[69]

So, contrary to the land ethicist who, for the sake of stability and integration, favors species over individuals and the strong over the weak, Segundo stresses bringing the unintegrated, the marginalized, the outcast, the weak, to integration. And contrary to the land ethicist, who sees simpler forms as biotically more integrative and so more valuable, Segundo sees more differentiated and complex forms as more integrated. Not only has human complexity reached a stage where we can destroy the biosphere, as many ethicists are rightly stressing today, but we humans can also consciously, in freedom and love, take on the integrative or evolutionary task. We are *a kind of* 'crown' of evolution; we cannot avoid and so must accept the responsibility of it.

Finally, the land ethicist is prepared to accept a certain amount of breakdown in complexity in order to regain a perceived biotic stability. Segundo thinks the biosphere is running down and will ultimately collapse. He admits that the very project of ordering and integrating uses and makes unusable the finite supply of energy, and so leads ultimately to its own breakdown. But we should continue our efforts for integration. Indeed, Segundo thinks it preposterous that reflectively conscious-free minds should be produced by evolution to participate in the evolutionary project and yet the project should, as it were, fizzle out; he concludes that the effort made toward integration by humans through their love will last forever, will have eschatological significance.[70]

Both Gustafson and the land ethicist start out in ethics with a concern for the whole in connection; they are radically nonanthropocentric and nonpartisan. The liberationist position I have been developing starts out with concern for suffering and oppressed humans and stresses the importance of negating the negation of the worst off in order to bring about the flourishment of all. It extends its concern to other species and the environment. It seeks to change humanly created social structures which destroy other species and the environment, structures such as factory farming and those which cause industrial pollution. And it seeks to change the conceptual and value structures on which these others are based, structures of dominance, exploitation, and competition. Once again, the use of the negative criterion makes ethics concrete and not dangerously utopian.

The liberationist approach I have been developing is anthropocentric and partisan. We cannot avoid anthropocentrism in the sense that we are the *measurers* for our ethical decision-making of what is good. Even if we accept a Law of God imposed from without, it is *we* who accept it, evaluating it as of God and as good. Put another way, we cannot avoid anthropocentrism in the sense that we interpret reality in terms of human experience and values. What experience, what values, can we use other than those which we have and can understand? But this is not to say that we need be anthropocentric in the sense that we are the *measures* of what is good, that humans are the most valuable beings and that human values are simply the values that are best for humans. And it is certainly not to say that everything else in the cosmos is a mere means to human ends.

We have already argued that because other species of animals have purposes, interests, emotions, etc., they have their own value and are appropriate objects of moral concern. While flowers, trees, mountains, and ecological systems do not have their own interests and purposes, they do have their own giveness and involve their own needs, directions, unfoldings, and connections, which are independent of us. Everything that is alive or even existent, and all the integrated networks of things, have their own integrity and are deserving of our respect. Everything has its own intrinsic value and nothing is a mere means to our ends. This is reflected, whether he intends it or not, in Segundo's view that the mind is striving for integration at every level and each level is analogous with every other. But while we must seek equality within the human sphere, we cannot avoid acknowledging hierarchy in our relations with other creatures and things. It is not simply a matter of recognizing a hierarchy in the sense of greater and lesser needs of different creatures and things. Nor is it a matter of always giving first preference to the beings with greater or more complex needs. As I have said we may decide it is wrong to kill an animal for food. But, as I have also said, we must save a drowning child before a drowning dog.

Not only are other things not mere means to our ends but it is conceivable that we would come across in history beings who seemed to be greater than ourselves. As far as we know, we have powers—to destroy and to create—much greater than other things we come across on earth. As consciously integrating minds and co-creators in the evolutionary project, we would not be responsible if we did not acknowledge this role of stewardship. But our very way of being steward, of performing the integrative function, must centrally involve recognizing and exploring the interdependence of all things and our interdependence with them. Our stress must be on seeking right relations and greater connectedness and integratedness with other species and the environment for the flourishment of us all, not on a hierarchy that must sometimes come into play. We can enter into community and can come to communicate with the rest of the living world to a significantly greater degree than most of us imagine. Only when we do this and when we take sides with our world against the human mentality and practice of exploitation, can we begin to discern what we ought to do when our needs and interests conflict.

CONCLUSION

An ethic of social solidarity is implicit in an ethic for which resistance to suffering and the option for the poor are foundational; it is supported and even required by the Christian scripture and our social anthropology, and it is demanded by the empirical situation of social suffering in the world.

The concern of this ethic is twofold: to transform oppressive social structures and personal relations into liberating ones. In practicing the kingdom of God, Jesus sought both to overturn oppressive structures, particularly politico-religious ones surrounding the Law, and also to mend personal relations and move toward an egalitarian community where all are included. This reflects an anthropology of the social individual, the individual who is essentially in relation to her or his own body, other humans, social structures and institutions, and nature. These and other forms of human relatedness remain ethically relevant through every changing historical context.

Because we are essentially related to our bodies and to social structures, that is, because we are embodied subjects and socially conditioned, our understanding, power, freedom, and responsibility are much more restricted than for a traditional ethic of the individual. We are conditioned freedoms. But the scope of our ethical sphere is greatly extended. We participate in creating our context and liberating our conditions for living, as well as more directly creating liberating relations with others. Our attempts to change structures and personal relationships are interdependent but the personal must be brought within the broader 'conditioning' sphere of the social structural.

While transforming oppressive structures and seeking right relations are the practical imperatives of an ethic of social solidarity, community is its goal. The kingdom of God is a community of people and dolphins and cedars and other things; it is not a set of structures for community. Mutuality, a relationship of giving and receiving based on equality and rooted in altruism, is the goal of most human community. It is the only relationship that is appropriate between women and men, the peoples of different races and ethnic groups, and the rich and poor who, if they are in right relation, will no longer be rich and poor. Stewardship, a relationship which includes reciprocity but also responsibility for nurturing, on the part of most adult humans toward other species and the environment as well as toward children and the severely mentally handicapped, is the goal of community between most humans and these groups. Stewardship too must be rooted in altruism on the part of humans. Humans as co-creators in the evolutionary project aim at maximizing integratedness for all. But this must involve giving preference, although not exclusive preference, to humans and those others with the greatest capacity for suffering and salvation. And it involves seeking integratedness by mending disintegratedness, by including especially the excluded.

NOTES

1. *God the Future of Man*, p. 159.
2. I do not comment on but accept, with an aim to building an ethic, liberationists' interpretations of specific passages of scripture. I defend their general hermeneutical approach in chapter 5 and allude to it in other places. But it

is worth noting here that, while to make a historical person, from another time, place, and culture, a central guide to ethics creates difficulties, it also has advantages. In our historically conscious context, we must show how we can understand the ancient story as intended by the authors of our texts, and even as it was first played out, and also how it can be genuinely relevant to us today. However, seeking guidance from a concrete witness, rather than relying entirely on more abstract and general philosophical argument, gives an ethic its own credibility and power. Perhaps ironically, story, which always tells of what is historical and particular, is more 'timeless' in its capacity to communicate than abstract argument, which is constructed to have a universal quality. This is because what we learn by transposing from others' contexts to our own is richer than what we learn from abstract argument, which does not fully capture what is relevant to any context. This phenomenon is demonstrative of both the fundamental historicity and unity of the human species and will be discussed in chapter 4.

3. I am attracted by "kindom" as a replacement for "kingdom" in order to overcome the latter's patriarchal connotations. But while, for this reason, I find any notion of "king" unattractive, I do not hear "kingdom" of God in just the same way. It captures the utopian quality of our vision of right order and community, and also God's power to transform what we do in a way which conforms to that vision. So I retain the traditional term.

4. Walter Rauschenbusch argues that an experience of social problems, and a secular ethical experience and practice of solidarity in response to these problems, can actually disclose a religious experience of the kingdom of God which will form the basis for a reinterpretation of the symbol of the kingdom of God. He argues that the kingdom of God, understood as a historical force set in motion by Jesus, is causally responsible for the social ethical experience so, while God encourages the ethical experience of solidarity in response to social suffering and the ethical practice rising out of it, revelation of God comes through the ethical experience and practice. This articulates the structure of the argument of Rauschenbusch's *A Theology of the Social Gospel* (Nashville: Abingdon Press, 1946).

5. Schillebeeckx, *God the Future of Man*, p. 78; Gutiérrez, *A Theology of Liberation*, p. 169.

6. *Jesus*, pp. 142–43; 162. Quotation at p. 142. (Exclusive language replaced.)

7. This theme runs through *The Historical Jesus of the Synoptics*. But see especially pp. 16–17.

8. *Jesus*, pp. 167–68. The parable of the laborers in the vineyard provides a prime example of this (Matt. 20:1–16).

9. *The Historical Jesus of the Synoptics*, pp. 158–59.

10. Sobrino argues explicitly this way. See "Jesus' Relationship with the Poor and Outcasts," p. 13.

11. See Gutiérrez, *A Theology of Liberation*, chapter nine, "Liberation and Salvation," pp. 149–87, especially p. 177; Schillebeeckx, the *Jesus* books, especially *Jesus*, p. 141 and *Christ*, p. 792; Juan Luis Segundo, *Jesus of Nazareth Yesterday and Today*, vol. III, *The Humanist Christology of Paul*, ed. and trans. by John

Drury, 5 vols. (Maryknoll, New York: Orbis Books, 1986), especially pp. 122–24, 130, 137, 160.

12. Soelle seems to be an exception. I shall discuss her eschatology in chapter 5.

13. *A Theology of Liberation*, p. 205.

14. *The Historical Jesus of the Synoptics*, pp. 90–91, 110–14.

15. Schillebeeckx, *Jesus*, pp. 162–63; Segundo, *The Historical Jesus of the Synoptics*, pp. 93–103. This will be discussed in more detail in chapter 4.

16. Quotations at *Jesus*, p. 166 and *Christ*, p. 795 respectively.

17. Juan Luis Segundo, *Jesus of Nazareth Yesterday and Today*, vol. I, *Faith and Ideologies*, ed. and trans. by John Drury, 5 vols. (Maryknoll, New York: Orbis Books, 1984), p. 46; *The Liberation of Theology*, p. 79.

18. *Jesus*, pp. 211–12, 145, 153. Quotation at p. 153.

19. *The Historical Jesus of the Synoptics*, pp. 90, 119.

20. *A Theology of Liberation*, pp. 231–32.

21. There is no inconsistency between this and Segundo's claim that the kingdom is bad news for the unconverted. The experience of the rich young man is a common one, the experience of having found what we have been seeking yet being unwilling to pay the price for enjoying it.

22. Gutiérrez discusses this view in *A Theology of Liberation*, pp. 229–30.

23. *The Historical Jesus of the Synoptics*, pp. 153–54, 182.

Schillebeeckx, arguing more on the basis of exegesis than on the logic of Jesus' life, says that the expectation of the end experienced by the early Christians, which influenced their scriptural texts, was based on their experience of the risen Christ and cannot be traced directly to Jesus' preaching. Jesus connected God's rule being at hand with his seeing it come about in his own action, but the sources do not suggest that he identified this with the end of the world. Schillebeeckx goes on to speculate, however, that such a view would not have been an unreasonable one for Jesus to have had. But he still supports the politico-religious interpretation of Jesus' mission. *Jesus*, p. 152.

24. At least some of this is implicit in Gutiérrez's thought when, on the one hand, he argues that "human reason *has become* political reason" and the political sphere is where critical freedom, "which is *won through history*," is exercised, and, on the other hand, he investigates our political anthropology as though it had a status about it of humanity truly becoming itself. In other words, through learning of our social conditionedness and our power to change our social conditions, we become subjects of history, able to redirect the course of history. See *A Theology of Liberation*, pp. 47–49. (My italics.)

Liberationists tend to use the term 'political' very broadly, almost to coincide with what I mean by 'social.'

25. *Christ*, p. 733.

26. Schillebeeckx's first anthropological constant coincides with the level of our most basic human needs on Lonergan's scale of values. Indeed, the progression of Schillebeeckx's constants from basic material needs to social needs incorporating other humans and social structures, to cultural needs (including the power to make meaning), to spiritual needs, parallels Lonergan's scale. And it is fitting that it should. Both are attempting to set out what is good and necessary for the humanum, although Schillebeeckx does not explicitly suggest that he is ordering his constants according to a scale. Schillebeeckx discusses his anthropological constants in *Christ*, pp. 734–42. He describes them as a system of coordinates . . . at p. 734.

27. Ibid., pp. 732–33, 742–43. Quotations at p. 733. The role of norms in ethical decision-making will be discussed in chapter 4, pp. 154–59.

28. To take a concrete example: On this view, because there are no absolute behavioral norms, there are no absolute prohibitions against using "artificial" means of birth control, still very much an issue in parts of the Third World, such as the Philippines. New possibilities for living are not ruled out a priori but are considered in terms of the various constants. We may consider what effect would using this or that means of birth control have on my body, on my relationship to other humans, particularly my partner and family, on my relationship to the wider society and nature in the context of population control? Are political and economic structures in place in my society to facilitate the successful use of contraceptives, and if not should they be? How does my tradition, my culture, my sense of the good relate to this issue? Normally, there will be pros and cons on any issue and here is where the need for balance and synthesis comes in. While Schillebeeckx does not directly discuss the use of anthropological constants in ethical decision-making, he does say: "Ideas about marriage, love and sexuality have shifted in our time . . . for the most part solely because science and technology have been able to provide means which were not at the disposal of people of former times." *Christ*, pp. 735–36.

29. Schillebeeckx, *Jesus*, p. 19.

30. Schillebeeckx explicitly says he is articulating only *some* anthropological constants. See *Christ*, p. 734.

31. For example, Kant's stress on our rationality and freedom was directly relevant to the Enlightenment's confrontation with the dogmatism of church and state and still holds important insights for us in connection with our autonomy. But insofar as these insights have not been incorporated within a broader framework of historical constants, but have been made to do all the work vis-à-vis contemporary social problems, Kant's rationality and freedom have hidden from us our historicity and relationality, our concrete *unfreedom* in the face of our social conditioning, and our limited capacity to transform those conditions.

32. Segundo, *The Historical Jesus of the Synoptics*, p. 37; Schillebeeckx, *Jesus in Our Western Culture*, pp. 5–6. My understanding of a transcendental deduction or argument is one which moves 'backward' from something which is given in experience to logically necessary conditions for that experience. The conditions are as certain and as universal as is the given in experience. Kant introduced transcendental arguments as a method of extending knowledge beyond the given in experience in response to Hume's reduction of knowledge to the given in experience. *Schillebeeckx suggests that experience itself can disclose its own conditions when he describes a disclosure experience as involving seeing within an experience a deeper dimension "that reveals precisely the deeper basis and condition of possibility of the secular event."* See *God the Future of Man*, p. 74. (My italics.)

33. See, for example, P. F. Strawson, *Individuals: An Essay in Descriptive Metaphysics*, (London: Methuen & Co. Ltd., University Paperbacks, 1964), chapter three, "Persons," pp. 87–116.

34. See, for example, *Christ*, pp. 736–37.

35. See, for example, Descartes' "Meditations on First Philosophy," *The Philosophical Works of Descartes*, vol. 1, trans. Elizabeth S. Haldane and G. R. T. Ross, 2 vols. (Cambridge: Cambridge University Press, 1969), pp. 131–91.

36. Ludwig Wittgenstein, *Philosophical Investigations*, trans. G. E. M. Anscombe (Oxford: Basil Blackwell, 1958). Material for the private language argument is scattered throughout the text but a central attempt by Wittgenstein to articulate it is found at numbers 243 to 282, pp. 88–97. There is no agreement even on how to formulate the private language argument, much less on whether it is valid. But it is the best known of a cluster of quite similar arguments offered by both continental European and Anglo-American philosophers, all of whom draw the same conclusion: Self-consciousness requires the consciousness of others, our subjectivity depends on our being intersubjective. However, while perhaps linguistic meaning must be public, seeking new expression to bring new indeterminate thought to determinateness must be accounted for as well. And that language must have begun at some time must be acknowledged. Thus, many argue, Wittgenstein's private language argument only precludes a logically private language, one no one else could understand. But then it remains the case that even creative thought and expression can take place only within a context which is at least potentially genuinely public, involving others. But this is to say that we must be fundamentally available to others; we must be fundamentally physical as well as mental.

37. *Individuals*, pp. 87–116.

In a similar vein, Jean-Paul Sartre argues that by 'the look' of the other, I come to recognize myself as an object for the other whom I thereby recognize as a subject and as a threat to the one I finally recognize to be myself as subject. See Jean-Paul Sartre, *Being and Nothingness: An Essay in Phenomenological Ontology*, trans. Hazel E. Barnes, introd. Mary Warnock (London: Methuen & Co. Ltd., 1969), "The Look," pp. 252–302, especially pp. 252–65.

38. We do sometimes experience dualistically. We may watch and protest our body deteriorating while our psyche remains intact until we die. Strawson suggests that while we must start out as mental/physical in order for the self-conscious subject to emerge, the mind may split from the body at death. It seems to me, however, that the experience of our mind as separate from our body is an experience of unwholeness and that a final salvation is more likely to include 'the resurrection of the body' for a 'new earth.'

39. *The Power of the Poor in History*, pp. 92, 193.

40. *Suffering*, pp. 70–74.

41. Beverly Harrison, "The Power of Anger in the Work of Love: Christian Ethics for Women and Other Strangers," *Union Quarterly Review* 36 (1981): 50.

42. Soelle uses the "net" symbol differently. She speaks of the net of neighborly love to express the sense in which there is nothing we do for each other that is lost or done in vain. See Dorothee Soelle, *The Strength of the Weak:*

Toward a Christian Feminist Identity, trans. Robert and Rita Kimber (Philadelphia: The Westminster Press, 1984), p. 32.

43. I deal with these important relationships briefly here to show that our social anthropology demands solidarity, equality, mutuality, and altruism. They will be further discussed in an ethical context in the next section of the chapter. See also Helmut Peukert, *Science, Action and Fundamental Theology: Toward a Theology of Communicative Action* (Cambridge: MIT Press, 1988) on how our communicative practice commits us, not only to truth-telling, but to equality, solidarity, and justice for all.

44. Peter Berger speaks to this issue proceeding from a desert island situation. He is convincing on how we produce and maintain institutions but not on how we change them. Here I begin with his line of argument and revise and expand it. See Peter Berger and Thomas Luckmann, *The Social Construction of Reality: A Treatise in the Sociology of Knowledge* (Garden City, New York: Doubleday & Company, Inc., 1966), pp. 53 ff.

45. Segundo, *The Liberation of Theology,* p. 125. The second and third sections of the next chapter, pp. 126–46, will show how we can be both conditioned and critical of our conditions, and how tradition can teach us to be creative.

46. This will be discussed on pages 98–102 of this chapter.

47. Throughout, I take the Christian term agape, and the secular term altruism, to mean the same.

48. H. Richard Niebuhr, "The Center of Value," *Radical Monotheism and Western Culture: With Supplementary Essays,* p. 105.

49. *The Historical Jesus of the Synoptics,* pp. 128–29.

50. *Jesus,* p. 606. Gutiérrez argues similarly. See *A Theology of Liberation,* pp. 176–77, 206.

51. "The Power of Anger in the Work of Love," p. 51.

52. Ibid., p. 50.

53. Barbara Andolsen, "Agape in Feminist Ethics," *The Journal of Religious Ethics* 9 (Spring 1981): 80. Harrison concurs that the situations where self-sacrifice is called for are extreme and the norm should be to engage in acts of love which bring mutual relationship to life. Ibid., pp. 52–53.

54. Central to the formation of sisters, brothers, and priests in the Philippines is "immersion" with the poor, which often involves living for some time in squatter communities. Something like this is essential today, for the non-poor, for our formation as Christians and truly human persons.

55. *Jesus in Our Western Culture,* pp. 55–63.

56. If altruism is a ground for hope that goodness will prevail, then a mutuality of free giving and receiving is doubly a ground for hope. And, of course, receiving is essential to our being able to transcend ourselves in giving.

I have not raised the most discussed issue regarding altruism, that is, whether it is possible. Some philosophers and psychologists have, in a rather a priori way, reduced all human motivation to self-interest, arguing that acts which appear selfless are really done for pleasure or honor or whatever else the agent might want for herself or himself in giving. In response, I would argue that we must distinguish the motive for which an action is performed from its perhaps known consequences. We may know that we will get joy out of something we do, primarily, for the sake of the other. Also, those who raise the question tend to assume that, in order for an act to be altruistic, it must be 'purely' selfless. Otherwise, it is actually selfish. Consistent with the view that we are mental/physical and have restricted freedom, I am not assuming we ever have pure motives, but rather, if we do we never know it. However, this does not preclude the possibility of acts which are more or less selfless, selfless to the extent to which they are directed toward the welfare of the other. Because we can, in stories and in life, distinguish cases of people acting more or less for the sake of others, then acting for the sake of the other has concrete meaning for us and there is no reason to believe it is not possible. In fact, as I have just suggested, experiences of doing for the other have such a profound effect on us it would be difficult to believe, existentially, that they are all illusory.

57. Catholic manual ethics, based on a rigid interpretation of natural law, attempted to deduce absolute moral norms from an unchanging human nature. For this view, too, what we ought to do was completely knowable and doable. We were called to be perfect.

Natural law theory will be discussed in the next chapter on pages 146–48. See especially footnote 49.

58. Personal ethics, insofar as it is directed toward transforming personal relations from oppressive ones into more liberated, egalitarian ones, in effect transforms structures of relationship. But, *by the distinction between structural and personal ethics, I wish to maintain the distinction between what is involved in the corporate action of challenging political or conceptual . . . structures directly and what is involved in relating to one another ethically on a personal level which, if it is innovative, will have an effect on structures.* The distinction between structural and personal ethics reflects the distinction between our being subjects of history and subjects in relation to one another as discussed in the context of our social anthropology.

59. Margaret Atwood, *The Handmaid's Tale,* (Toronto: McClelland and Stewart Ltd., 1985), pp. 182–91.

60. See Mary Midgeley, *Beast and Man: The Roots of Human Nature* (Sussex: The Harvester Press, 1978), pp. 215–16, 227–31, 277–80, for more developed examples of how other species demonstrate long-term interests and purposes, complex emotions, insight, linguistic understanding, and self-consciousness. See James Rachels, "Do Animals Have a Right to Liberty?" in Regan and Singer, *Animal Rights and Human Obligations*, pp. 214–18 for discussion of the rudiments of a moral sense in rhesus monkeys.

61. Richard Ryder, "Experiments on Animals," in Regan and Singer, *Animal Rights and Human Obligations*, p. 35.

62. Jeremy Bentham, "A Utilitarian View," from Jeremy Bentham, *The Principles of Morals and Legislation* (1789), chapter seventeen, section 1, in Regan and Singer, *Animal Rights and Human Obligations*, p. 130.

63. These cases are very different from those of the relationships between the poor and rich; blacks, browns and whites; women and men, where mutuality must be aimed at.

64. Gustafson, *Ethics from a Theocentric Perspective*, vol. 1, chapter five, "God in Relation to Man and the World," pp. 195–279. Concerning his views on liberation theology see pp. 15, 22–25, 53–55, 72–73. Also see *Can Ethics be Christian?* (Chicago: The University of Chicago Press, 1975), pp. 124–27, 131–44. He speaks more positively about liberation theology in his more recent book. On our choosing against human interest see *Ethics from a Theocentric Perspective*, vol. 1, p. 202.

65. Aldo Leopold, *Sand County Almanac* (New York: Oxford University Press, 1981), pp. 224–25.

66. J. Baird Callicott points out the tension between mainstream environmental ethics and the animal liberation movement and interprets and defends Leopold along these lines. See Callicott's "Animal Liberation: A Triangular Affair," *Environmental Ethics* 2 (1980).

67. See for example, Garrett Hardin, "Lifeboat Ethics: The Case Against Helping the Poor" and Joseph Fletcher, "Give If It Helps But Not If It Hurts," in William Aiken and Hugh La Follette, *World Hunger and Moral Obligation* (Englewood Cliffs, New Jersey: Prentice-Hall Inc., 1977), pp. 11–21 and pp. 103–14 respectively.

68. Minimally, for Segundo 'mind' is "a system that receives and processes information to serve the totality of the organism." See *Jesus of Nazareth Yesterday and Today*, vol. V, *An Evolutionary Approach to Jesus of Nazareth*, ed. and trans. John Drury, 5 vols. (Maryknoll, New York: Orbis Books, 1988), p. 34.

69. Ibid., pp. 15, 42–60. In defense of his own evolutionary theory Segundo argues, in effect, that if Darwin's theory of natural selection, which features chance, were correct, evolution would oscillate between greater and lesser complexity; if Lamarck's theory of the inheritability of acquired characteristics, which features purposiveness, were correct, change and the move to greater complexity would happen so quickly that real integratedness could not take place and all would collapse. Thus illustrates the need to combine chance and purposiveness.

70. Segundo does not suggest that anything in history outside of humans and their projects have eschatological significance. But given the argument of this chapter, it is appropriate to suggest that the earth and all its creatures should be taken up eschatologically. This is fitting to our essentially mental/physical and relational character and to Segundo's evolutionary theory where mind is at work from the beginning, and each stage is analogous to every other. And it is fitting to Segundo's stress on a continuous eschatology.

4

A Liberationist Ethic Is an Innovative Ethic

INTRODUCTION

Given that our experiential starting point in ethics is not of a pre-established order embodying a blueprint for right action, but of disorder and no blueprint, ethics must be creative, innovative.[1] It cannot involve mere application of principles or obedience to norms that are handed down by religious, cultural, or philosophical tradition. Rather, it must involve our responding to the disordered, suffering cosmos, first through our innovative practice, out of which new and revised norms will emerge. We have seen that, for Schillebeeckx, it is through the negative contrast, experienced most acutely by people actively engaged in confronting the world's problems, that humans recognize and rebel against new sufferings and first find right practices; theoretical reflection, critical examination, and official formulation come afterward.[2]

The content of a liberationist ethic also requires that it be innovative. Because it compels us to resist suffering, there is no end to what we can do. And to discover what is best to do in different situations requires discernment and trying different things out. Because a liberationist ethic demands that we seek structural change, it cannot rely on already existent frameworks of social organization or even of thought and value, but must seek out their oppressive tendencies and search for ways to transform them. Because it strains to attain at the personal level, even before it achieves at the structural level, right relations between rich and poor, women and men, it must be experimental and risk-taking. Because it extends its concern to include other species and the environment, a liberationist ethic requires enormous imagination.

In this chapter, we will explore why innovativeness in ethics is necessary, how it is possible, how to go about it, and how to be respon-

118

sible in doing so. This will involve considering the relationship between practice and norms for right practice, which involves, in effect, the relationship between practice and theory within the sphere of ethical life. By considering a liberationist interpretation of Jesus' relationship to the Mosaic Law, I will show why innovativeness in ethics is necessary, and something of what it involves. Jesus demonstrates that the Law will oppress if we interpret it legalistically. We must fearlessly and freely seek out new forms of practice for our context which express the Law's, or our ethic's, fundamental value. I will then show how an innovative ethic is possible by stepping back and developing an anthropology and epistemology appropriate to Jesus' and our ethical innovativeness. This will involve understanding ourselves and our innovative learning on a gestalt and evolutionary model for which knowing how or practical knowledge is prior to knowing that or propositional and theoretical knowledge. And it will involve showing that our experience of reality is not determined by our frameworks of thought and practice. Because learning how—to integrate our practice with our value—requires human models who show us how an innovative ethic lends itself particularly well to an ethic of discipleship. We shall explore Jesus' showing us how. Finally, to demonstrate that this ethic is responsible as well as innovative, I will discuss guides for ethical decision-making. This will locate a liberationist ethic vis-à-vis mainstream personal ethics of deontological, teleological, and proportionalist types.

JESUS AND THE LAW

A liberationist interpretation of Jesus' relationship to the Law stresses that, for Jesus, ethics does not involve obedience to a set of pre-established do's and don't's motivated by reward and fear of punishment. This leads, inevitably, to manipulation not only of the Law but of the gods. And it leads to the oppression of the socially deprived by the custodians of the Law. For Jesus, the Law promotes an ethic which must be creative, innovative, and risk-taking in order that every threat to the humanum might be overcome. This implies that we cannot rely, in ethics, entirely on established norms of behavior, but that we must develop new practices in response to new, largely negative, experiences, out of which we may formulate new norms for practice.

Jesus' Encounters with the Pharisees; His Opposition to Legalism[3]

While the Pharisees allow the law-abiding Jew to respond to a human emergency on the Sabbath, they object to Jesus' curing the sick and disabled and to his not discouraging his disciples from plucking corn on this day. By his practice more than his words Jesus points out the acutely contradictory position of the Pharisees. The Sabbath was introduced in the first place out of concern for those whose daily life was a grind and was only later, in the creation stories, given theological underpinning. But the Sabbath, together with every aspect of the Law, eventually became 'fenced around' with a multiplicity of rules, and developed into a 'divinely' sanctioned institution, sacred, absolute, and acutely oppressive.[4]

When, on one occasion (Mark 3:1–5), Jesus challenges the Pharisees as to whether it is permitted to do good on the Sabbath, they do not answer. Schillebeeckx's explanation for their silence is that they recognize their hypocrisy, that their practice is in conflict with their belief, that while the Law is about human flourishing, 'the fence around the Law' prevents it from accomplishing its aim. *Schillebeeckx's Jesus is trying to retrieve the point of the Law, to show that the Sabbath must be understood as a time for doing good, that the proper meaning of the Law is freedom to do good.*[5] *For Segundo, the Pharisees do not answer because they do not really understand the question. For them, the intricacies of the Law define what is good; it is the yardstick of the good.* But Jesus' question presupposes that we can know what is good independent of the Law, that we must evaluate the Law according to our human experience of what is good. "The Sabbath was made for humans, not humans for the Sabbath" (Mark 2:27); the Sabbath is relative and human welfare is absolute.[6] Where the Pharisees have gone wrong, from Segundo's point of view, has been in treating instruments, means, ideologies, in this case a specified set of do's and don't's of the Mosaic Law, as if they constituted an end, an ultimate value, something in which we place our faith and which God revealed as absolute. But, while a set of behavioral rules will be effective in one set of circumstances, they will not be effective in another.[7] Segundo complements and extends Schillebeeckx's understanding by explaining a mechanism for self-deception that is at work and which makes the contradictory situation of the Pharisees possible.

Segundo argues that Jesus' response to the Pharisees' accusation that his works of mercy have their source in Satan (Mark 3:22–30),[8] makes even more explicit his view that the Law, something imposed from the outside, cannot define what is good, but rather, good must interpret the Law. He argues that what counts is the good that is accomplished, not the credentials of the agent. An agent's blaspheming against some god or other is not of great importance but blaspheming against the Holy Spirit, that is, against God's value and God's salvific acts which are mediated by humans, is of deadly consequence. Nothing, including the Mosaic Law, could count as a sign from heaven, as having a stamp of 'heavenly' authenticity, except the kinds of signs Jesus already gave us, the signs of fundamental concern for human welfare. Overall, Schillebeeckx is more concerned to stress that the true Law of God is to act for human good and Segundo's main concern is to argue that human good is the criterion of authentic religion. Again, the views are complementary.

Jesus' View of the Law in the Parables; Gratuitous Love, not Calculated Giving

Schillebeeckx describes how a number of Jesus' parables show that the erroneous view of the Law, as involving absolute do's and don't's, forms the basis for a system of precisely calculated rewards and punishments. And the parables reveal a new view of the Law involving gratuitous and 'excessive' love. In the story of the Pharisee and the Publican (Luke 18:9–14), the Pharisee, who declares himself righteous before God because he had obeyed the established rules, is renounced, while the publican, who does not even know the rules but who seeks God's forgiveness for his sinfulness is proclaimed justified. The spurning of the mentality of calculated reward is expressed most shockingly in the parable of the laborers in the vineyard (Matt. 20:1–16), where those who work for an hour receive as much pay as those who work a full day. The excessiveness of God's love is expressed most strongly in the stories of the Prodigal Son (Luke 15:11–32) and the Good Samaritan (Luke 10:29–37). The father of the prodigal goes out to welcome his son, robes him in his best clothes and prepares a great feast. Not only does the good Samaritan help the wounded man whom the clergy had passed by but he also puts the man on his horse while he walks, and he pays for the man's recovery. *Schillebeeckx insists that the logic for living expressed in these parables, including the "astonishing, 'excessive' compassion" they reveal, is "a concrete possibility in life." Jesus, himself a parable of God, demonstrates this.*[9] Finally, we can see that because the parables oppose the blind following of already prescribed rules and the calculating mentality that this requires, and because they demand unmeasuredness and even 'excessive' giving, they demand innovativeness in ethics and the risk-taking this entails.

Although Segundo agrees with all of this, there are some things he says which may lead us to believe that he does not. He argues, for example, that while Jesus may have appeared to criticize the attitude of the priest and Levite, the good Samaritan was in a position to help the wounded man only because he had, in his life, ignored many others in need. Otherwise he would not have had horse or money. We cannot help every needy person we meet. To attempt to do so is merely to waste our limited time and energy and to succeed in helping no one.[10] *Segundo is, in effect, warning us against turning a parable into a legalistically interpreted Law.* But, in order to see that this does not conflict with Schillebeeckx's call to excessiveness as a concrete possibility, we shall turn to their discussions of the Sermon on the Mount.

Jesus' Positive View of the Law and the Sermon on the Mount

Consistent with Schillebeeckx's insistence that we are called to live the radicalness depicted in the parables, liberationists agree that we must not soften the imperative to love in the Sermon on the Mount. We must not weaken it to a mere loving disposition or set of rules for right practice or to the status of mere advice which is not binding. Responsible and creative engagement in the incompletable, ultimately humanly impossible task of the kingdom is not something for saints and heroes only but for all of us.

According to Schillebeeckx, the Sermon on the Mount must be understood as a "critical, utopian stimulus" for ethics. It is involved in every context but it always contains "a surplus" and we never completely capture it, even when we attempt to revise our structures in accordance with its goals.[11] What Schillebeeckx is getting at is that in our changing history new structures will always become outdated. And old, resolved negativities will give rise to new ones. Old ways of thinking and acting will always have to give way to new ways which cannot be laid down in advance but which we must discover. However, while the message of the Sermon cannot tell us what to do in any context, it can and ought to act as a critical, guiding force for every context. It does so by providing us with a structure of values, general directions for practice, and the requirement that our values and practice be integrated. In the Sermon, Jesus provides us with a model and criterion for deciding what to do, but does not tell us what to do; this demands a "new creative response" to new situations.[12] Schillebeeckx gives examples from Paul such as his allowing exceptions to the command against divorce in a way appropriate to the welfare of his society. He adds his own twentieth-century insight that, because marriage is itself a cultural phenomenon, what may not be dissolved is culturally relative, so that both seeking reasons for divorce and vetoing second marriages miss the point.[13]

Once again, Segundo may give the appearance of subverting the radicalness of the gospel message because he denies that the Sermon on the Mount necessarily calls us to turn the other cheek or, indeed, to reject violence. But his reason for this is that the Sermon does not tell us what to do. Furthermore, he argues, overt behavior cannot be morally evaluated in isolation. Its worthiness is relative to that of the intended project into which it is integrated. To concentrate on isolated actions, mere externalities, is legalistic and mistaken. To turn to the root of our action in our attitudes and intentions is at the heart of the Sermon's message. Not only killing and adultery but anger and lust are to be overcome. But this is not to say that only attitudes count, nor is it to say that Jesus, in effect, adds inner do's and don't's to the external ones of the Pharisaic interpretation of the Law. Nor is it to say that the integrated self as such, the 'beautiful me,' is what counts. Our integrated action must be geared to the ends of love and human flourishment. This means that Jesus is not renouncing all anger any more than he is renouncing all killing. He expressed anger and a modicum of violence on the occasion of the cleansing of the temple and he was not repentant for it. The impossibility of spelling out in advance just what kind of love we are to engage in has the advantage of leaving us

> free to operate imaginatively and creatively, to figure out what would be the most effective and comprehensive sort of mutual love at a given moment in history. . . . Jesus is calling attention to a gratuitous sort of love that almost seems to be a useless luxury—and that is all.[14]

The specific kind of love that Jesus preached and practiced expresses his way in his situation of being most effective in love.

It is clear from all of this that Segundo's pointing out the limitations of the good Samaritan cannot be in conflict with Schillebeeckx's pointing to the Samaritan's gratuitous and excessive love. Our love is gratuitous and excessive if we give unmeasuredly, neither measuring the other's need nor measuring or even expecting reward for ourselves. But we must at least attempt to make our love effective, and so we must discern and make judgments about which of competing needs we shall address. Once again, Schillebeeckx and Segundo complement one another, each bringing a necessary aspect of Jesus' message to the fore. *Segundo makes us aware of the limitation of our very historicity, not in order to smother our possibilities but to free us to be effective. Schillebeeckx brings to life, to some degree, the experience that Jesus himself instilled in people, of the kingdom that was possible for them to practice.*

Political Significance of Jesus' Relationship to the Law

Jesus objected to the oppressive ways in which the Mosaic Law was interpreted and enforced when it was intended and claimed to be for the good of the people. And he objected to the Temple, the "house of prayer," being turned into a "robbers' den." Both what he said and did and the authority he claimed in speaking and acting constituted a "mortal threat" to the religious establishment. And for this Jesus was executed.[15]

While liberationists agree that it was Jesus' conflict with the religious leaders of Israel and not a conflict with the Roman overlords that was the reason (although not the sole cause) of his being executed, they also insist that this conflict was more than a narrowly religious one. Jesus only bothered to confront the religious authorities because, through their use of the Law, wittingly or unwittingly, they were oppressing the ordinary people, making them outcasts in their own culture. The poor people of Jesus' world were not instructed in the intricacies of the Law, so they did not know it and could not obey it. But, for this reason, they were judged by the religious authorities to be unworthy, unclean, "sinners." Segundo argues that this sanctioned a class structure within the Jewish society which affected every aspect of people's lives.[16] Liberationists agree that Jesus struck at a more fundamental kind of oppression than any the Romans could lay on the Jewish people because the oppression under the Law was hidden and, indeed, sacralized, made to appear as though it were good, what people 'deserved', and God's will. This, of course, served to doubly oppress people, to oppress them objectively, in terms of their status and opportunities in society and in terms of their position before God, and to oppress them subjectively, in terms of their self-worth. Jesus was executed, then, not only because he threatened the authority of the religious leaders qua religious but also because he threatened their social power. And he unmasked not only hypocrisy and self-deception in narrowly religious matters but also a this-worldly greed.[17]

However, why Jesus was such a threat to the religious leaders of his time, and why his message is an equal threat to people in positions of power today, religious and nonreligious alike, is not only because he unmasks structures which serve the self-interest of the powerful—although this is sufficient reason to make him a threat. *Even more threatening, he does not replace one set of do's and don't's, one set of controls, with another, which, ironically, precisely because they can be completely grasped and controlled, can also be used to control and manipulate not only other humans but also the gods.* By rejecting the Law as a set of clear-cut rules, Jesus rejected the view of it as a contract which restricts God more than humans and which can be used by humans to make God in their image. Jesus' demonstration of his own human freedom and his innovativeness in relativizing all rules to the criterion of love for the other, especially the other in need, undermines the security of any religious—or secular—establishment which thinks it controls God or gods.[18]

The Anthropology Jesus Displays vis-à-vis His Innovativeness

Jesus demonstrates a number of fundamental human qualities in the attitude he takes to the Law. He shows himself to be one who *experiences* most acutely what is going on around him and who attends particularly to the sufferings and oppressions that must be overcome in order to bring God's rule and kingdom closer. He is an active *interpreter:* Rather than passively accepting the established interpretation of the Law, and thus following the course of least resistance, Jesus actively seeks its inner meaning, its spirit. He discerns its spirit through the acute contrast between his experience of God's excessive love and compassion for humans and his experience of the suffering and deprivation of many around him. To interpret presupposes bringing values to one's interpretation, being an evaluator. Because Jesus does not accept the established interpretation of the Law as a set of fully spelled-out rules which fit every circumstance and are not in need of interpretation, but because he interprets the Law in an open-ended kind of way and in keeping with his own experience of the good, he is an *evaluator* of the Law in a strong, deliberate sense. Jesus is an *actor*, one who acts on his evaluations. His action is not, as it were, passive. Rather, he upsets the established order when he cures on the Sabbath, turns over the tables in the temple, talks theology to women. In all of this, we see that Jesus is *both free and responsible*. He is free from a 'letter' of the Law composed of restrictions imposed from without and which conflict with what is authentic and important. And this makes him free to pursue the 'spirit' of the Law which conforms to a liberated and flourishing humanity. He thus takes responsibility for how he interprets and what he does.

All of this implies an *innovativeness and creativity* on Jesus' part, which involves a certain *know-how*. We can make use of Segundo's distinction between faith and ideologies here. Jesus recognizes that the point of the Law is human welfare. This is his value and goal, his anthropological faith which he takes as absolute. And the system of norms that the Law expresses, he treats as a relative system of means, an ideology which is as valuable as it contributes to this end. In his treatment of the Law, he shows that the main creative task of ethics is to integrate our means with our fundamental value, to let go of or revise outdated interpretations and norms for right practice and to seek new ones which will make our value alive in a changing context.[19]

ANTHROPOLOGICAL AND EPISTEMOLOGICAL PRESUPPOSITIONS OF AN INNOVATIVE ETHIC

Jesus' relationship to the Law demonstrates, not only that it is necessary, but also that it is possible to work out in creative ways how best to serve the humanum in an ever-changing context. But there is enormous theoretical difficulty in understanding how creativity and the freedom that it requires are possible, how we can genuinely take our historical context into account in our ethicity. Neither traditional empiricist nor rationalist epistemologies and anthropologies can account for these or, indeed, for how learning, the *becoming* of knowledge, is possible.

The first part of this section will propose something of a gestalt model of learning, where, by means of both acting and allowing on our part, outdated forms of thought and practice disintegrate and new ones emerge. This involves a kind of 'knowing how' which is prior to 'knowing that,' a practice which is prior to theory and norms for practice.

But also, if our ethics is to be creative and if genuine learning is to be possible, then reality must be able to open up new experience and new practice which is not completely governed by our already-given interpretations and systems of norms. The second part of this section will use George Lindbeck's cultural-linguistic model of interpretation as a foil for exploring the ways in which experience and practice must be prior to theory and norms.

Innovative Learning and the Priority of Practice

We have been arguing throughout that experiences of negativity, whether they be of massive poverty or the destruction of our ecology, place an ethical demand on us to change our practice and interpretation so as to overcome the negativity. Experience of negativity is an important guide to right practice and understanding because it demonstrates where our interpretations and projects do not take proper account of the reality which exists independently of us. This is as true for science as it is for ethics.[20] Negative experience often requires more than superficial 'corrections.' It often requires creative shifts in practice and thought.

Philosophers have argued that neither rationalist nor empiricist epistemologies can account for the creativity required for learning or discovering something fundamentally new. Rationalists, too richly armed with innate ideas, must already know what they are looking for, and empiricists, too meagerly armed with 'blank sheets,' cannot recognize what they are looking for even if they discover it.[21] Applied to ethics, we can say that rationalists, armed with a priori principles from which they deduce what to do, cannot account for the requirements of a changing history and so cannot respond to negativity. And empiricists, unarmed as they are, cannot respond to negativity in a way which is consistent with permanent grounded values. Indeed, empiricists cannot account for value at all.[22] Analogous to Segundo's view that the flexibility and integration required by evolution involve both purposiveness and chance, so too innovative learning requires both bringing our knowledge and purposes, questions and values, to bear actively on a negativity, and also waiting on the world to act on us in directions we can encourage but not force or completely predict but which we must respect.[23]

We do not merely respond to 'raw' stimuli or apply a priori categories but adapt to the world's impingement in ways that protect our integratedness and directionality, and that may also require reintegration and revised directionality. We actively engage the world by interpreting it and acting on it in terms of our values and interests. It is only *because* we interpret and act on reality, that reality can be known to us at all. But, of course, we cannot interpret or act on the world in any way at all. And when reality responds negatively to our practice and interpretation, we ignore it at our peril.[24]

When reality negates features of our practice and conceptual framework we do, or ought to, move from determinateness, clarity, certainty, to indeterminateness, unclarity, uncertainty in their regard. It is not that we have had everything all wrong but rather that some things have gone askew; our practice and understanding have not kept pace with changes in the situation. We are, as it were, surrounded by data which does not quite fit together and by models, principles, and norms that do not fit the data. Often our understanding of our problem is almost as indeterminate as its solution; we do not know just what our problem is until we know its solution. Often there is no single solution to our problem and no single articulation of it. Both our ethical and scientific histories can move in many directions. Reality provides us with genuine opportunity for creativity.[25] We can, within limits set down by reality and by our own and our inherited experience, genuinely make new meaning. The move from indeterminateness to determinateness, which is a move to a new focus or integration, requires both active seeking or purposiveness and allowing a new gestalt to form which seems to involve chance. To try methodically to put the pieces together is not enough. We have to wait on their coming together. But it is important to allow ourselves to move into this vulnerable position of indeterminateness when reality challenges. Clinging to outdated solutions only creates negativity and disintegration.[26]

That we are not in complete conscious control of our innovative learning but that it has a tacit dimension which requires allowing things to fall into place is important. This tacit dimension involves know-how or practical knowledge which cannot be captured in a sum of propositions or rules. Games which involve physical skill provide an obvious example of practical knowledge. The tennis player attends from the direction of the breeze, the surface of the court, and even his bodily movements and predetermined strategy, and he attends to the play, the overall project in which he is engaged. Yet, while he is not attending to all these other things, he must be taking them into account. Gilbert Ryle[27] argues that this sort of practice clearly involves intelligence, the applying of criteria, thinking what one is doing, and not simply rote response. But this does not involve doing two things, having propositions or prescriptions running through one's head followed by a certain behavior, doing a bit of theory followed by a bit of practice. The thought is in the practice. The implications of this become apparent if we take a more 'intellectual' example such as Ryle's classic case of the chess player. The chess player may reflect before making an intelligent move but often does not. If to make an intelligent move required bringing some rule of strategy to mind, how would she guarantee that she had brought the appropriate one to mind? To posit the bringing to mind of a prior rule would obviously lead to an infinite regress of reflectings on rules. In any case, to bring the appropriate rule to mind is not enough. She would have to know how to apply it appropriately in this situation, and further rules could not tell her this. No matter how many rules we know, how many strategies we have memorized, we cannot formulate recipes for recognizing when to use and change a strategy, for formulating a new strategy to fit new circumstances, even for recognizing what is the strategy of our opponent. Genuine, intelligent knowing-how involves constant innovativeness, taking an intelligent but partly tacit account of a constantly changing situation and being able to adapt to it for the sake of an end. All of this explains the possibility of the 'holy fool,' an ethical example. The 'holy fool' may be contrasted with the highly articulate person, who, for example, knows that she is unreliable at the reflective, propositional level but who is blind to it at the practical level, who systematically makes promises believing that she will keep them and who systematically fails. The 'holy fool' on the other hand, is so lacking in self-concern but so concerned for and in tune with the needs of others, that she almost always brings about good quite oblivious to what are her criteria and often quite unable to adequately articulate them.[28] While to romanticize inarticulateness is not helpful, the contrast here demonstrates where value and goodness really lie.

Knowing-how cannot be captured as a sum of propositions; indeed, propositional knowledge or knowing that presupposes knowing-how. Theory, theoretical knowledge presupposes theorizing which, of course, is a form of practice. But even theorizing requires a base in experience and in prior nontheorizing forms of practice which the theorizing is about. *We engage in logical and scientific and ethical practice before we theorize about these things or formulate propositions or principles about them.* Theories and principles and even experience and practice may become sedimented, ritualized, absolutized, leaving no room for innovation. But because our relationship to reality changes and requires our innovation, to allow sedimentation will bring about a disastrous lack of fit between the requirements of reality and our ethical and cognitive response. *While both practice and theory can be sedimented or innovative, theory and theorizing presuppose experience and practice; new theory and new theorizing presuppose new experience and new practice.* We are engaged thinkers before we are disengaged thinkers; we are actors before we are contemplators. Because we are mental/ physical, we think/behave before we learn to separate our thinking from our behavior by reflecting on what we do. And innovativeness requires this.

Four Ways in which Experience and Practice Are Prior to Theory and Norms for Practice: A Liberationist Response to Lindbeck's Cultural-Linguistic Model

In the last chapter we stressed the social character of our anthropology and ethics. In this chapter we have begun to stress the importance of knowledge as a practical skill and how this kind of knowledge is prior to propositional knowledge. We have argued that language is central to our sociability, but it is also a central form of our practice. From this, it may appear that the liberationist perspective has much in common with George Lindbeck's cultural-linguistic approach. This approach sees religion and ethics as social phenomena and practical skills we are trained in, on the model of language. However, for Lindbeck, the cultural-linguistic framework or tradition into which we are born has priority over experience and practice which, on a strong interpretation, lays him open to charges of cultural determinism, behaviorism, cultural relativism, fideism, and idealism (although not solipsism). I shall argue, by contrast, that there must be a certain priority or at least independence of experience and practice vis-à-vis the cultural-linguistic framework in order that we may avoid the various 'isms' and in order that ethics may be truly innovative. Using Lindbeck as a foil will help show that to posit the priority of practice to theory is not sufficient in order to capture the creativity and freedom necessary to the liberationist perspective. *Priority must be given to new practice which must be based on new experience of a reality which, in some spheres, challenges and negates, and thus demonstrates that it is independent of the cultural-linguistic framework.* The productive force of the negative contrast experience, i.e., the imperative to resist suffering, and the operation of the hermeneutical circle of learning, depend on this.

Lindbeck's View

Hermeneutics. For Lindbeck, the original stories found in the sacred texts of a religion provide "the interpretive framework within which believers seek to live their lives and understand reality." The stories provide the rules for religious and ethical practice which issue into experience and belief. Thus we ought to start in ethics and religion, not with contemporary secular experience but with our sacred texts; we ought not to seek our stories in the text but to make its stories our own. "It is the text, so to speak, which absorbs the world, rather than the world the text." And it seems to be assumed that the text will disclose its meaning if we but attend to its literary structure. Lindbeck admits that his model of religion will stress debate about conceptual issues more than issues of substance, such as those which concern liberationists. But rather than attempting to make religion popular by accommodating it to the interests and norms of secular society as the liberal does, Lindbeck thinks religion should attract people by example and initiate them into its traditional ways. Even if this means fewer will respond, truer and more deeply committed Christians may be formed.[29]

Priority of the cultural-linguistic context. Key to Lindbeck's position is that, while there is a reciprocal relationship between the religious text, or, more generally, the cultural-linguistic context and experience, the former and not the latter acts as "leading partner." On his view, "human experience is shaped, molded, and *in a sense constituted* by cultural and linguistic forms." Inner experience is primarily a *product* and even a *by-product* of the cultural-linguistic context. Thus, the traditional relation between the inner and the outer is reversed. He argues that "it is necessary to have the means for expressing an experience in order to have it, and the richer our expressive or linguistic system, the more subtle, varied, and differentiated can be our experience."[30]

No universal core religious experience. Because religious experience arises out of a text, Lindbeck denies that there is a universal core religious experience. He argues that love, for example, can have but a 'family resemblance' and has no common essence as used by Buddhist, Christian, and humanist. He states without evidence that different religions often produce "fundamentally divergent depth experiences of what it is to be human." Not only does he deny that all humans look out onto a common reality, but also he assumes that there are no linguistic or other anthropological universals.[31]

Change in a religious tradition. Given the priority Lindbeck claims for the cultural-linguistic framework, we are forced to ask how does the framework get off the ground in the first place and how does change in it take place? Lindbeck makes no attempt to answer the first question but he does offer a response to the second. He argues that change in a religious tradition and in a cultural-linguistic framework takes place not in response to new experiences but because the religious or more general interpretive scheme becomes inappropriate to a new context. He explains that the clash between the framework and the new context produces a negative experience which stimulates prophets to seek new concepts which, in turn, produce new religious experiences.[32] But what is the new context if it is not a change in reality which is not governed by our framework of interpretation? And what is the negative experience if it is not the experience of that reality saying "no" to our interpretation, an experience which is not completely governed by our framework but rather demands that we creatively seek change in our framework? Lindbeck's language sometimes suggests determinism, where change takes place through the clash of two systems of which we are but the passive recipients. It sometimes suggests what he denies, that our new experience is not "constituted" by our framework but encourages us to make changes in the framework.

On truth. Another connected difficulty for Lindbeck involves whether we can come to experience and understand other frameworks than our own and whether we can adjudicate between them. What constitutes truth for Lindbeck? Within a framework, truth involves not just coherence of a propositional sort, but integration of practice and experience, of form of life, based not on axioms and definitions but on stories that hold a logic for right living. But because the very meaning of propositions is dependent on this wider behavioral context, the non-believer who does not or has not practiced a religion cannot understand its propositional claims. Different religions

> may have incommensurable notions of truth, experience and of categorial adequacy, and therefore also of what it would mean for something to be most important (i.e., "God").

Then, notions of goodness and ethics would also be incommensurable. Lindbeck argues that some religions correspond better than others to an extra-systematic reality and to the nature and will of God. But he gives us no criteria for adjudicating among religions. Yet later in the text he denies that his position is relativist or fideist. There he argues that religions can be compared on an ad hoc basis but not according to universal norms.[33]

A Liberationist Response

In general, the liberationist rejects Lindbeck's view that the cultural-linguistic framework has priority over experience. The liberationist can sympathize with, gain from, and even contribute to Lindbeck's claim that the text provides a grammar or logic for living but not a content to be mimicked.[34] But for the liberationist it is crucial that we do not start with the ancient text but that we bring our contemporary experiences of suffering to the text and test what it has to offer by how genuinely relevant it is to our experience. *This is not to accommodate but to challenge the status quo and to refuse to escape into Lindbeck's 'safe' religion* which, as Lindbeck himself admits, engages in conceptual analysis while avoiding contemporary problems. Indeed, in seeming simply to opt for an ancient text, rather than, for example, to opt for the poor, Lindbeck is in danger of being not only irrelevant but arbitrary, promoting closed and rigid religious communities which train us before we can question and deny us any very clear tools for questioning.

Liberationists agree and disagree with what Lindbeck says about a common core experience of God. Because they think all experience is interpreted they are likely to deny that there is such a common experience. But, even if they think there is a universal feeling of, for example, trust in the whole, they do not base religion and ethics on it. Segundo points out that such a feeling is so general as to admit of contradictory interpretations and practices. Christian love, for example, means support for the status quo, an easy peace for some, support for the marginalized, and justice through conflict for others. For liberationists, what counts fundamentally is whether people, whether they be Christian, Moslem, or atheist, live by the same value of liberation, especially for the worst off.[35] This, of course, conflicts with Lindbeck's view that agreement or disagreement is (or ought to be) relative to the text from which people proceed. The liberationist thinks, in spite of our deep cultural differences, that there are similarities in the sufferings and a commonness to the world we experience, which make dialogue and agreement possible, regarding not only fundamental values but policies for practice. And this is crucially important for solving global problems such as poverty and pollution.

For liberationists, new, particularly negative, experiences demand change which will involve new practice and understanding and a revision of our framework. We bring our preunderstanding, our cultural-linguistic framework, to our experience, but the experience and our response to it in part transcend the framework and are not determined by it. There is a genuine dialectic between new experience and practice on the one hand and our framework on the other. More than this, there is a genuine hermeneutical circle between these, which enables learning. A newly revised framework resulting from a prior new experience and practice may play a role in the very having of a new later experience. But a new experience of external reality can still negate, and so transcend, the framework.

Liberationists are in partial agreement with Lindbeck's view that we do not understand even the propositions expressed by those engaging in a form of life not our own. They agree that we do not at all fully understand the option for the poor or what it is to follow Jesus if we have not engaged in these practices. Right practice precedes correct understanding. But, if asked, they also would argue that, through observation, imagination, empathy, and recognizing similarities between the framework of the other and our own, all of which are *made possible by a commonness in our humanity opening onto a common world,* we can, *to some extent,* understand the other from that other's perspective. This is implicit in the view that reality teaches us by negating our frameworks when our frameworks are not true to reality.

Four Senses of Priority

Discussion of the differences between Lindbeck and the liberationists has revolved around the issue of priority between the cultural-linguistic framework on the one hand and new experience and innovative practice on the other. But just what can be meant by priority has remained vague. I shall suggest four different things that can be meant and then go on to discuss what would be the liberationist position on each of them.[36]

(1) The most obvious sort of priority is *causal or genetic priority* where either experience and practice is considered to be temporally prior to and to causally bring about the cultural-linguistic framework, or vice versa.

(2) A second sort of priority, which we may entitle *logical or conceptual priority*, considers whether using language and engaging in the various disciplines, including theology, and in religious and ethical practice are primarily about experience and are expressions of experience, or whether humans engage in these things primarily for their own sake and not to express something else.

(3) We may distinguish *existential priority* where, for the one perspective to be authentic, practice and belief must be based primarily on the authority of experience and not on the authority of the cultural-linguistic framework. For the other perspective, experience is the product of noninnovative practice which, together with its systematization in religion and morality should be understood as a skill we are trained in. On this view, the Christian comes to experience salvation, say, by following Jesus, in the sense of engaging in an imitative practice.

(4) We may speak of an *epistemological priority* according to which, for the one perspective, we can know or experience more than we can tell and for the other, we can tell more than we know or experience. According to the first perspective, at least sometimes, our experience is richer than or different from our conceptualizations and we must seek better expressions of our experience. Whatever the origin of experience, the quality of new experiences is not determined by the cultural-linguistic context. On the second perspective, the context enriches experience by allowing new discriminations. What can be experienced

is circumscribed by what can be expressed. What is experienced by any given person at any given time is circumscribed by what can be expressed by that person at that time.

Regarding the *first* alternatives, it is true that the cultural-linguistic context may and undoubtedly will cause some experiences or others. But the issue is whether the context is the leading partner vis-à-vis experience. If so, we have no explanation for how the cultural-linguistic context itself comes about and we have serious problems regarding how social change takes place. Also, to the extent to which we argue for the causal priority of the cultural-linguistic framework, to that extent are we committing ourselves to the view that we are culturally determined in our experience of, practice in response to, and thought about the world and ourselves. We are as determined in our practice as in our experience and thought because, while on this view experience and thought are the by-products of our practice, our practice itself is not innovative but is the product of training in the way of the context. *Without there being 'room' in the scheme of things for experience, however indeterminate, which is not circumscribed by the cultural-linguistic framework* but which responds to changes in a changing environment and which seeks changes in the cultural-linguistic framework, *there is no room for innovative practice, for freedom to operate in integrating practice and value. Without this space between the framework and some experience, we have no access to reality except as circumscribed by the context, and so no means of adjudicating the context or initiating change.* While we can agree with Schillebeeckx and the other liberationists that all experience is interpreted and that we never confront reality raw, in order that there be a genuine dialectic, a mutual influence, between what is given from the side of the self and of reality, experience must be able to find the cultural-linguistic context inadequate and so must, to an extent, be able to escape it. As we have already seen, negative experience questions our frameworks and interpretations. So all experience cannot be completely governed by our frameworks and interpretations. If there were not "room" for new experience and practice, then response to the imperative to resist every threat to the humanum would become impossible.

Regarding the *second* alternatives, I would agree with the perspective that gives priority to the cultural-linguistic framework to the extent that, because we are fundamentally social, we are fundamentally communicators, which in our case means language-users. We often talk and participate in various common forms of life more for the sake of sociability than for the sake of communicating or accomplishing something else. But it is also true that knowledge is based on experience and experience is its test. *The various intellectual disciplines and theories, as well as religious and ethical practice, are fundamentally about our experience of the world and ourselves in it, and they are for the sake of exploring, explaining, and changing experience or they are empty.* However influenced is our experience by our framework, we build and rebuild the framework to reflect not only experience as it is but as we perceive it ought to be. To harmonize our experience with the cultural-linguistic framework is to support the status quo and encourage determinism, whereas to seek changes in the framework so as to fit actual and aimed-at experience involves freedom and innovativeness. While the cultural-linguistic framework is not only for the sake of experience, aimless communicating is trivial by comparison to theorizing and otherwise engaging in building the framework to conform to our purposes, which are tied to experience.

Regarding the *third* alternatives, from the experientialist point of view, if belief and action are to be authentic, to be truly human and not a more-or-less rote response to some external authority, they have to be grounded in our experience of what the world is and how it ought to be. Although there is an interdependence between experience and the cultural-linguistic context, *if the latter does not encourage our belief and action to be true to an experience which is not simply handed down by our tradition, then, although we are social and need some cultural-linguistic context or other, the one we have becomes an external authority which is oppressive rather than liberative.* This is not to deny the importance of learning-how, the skill involved in religion and morality; but it is to resist blind training in that skill, behavior modification, rather than initiation into a creative know how which exercises our freedom and, in response to negativity, aims at bringing what is the case closer to what ought to be the case. Nor is this to deny that we learn the full meaning and value of, say, the Christian faith, only by engaging in its practices, by living it; but there has to be something which attracts us and holds us which is not strictly internal to the system itself. Human authenticity requires that we test our framework by our experience.

Regarding the *fourth* alternatives, understood properly, we both can know or experience more than we can tell and we can tell more than we experience. But, while we can learn from language to discriminate subtle colors or emotions, say, *it is only, initially, because someone experienced the need for a new discrimination, experienced, indeterminately, something new, and sought to map it into the logic of the language, that there* *are the discriminations in language which we can learn.* There is quite another sense of knowing more than we can tell: practical knowledge, knowing how to swim or play chess, is a knowledge which cannot be spelled out in propositions.

I conclude that while social conditioning is necessary for our liberation as well as being a cause of oppression, while our very subjectivity is partially but fundamentally dependent on this conditioning, our experience, belief, and practice are not completely circumscribed or determined by that conditioning. A dialectical interaction is involved whereby new negative experience, guided by reality, and new creative practice in response to this experience, compel us to change our framework which then, in its revised form, contributes to the way we approach reality. While there is a strong interdependence between our new experience and with it our innovative practice on the one hand and the cultural-linguistic framework on the other, in the dimensions of priority I have distinguished, new experience and practice do have priority over the given framework. Neither cultural determinism nor cultural relativism and fideism threaten an innovative and responsible ethic.

Similarities between the Cultural-Linguistic Model and the Cognitivist Model

Ironically, Lindbeck's cultural-linguistic model of religion, ethics, and interpretation tends to have some of the serious drawbacks of the traditional cognitivist model. The cognitivist approach understands religion and ethics as involving, primarily, the communication of informative propositions and ethical principles which, respectively, have an objective and nonrelative truth-value and imperative for right practice. On this view, orthodoxy is prior to orthopractice. It recommends the handing down of 'eternal' truths and norms which we are to accept and apply to our own historical situation. The authority of tradition predominates over what Schillebeeckx calls the authority of experience. While the cultural-linguistic approach appears very different because it stresses practice over propositions and theories and, for all practical purposes, relativizes truth and right conduct to a language and culture or a story and religion, for the cultural-linguist too the authority of tradition predominates. In this case, of course, the tradition does not represent absolute and unchanging truth, although we seem to have to relate to it as though it did. In both cases we are locked into a system imposed on us from the outside. For neither are we genuinely creative and free moral agents who must work out what to do in a changing history. *Thus we see clearly that it is not sufficient to give priority to practice over propositions, theories, and norms. We must give priority to new experience and new practice over new propositions, new theories, and new norms.*

AN ETHIC OF DISCIPLESHIP

A liberationist ethic, because it is a creative ethic for which knowing-how is important, lends itself to an ethic of discipleship. We may ask, how is this possible? How can an ethic which stresses creative discovery of what we ought to do be an ethic of following another? This section will argue that we can learn from our experience of others which values are worth living for. Ironically, it is precisely because learning right practice involves know-how or creative skill that the example of others is important—to show us how. If learning right practice were a matter of learning a set of rules, a computer printout or a stone tablet would do as well.

Learning Values and Human Models

While the productive force of the contrast experience involves a tendency to resist oppression, it is clear that not everyone accepts it as a fundamental value. We can learn this value from our experience of the oppressed and those who are in solidarity with them. But we can look to other models as well, models representing money or fame, say. While we cannot get a preview of what our life will be if we opt for this or that value, we can and do extend our own experience by looking to the lives of others, particularly lives already lived.[37] We learn what will be our overriding value and goal, that in terms of which our life will be integrated and toward which it will be geared, from people more than from philosophical argument and handed-down statements of values and principles. The reason for this is, in part, because we trust people more than ideas. People attract us, move us, and interest us more than ideas. So we learn from them. Also, in people we see values contextualized or given meaning and concretized or given existence. Only then do we really know what we are giving assent to.

Abstract principles and rules cannot capture the integratedness of value, intention, action, goal, and consequences in a context in the way that the story of a human life or even a slice of a human life does. We are moved by stories about people in much the same way as by direct encounter with them, and it is appropriate that we should learn fundamental value from the story of Jesus, of a life already lived.

Schillebeeckx recognizes the power of story to transform. He frames his book, *Jesus*, with two stories of crippled men. He relates the story from Acts 3 and 4, which tells of a man who daily begged for alms at the temple gate and was cured *through Peter's calling on the name of Jesus*. But magic turns to miracle when Schillebeeckx interprets that the man was cured *when he heard from Peter the story of Jesus*. The second story relates how a paralyzed man, while telling the story of his mentor who would leap and dance during his prayers, found that he had to *show how* the master had done it—and so the crippled man was cured. Here, the very telling of the story becomes the practice of its content. Between these stories Schillebeeckx offers us his own attempt to bring the story of Jesus alive for our generation.[38]

Learning How to Integrate Practice with Value

We take our fundamental value, that in terms of which we live our lives, to be lasting. And what really *is* of fundamental value, which we can articulate in terms of human and cosmic welfare, does not change with a changing context. This is why we can learn what is of fundamental value from people who are long dead. But, as the discussion of Jesus and the Law demonstrates, forms of practice are relative to our historical situation. *A central problem of ethics, then, is to find forms of practice which will make our value alive in our context. This involves knowing how, and we learn how by and large by being shown how, by the example of others.* But can we say more about Jesus' showing us how?

In Segundo's technical language, Jesus, in effect, distinguishes faith, his ultimate value, from ideologies, the systems of means he employs in order to make his value felt in history.[39] Let us consider this. While Jesus was not explicitly attuned to the relativity of our existence in the way that our modern historical consciousness has allowed, his whole life was geared toward preaching and practicing the kingdom of God for all, through alleviating the physical, psychological, and social sufferings of the worst off in his society. His aim was practical, to offer partial salvation and the hope of eschatological salvation by responding to concrete historical need. His method was to achieve positive ends by seeking to alleviate the suffering that he found. This required that he relativize everything else, especially the static rules associated with the Law which, in his context (although perhaps not in an earlier age), served to cause rather than to alleviate suffering. From a liberationist perspective, the means Jesus used, the ideology he created, which included a whole interpretation of reality as well as a system of practices, was primarily political. By curing the sick, talking theology with women and having meals with sinners, he demonstrated God's love for society's outcasts and marginalized while, at the same time, by confronting the manipulators of the Law, he exposed their systematic sacralization of oppression. By these two connected means he sought to overcome oppressive structures.

But what are we to learn from this? Are we to treat Jesus' using a political ideology for the sake of liberation as an example for us to find a system of means appropriate to our context? Or are we to accept Jesus' political ideology? Or can we learn something which is more instructive than the first and less imitative than the second? Segundo suggests that Paul did not adopt Jesus' political ideology but developed a broader, anthropological system of means appropriate to his more universal context, embracing as it did both Jews and Gentiles. This anthropological ideology speaks of humans as divided selves who cannot accomplish the good that they intend because, driven by both greed and the need for the security of self-righteousness, they become immersed in self-deception. But, even when they are in good faith, freedom normally does not function; they are "helpless 'creator(s)' in a world already made"[40] according to its own laws, which conflict with our freedom. But Segundo suggests an even broader evolutionary ideology to be most appropriate for our time, one which seeks flexibility in solving our complex global problems, by making use of both negentropy and entropy, purposiveness and chance, acting and allowing, for the sake of greater integration of the social and natural world.

Thus, determining what we ought to do in ethics involves learning, not so much facts or rules, propositions or prescriptions, but learning to learn,[41] learning how to go on, learning how to integrate our interpretation and practice with our value in light of a changing situation which offers new difficulties and possibilities. Learning to learn, creating new ideologies, involves a hermeneutical circle moving from new experience, usually of negativity, through new, tentative practice, to new, systematized, interpretations of reality and norms for right practice which will be appropriate to our lasting value and goal. And these norms and interpretations come to form part of the preunderstanding with which we approach reality once more.[42] But can we be more precise?

While there is no deductive route from one of these ideologies to another, they are connected. The anthropological ideology reveals the universal mechanisms at work in Jesus' political exposé. The religious leaders deceive themselves in their misuse of the Law in order to both satisfy their greed for power and wealth and appear righteous. And Jesus, in spite of his good faith and creative use of the Law, seems to fail overall in his project of the kingdom. Forces outside his control are more powerful than he. The evolutionary ideology demonstrates that the gap between what we will and what we accomplish has a base in the workings of nature itself. Most people, most of the time, will take the course of least resistance, of the status quo, what, in evolutionary language, is called entropy. But even if, like Jesus, we make a great effort to balance negentropy and entropy, whatever gains we make will not be lasting. Thus, we can reinterpret Jesus' own story in more and more universal terms as we move from one ideology to the next. And we can see Jesus as salvation-bringer in each. Indeed Segundo thinks, in creating ideologies, if we take Jesus as our model, we are also creating Christologies.[43] But Segundo does not really intend that ideologies which are Christologies should be as closely connected as I have suggested his in fact are. According to Segundo, Jesus uses a political ideology for his context and he intends only that the other ideologies should capture what Jesus would have done in these other contexts. Paul creatively looked for analogues between Jesus' context and Jesus' salvific response to it on the one hand and his own context on the other, in order to discern what would be a salvific response to his situation, along Jesus' lines of value and creative practice. Paul transposed from Jesus' context to his own. For example, he made a connection between the Satan in Jesus, which enslaved individuals, and Sin, the universal enslaving mechanism which comes between conscious intention and actual performance. The evolutionary view clearly connects entropy, the tendency in nature toward disintegration, with Sin.

Thus learning from Jesus how to integrate practice with value involves more than treating him as an example of one who did this. It involves being concretely guided by the inner logic of Jesus' life.[44] *And we do this by seeing analogues between and creatively transposing from his context to our own; this is discipleship.* But it is significant that we learn how to go on integrating practice with value, not only from Jesus, but also from others who form a tradition with him. Without the example of others, we would be inclined to absolutize Jesus' means and to see him as replacing an old Law made up of one set of rules with a new one made up of another set.

Discipleship and a Christian Ethic

We began this section with the concern of how, if a liberationist ethic is a creative ethic, can it lend itself to an ethic of discipleship, of following another. We have shown that learning from other people is important to a creative ethic. We learn or choose what will be our most fundamental value on the basis of the lives of others, and we learn from others how to integrate our practice with our value. Disciples of Jesus see in his fundamental value their own and they see in his free and creative way of relativizing practice to value an invitation to do the same. Even more than this, they may learn something of how to interpret their context and find right practice by creatively working out how their context compares with that of Jesus. They may at least get glimpses of how to live in accordance with the inner logic of Jesus' life.

Some may still ask whether all of this is sufficient for an ethic of discipleship to Jesus. Does not discipleship to this unique person yield something unique, a unique Christian ethic? For others, however, with the introduction of a kind of transposing between Jesus' story and our own, a liberationist ethic may suddenly appear too narrowly Christian. Do we have to be disciples of Jesus in order to accept a liberationist ethic?

People who are not disciples of Jesus subscribe to the liberationist value and creatively seek to integrate their practice with that value. But is there anything unique about the inner logic of Jesus' life which the Christian will bring to her or his context? A central feature of Christian discipleship stemming from scripture and tradition, and also highlighted by liberationists, is that of following Jesus in suffering and even to death. But before we ask whether there is something distinctive, even unique about this, we must ask how do we make consistent with our aim of efficacious love, of effectively seeking to make our practice reflect our value, discipleship to one who came to be rejected by his friends as well as his enemies, and was executed? Sobrino sees Jesus' call to discipleship as having two stages. In the first stage he calls disciples to make a fundamental break with their values and possessions and to use their power effectively for God's kingdom. Later, when Jesus seems to be a failure and God's kingdom seems not to be coming into view, hope has to be hope against hope, and trust in God must be in spite of the evidence. This second stage involves an epistemological break whereby the demand on the Christian must be understood not only to surpass natural understanding but to contradict it. Discipleship means "no longer service to the kingdom that flows from a logic prior to Jesus" but "following the concrete person of Jesus" in the context of his seeming failure. There is "a shift from a line of action based on the universality of certain values (those of the kingdom) to a line of action based on a specific and particular reality (Jesus' own line of action.)" The first phase presupposes a God already known, the second involves following Jesus into the unknown, against natural 'common sense.' Loving efficaciously gives over to an apparently powerless love which manifests itself in suffering. The sacrifice of possessions becomes sacrifice of self.[45] However, our experience of the love of others and our own practice of love and justice in the face of persecution provide some grounds for hope against hope.[46] The experience and meaning of salvation are learned through the experience of suffering in our practice for others.

Is the ethic of Christian discipleship, then, unique, because it is radically attached to the person of Jesus who calls us to follow him against all logic? Sobrino is not suggesting that following Jesus is against *all* logic because, as we have just pointed out, he does admit that there are experiential grounds for hope in the context of suffering and failure. But he does think a new upside down logic comes to bear with the introduction of suffering and failure, one which we can only *see* as a logic in the context of following Jesus. I would argue, however, that *the demands of the kingdom, to give up status and possessions and to befriend the outcast, already constitute a radical break with the established order. And powerlessness and suffering are almost inevitable consequences of this.*

While we have associated knowing how to integrate practice and value with efficaciousness, in the ethical context it almost inevitably involves struggle, opposition, rejection, failure, and suffering on the way to a success which will always be incomplete and temporary. New sufferings will emerge as old ones may be resolved, and this is partly because new ideologies and social structures will become old, outdated, but resistant to change. Liberationists stress the predominance of suffering in history, a suffering "which dogs our best intentions and achievements."[47] And they agree that this will not change. The fundamental disorder, disjointedness, in which we find ourselves in history will not be made right in history. But we are not on a treadmill; we are not in a Sisyphus type of situation, persistently making efforts against an evil which is greater than ourselves, and always ending up back where we started. We partially succeed in overcoming concrete sufferings. Societies even progress to some extent and become more sensitive and responsive to what makes for liberation in certain spheres such as, for example, human rights. But partial success in the medium term costs in terms of some people's rejection and failure in the short term. And the need for new change does not cease.

The suffering, rejection, failure, and move to powerlessness which Sobrino associates with discipleship to Jesus is implicit in, or at least the inevitable consequence of, learning to learn and creating ideologies for the end of liberation, which Segundo associates with discipleship to Jesus. And while learning to learn and creating ideologies involve more than is included in the negative contrast experience itself, to be propelled to act out of that experience will, inevitably, lead to the demand for innovation and change, the demand for learning how to go on, which results in rejection and failure. Just as Jesus is a paradigm example of one who lived out of the negative contrast experience, he is a paradigm example of one who can show us how to go on, and his suffering, rejection, and failure actually give evidence to this. And if we combine Jesus' value rising out of the negative contrast experience and his showing us how, so that we are guided by the logic of his life, by transposing from his context to ours, then we will be learning from him how to go on, following him, in a profound sense. Also, finally, in order that it make sense to make the effort to go on, in order that our situation not collapse into that of a Sisyphus type, we have to have hope, or, often, hope against hope, for the concrete transformation of this situation of suffering now. And any hope we have that, 'in the end of the day,' goodness will prevail, will necessarily be a hope against hope. The salvific experience of the effort itself and the partial success we have are sufficient to give us hope, even though it may be a hope against hope, that the suffering before us can be overcome. But the Christian Easter experience, an experience that goodness does prevail overall, that Jesus' life and death are not only good and right but also that his value will govern and his efforts will succeed 'in the end of the day,' is a very powerful ground for hope both for today and for the absolute future. People who are not disciples of Jesus join and are effective in the struggle for liberation. But those who are not disciples of Jesus or someone like Jesus, in the Easter experience he stimulates in Christians, cannot have the same experientially based hope that goodness will prevail ultimately and in a way which transcends history.[48]

AN INNOVATIVE ETHIC IS A RESPONSIBLE ETHIC

It is not enough that ethics be creative and innovative; it must also be responsible. A liberationist ethic is a responsible ethic in a number of ways: It respects our freedom to learn from our experience what should be our ultimate value and it respects our innovativeness so that it is up to us to determine how we should integrate our practice with that value. In this sense, it is an ethic which demands that we take responsibility for our ethicity. It is also an ethic which demands that we take responsibility for our world, for responding to the oppression of people and the exploitation of the environment, and for changing the social structures necessary for this. Finally, a liberationist ethic, although demanding creativity on our part, is not anarchical but responsible because it gives us guides for ethical decision-making.

We have already discussed how a liberationist ethic demands that we be responsible for our very ethicity and for our world. In this section we will be concerned with responsible decision-making, with aspects of how a liberationist ethic guides innovativeness. The last section's discussion of creating ideologies in order that we may find forms of practice which correspond to our value was particularly relevant to structural ethics. This section will look at issues more commonly talked about in the context of personal ethics, issues such as where intentions, motives, consequences, and norms fit into our ethical decision-making. This will, to an extent, locate a liberationist ethic vis-à-vis natural law theory, utilitarianism, and proportionalism.

Natural Law, Utilitarianism, and Liberationist Ethics

Natural law theory, the view that there is a moral law in nature which participates in the eternal law of God, has had, historically, many strengths. It bases ethics on what we are rather than on something, such as the Mosaic Law, which is extrinsic to us; it gears ethics toward human flourishment as its goal; it places ethics within the domain of reason; and it makes ethics universal, the same for all, because we have the same nature. On its physicalist interpretation, according to which we can read off what we ought to do from our unchanging biological nature, it yields absolute behavioral norms which give us certainty in our moral life. But then, for example, masturbation, homosexual acts, and using contraceptives must be deemed intrinsically wrong because they frustrate the finality of the natural faculty of reproduction. And, because these acts directly offend against nature and the eternal law of God, it would seem that they are worse than, for example, rape, incest, and adultery! On the physicalist interpretation, an originally teleological ethic, concerned with achieving the goal of human flourishment, becomes rigidly deontological—with profoundly counter-intuitive results.[49] An attempt was made to reintroduce some flexibility into natural law theory by means of the principle of double effect which allowed the performance of an act with evil consequences if the act was not intrinsically evil, the evil was unintended and not the direct consequence of the act, and the good resulting outweighed the evil. But the results were still counter-intuitive. For example, this principle allowed the removal of the cancerous uterus of a pregnant woman with the effect that the fetus would die, but it did not allow the direct killing and removal of the fetus so that the uterus could be treated and the woman would, perhaps, be able to become pregnant again. *Humanae Vitae* relied on a physicalist interpretation of natural law and many Roman Catholic moral theologians, frustrated by playing with absolute rules to get results which would make for human flourishment, and often failing, eventually gave up all the requirements of the principle of double effect except the last, that the good resulting from an act should outweigh the evil. They became proportionalists.[50]

While we may have difficulty seeing any *connection* between a liberationist ethic and the natural law tradition in ethics, we may have difficulty seeing any *difference* between liberationist ethics and one of the archenemies of that tradition, utilitarianism.[51] They are similar in their stress on altruism, on the alleviation of suffering and, implicit in this, on the consequences of actions. But while the suffering with which the utilitarian is concerned tends to be quantifiable and associated with physical pain such as for food and shelter, the suffering with which the liberationist is concerned includes, as well, lack of freedom, self-respect, and the respect of others. Also, the utilitarian does not normally associate suffering with oppression and social structures. Thus, while both liberationist and utilitarian take the consequences of actions very seriously, the content they take to be relevant differs. The utilitarian aims at maximizing the overall quantity of happiness (or minimizing overall pain) at whatever cost to some groups or individuals, whereas the liberationist goes out to the worst off first. The former thus flaunts our ordinary understanding of justice whereas the latter aims at justice. The consequences are all that count for the utilitarian whereas, for the liberationist, intentions, motives, and personal qualities also count morally.[52] As we shall see, the *differences* between liberationist ethics and utilitarianism reflect important *similarities* between liberationist ethics and natural law ethics.

Ends, Means, and the Issue of Violence

We identify the principle, 'the end justifies the means,' with utilitarianism, and we tend to understand by it that we are justified in using any means to attain our end. Yet Segundo's distinction between faith and ideologies is a distinction between absolute end and relative systems of means we use to achieve that end. Schillebeeckx too argues that our forms of practice are relative to our fundamental value and goal. Liberationists insist on the relativity of means on the basis of the moral relevance of our changing historical context. Our historicity contradicts a given blueprint for right practice and demands innovativeness in ethical decision-making. But, then, are liberationists subscribing to the principle that the end justifies the means?

Segundo explicitly says that, while it is scandalous, it is also obvious that the end justifies the means.[53] But what he means is, not that *all* means to an end can be justified in a given context, but that *any* means can *only* be justified by its end in a context and cannot, say, be self-justifying.[54] Also, importantly, he argues that, as much as possible, we should seek means which *resemble* our ends.[55] To achieve the ends of justice and peace, we should seek the means of justice and peace.

But it is often difficult to find means which resemble our ends because the means must fulfil two sets of criteria which do not rest easily with one another. On the one hand, they must be effective, genuinely lead to our ends; on the other hand, they must be possible in the given empirical situation.[56] But the greater the gap between what is the case and what we think ought to be the case, the less will what is the case yield means which resemble what we think ought to be. Even if there are elections in poor countries which are controlled by local oligarchies, it is often virtually impossible to use the democratic process to bring about change. The rich kill, buy votes, and falsify results to maintain their power—and they are the only candidates.

In order to find means which resemble our ends we must be creative and flexible. We ought to avoid excessive purposiveness which relies on the shortest, most direct routes to our goal, as the routes of violence and manipulation often are, to bring about social justice. But neither should we be passive, merely letting things take their course. Maintaining our ultimate goal, of resisting oppression, say, as nonnegotiable, we should seek intermediate goals from within the situation with which reality presents us. If pressing for the implementation of existing tax laws would be effective but pushing for their reform would lead to repression, normally we should seek the former and wait on 'chance' to change the situation and make possible the latter. And, while we can encourage 'chance,' that is, shifts in a situation which will open opportunities for liberation such as the coming to power of a Gorbachev in a repressive regime, we cannot force it. By using the means available in seeking change, we are being, as it were, ecological, which often involves 'going slow.' But, importantly, this does not mean our goals cannot be radical.[57] And it sometimes happens, of course, that, often after a long process, radical change takes place abruptly.[58]

How do we encourage the seeking of means which resemble our ends? Segundo associates the person who seeks to integrate means and ends with the optimist, the person who tends to interpret life with a stress on its positive events. And he associates "calculating, manipulative reason," where means contradict ends, with the pessimist. But optimism can be taught. We can become attuned to a history of optimism through what Schillebeeckx describes as the history of peoples who have kept the hope of salvation alive amidst overwhelming suffering. Indeed, Christian hope commits the Christian to optimism.[59]

A central moral issue for liberation theologians of the poor is that of armed struggle, the use of direct violence, against the institutionalized violence of oppressive structures which kill the poor through hunger and sickness, and which are themselves held in place by direct violence and the threat of direct violence. Precisely because of the structural character of the causes of oppression, blame is both widespread and limited although, in poor countries, where the gap between the powerless masses and powerful few is acute and obvious, the extreme evil of some individuals' and groups' projects is very visible.

But, as well as the difficulty in determining to whom one can, in justice, direct one's violence,[60] there is the difficulty of effectiveness. We have argued that our means should resemble our ends. We should use just and peaceful means to attain a just and peaceful end. This is particularly important in the context of a protracted project, a long struggle, in order that we do not do untold harm to individuals and society and, connected with this, that we will be given hope and encouragement by our very engagement.[61] Indeed, *if, over the long term and on a large scale, we use means which contradict our ends, our means will tend to undermine our ends.*[62] Segundo particularly argues against manipulation of people, which he associates with armed struggle. Massive manipulation leads to massive distrust, which leads to the breakdown of the "social ecology" (the systems of social relations of a society), to the point where, not only the media, courts, and business no longer function, but neither, finally, does the family. He thinks that the social ecology is in less danger from even quite repressive regimes and implies that its breakdown is to be avoided at almost any cost.[63]

Segundo may underestimate the social destructiveness of some regimes. Spying on one's neighbor is a fine art in China and led to family members betraying one another after the massacre of protesting students at Tiananmen Square in 1989. Ferdinand Marcos profoundly damaged the social ecology of the Philippines by institutionalizing corruption in every sphere of Philippine social life, right down to the level of the local *barangay*.[64] From an ecological perspective we can say that long-term, large-scale, direct violence against an oppressive regime is almost inevitably excessively purposive and very destructive. But armed struggle need not always be both long term and large scale. The former is obvious but, regarding the latter, armed revolutionaries *may*, together with those who do not take up arms, spend most of their time consciousness-raising, organizing, and helping farmers in the field.

A great many other considerations must be taken into account in determining whether, in a given context, an armed struggle is morally justified. The brief discussion here is intended only to provide a relevant example for the discussion of ends and means. From a liberationist perspective, there is no absolute prohibition against direct violence in response to institutionalized violence because there is no absolute prohibition against particular systems of means or behavioral norms. The issues of effectiveness, and at what cost to individuals and society in terms of integrity, justice, human life, and the economy (in terms of both dignity and welfare values), are crucial. It should be stressed, however, that institutionalized violence is always supported by the threat of direct violence. Massive protests in poor countries are most often met with violence. And active nonviolence is not always appropriate. But after the period of violence in poor countries, there seems to be a growing movement toward preparing the powerless for self-determination by experimenting with new structures of social relationship within the spheres of their control and negotiating with the powerful.[65]

Dignity Values and Welfare Values: Liberationist Ethics and Proportionalism

Because they are responding to material poverty, it is possible to get the impression that liberation theologians of the poor are only concerned about material welfare. However, as we have stressed, liberation involves overcoming subjective as much as objective oppression, the oppression that denies people their self-respect and self-determination as well as that which denies them health and possessions. Liberation involves recognizing the interdependence between these. When the destitute come to have a sense of their own worth they actively seek and demand change in their living conditions. Changed living conditions help them and others to recognize their worth.

The importance of the subjective side of liberation is connected with the importance of seeking means which resemble our ends. Segundo describes the latter as the attempt to integrate the reasons of reason with the reasons of the heart.[66] This has to do with seeking actions which flow from the heart and from our intentionality. It involves seeking integration of the outer and inner self, and integrity. The importance of seeking means which resemble our ends, then, is not only in order to accomplish our objective goals but to respect our subject, which is also a goal.

We begin to see that liberationist ethics is much richer than utilitarianism. Indeed, it is importantly similar to the proportionalist approach that grew out of natural law theory. For the proportionalist, there is but one criterion of morality, that the balance of good over evil resulting from an integrated act must be at least as great as any alternative *where what counts as good includes dignity values as well as welfare values.*[67] Dignity values involve attitudes, motives, virtues, that is, the inner resources out of which our actions ought to flow. They include, for example, love, trust, integrity, self-determination, justice, and mutual respect, values which are mainly relational. Thus, they are not geared primarily toward self-perfection but building community. Welfare values involve quantifiable human needs such as for food, shelter, and access to medical care. *Dignity and welfare values are parallel to subjective and objective liberation; subjective liberation reflects respect for dignity values and objective liberation reflects respect for welfare values.* The proportionalist, like the liberationist, seeks means which resemble ends but permits means which contradict ends; for neither are there absolute behavioral norms. And for both, neither intentions, acts, nor ends taken in isolation but rather the integrated project based on fundamental values and flowing from intentions and toward goals, count ethically. Also, both maintain the distinction between the goodness of a person and the rightness of an act, a distinction which utilitarian and deontologist collapse in opposite directions.

Due to the combination of their more-or-less Marxian/utilitarian and Christian heritages, but also due to the subject of their concern, namely human liberation, liberationists seek both welfare and dignity values. Due to their concern with liberation and their understanding of the human person as fundamentally mental/physical, they see these values as interdependent. The heritage of proportionalists in, particularly, the physicalist strand of natural law ethics, combined with the principle of double effect and, with these, the subject of their concern in sexual and other 'personal' issues, was one which stressed dignity values. Welfare values, often thought of as concern for consequences, have more or less been added on. Proportionalists tend to see conflict between dignity and welfare values and the ethical task is to weigh the interests of each in determining what to do.

Classic dilemmas demonstrate: (1) An explorer who stumbles upon a remote village is given the option by the local leader of shooting an innocent peasant, or refraining from shooting with the consequence that the leader will shoot twenty peasants. (2) In the context of the rape of a white allegedly by a black, the sheriff of an acutely racist town can prevent the lynching of a number of blacks only by framing a black he has no reason to believe is guilty. The utilitarian option, for which only welfare values count, would likely be to shoot the peasant and frame the black. The deontological option, for which only dignity values count, would likely be the opposite. The proportionalist weighs, in each case, dignity values against welfare values. But we can ask whether there is a way of seeing these dilemmas which respects the interdependence of welfare and dignity values stressed by the liberationist.

There are some situations, and perhaps these are such situations, in which liberationist and proportionalist can go either way. We can develop morally powerful stories in which the explorer and the sheriff refuse to participate in the evil perpetrated by another, because to participate in wanton killing or to frame for a heinous crime innocent and oppressed people is to act against and to serve to undermine the deepest of human values. The agents may see themselves as providing an example to towns that are profoundly corrupt to show that racial and class bias, involving killing innocent people either for sport or out of revenge, are completely evil. They may hope that if they do not act neither will those who are bent on evil. They may see their act of refusal as simply symbolic, a joining in solidarity with decency and justice wherever and whenever it appears, with the hope that eventually, even if not in any direct way causally related to their refusal, goodness will prevail in these towns and everywhere.[68]

We could also tell a story involving the moral courage of explorer and sheriff who 'get their hands dirty' in order to save as many innocent people as they can. The point would not be that the agents have moral courage but that they go out to other human beings, *saving the lives and thereby respecting the dignity of as many as possible* which also demonstrates moral courage. It would be appropriate for the agents to express profound regret to their victims that they could not take their victims' places. It may be important that the sheriff assure his victim that his reputation would be redeemed. Indeed, whichever way the stories go, it is appropriate that the agents experience and express uncertainty and regret toward the victims.

Whether or not liberationist and proportionalist can come down on either side of these particular dilemmas, if there is not a pre-given blueprint for right action, and if we are not causally determined, but if our future is open, if we are genuinely called to make meaning, and if we are social and relational, then it will be inevitable that there will be many moral situations which are open to moving one way or another. *It is not so much that in situations of dilemma conflicting values have equal weight—we could argue in particular cases that human integrity and trustworthiness may be gained rather than lost by acting for the welfare of the most people or, indeed, that greater human welfare is endangered by submitting to extortion—but, because these stories are slices out of the whole connected human history whose future is open-ended, to be continued by others, they lend themselves to conflicting perceptions. Making meaning and community and the kingdom is an ongoing project where creativity is required at every step to turn events toward the good.* This is not to ignore our responsibility to consider the multitudinous issues which genuinely are relevant to moral decision-making and it is not to lead us to think it is up to others to make meaning from what we have done. On the contrary, we must make meaning of the situation which we did not produce, but we cannot control what will be done with the situation we create. Our ethical life in history is thus open to the future. But to make meaning, to properly consider all the relevant issues in ethical decision-making, it is not, as Edward Vacek says, a sophisticated computer we need but wisdom, a "well-ordered heart" characterized by compassion and depth of feeling and sensitivity to "relative importances."[69] Also, finally, while we must reject subjectivism in ethics, we must also recognize that each person's integrity is different. In integrity, some will step outside the established structures to seek change, and others will attempt change from within. This is not to say some will be radical and others will be reformers. We must be radical and, while we may use different means, we must seek the same fundamental change. Society and the kingdom need both sorts of people, which is to say that they need different and even opposing responses to some situations.

Thus, finally, *proportionalism and liberationist ethics merge in their giving equal respect, in ethical decision-making, to dignity and welfare values.* Indeed, proportionalism can be brought within the embrace of liberationist ethics, stressing as it does what tradition has considered to be mainstream "personal" issues.

The Role of Norms in Liberationist Decision-making

Both Schillebeeckx and Segundo speak negatively about natural law ethics on grounds of its being static and ahistorical. But some theologians have attempted to develop a new, dynamic understanding of natural law that embraces the need for creativity on our part.[70] Indeed, as we have seen, Schillebeeckx attempts, through his anthropological constants, to capture, by a loosely phenomenological and inductive method, constancies in our very historicity. Segundo proposes, by his distinction between faith and ideologies, a constant learning process, a know-how, in ethics, according to which our changing practice and perception are integrated with permanent value. This chapter and the previous one have demonstrated the importance of our sociability and creativity, aspects of our anthropology, for ethics. We should not renounce natural law theory too quickly. We must reject the presupposition of an eternal law of God written into nature which provides us with a blueprint for right action. Rather, we must insist on starting in ethics with our experience of disorder, disharmony, unmeaning. Indeed, reason must be guided in ethics by experience, especially negative experience. Both natural law theory, in the strand which connects God's law with reason, and a liberationist approach seek the goal of human and cosmic flourishment. Both see flourishment as complex, as including respect for what I have called dignity values as well as welfare values. We should be guided in what we ought to do by what we are. While a claimed strength of natural law theory has been its capacity to deduce, from our unchanging nature, absolute behavioral norms, a liberationist approach rejects this. It is central to liberationist and proportionalist approaches that, whatever our anthropological constancies, precisely because they are unchanging, they cannot yield behavioral norms which must be changing. Our changing historical context demands it.

Values can be expressed as norms: Do what is right and promote the good; act justly, mercifully, and courageously. They seem to be universal, the most general of them tautological. But they do not tell us what to do, what constitutes acting rightly and justly now. The categorical imperative, the principle of utility, and the principle of double effect are intended to be universal and are designed to yield behavioral norms but, due to their incapacity to consider some morally relevant factors, they often lead to deeply counter-intuitive results. The liberationist principle to resist every threat to the humanum and cosmos provides guidelines for priorities but does not yield behavioral norms. Behavioral norms may vary radically in the degree of their generality or specificity, ranging from a prohibition on killing, to killing the innocent, to directly and intentionally killing the innocent. . . . The more the context is built into the norm, the fewer will be the exceptions to it but the closer it will become to a description of a situation, the telling of a story, and the less generally applicable will it be. However, while there is an obvious difference in content between norms expressing values and those expressing behavior, in terms of universality there is not always as much difference between them as we might expect. The prohibition on intentionally and directly killing the innocent against their will is almost as universal as the imperative to act justly. We may, on occasion, have to kill an innocent to prevent something worse, and we may, on occasion, have to waive justice for the sake of mercy and love. And while no articulable behavioral norms are absolute, some behavioral norms are always morally relevant.

But precisely why can there be no absolute behavioral norms? The point is that if there are any we cannot know them because it is impossible to specify every exception to them. We cannot imagine all the possible situations in which the norm might, or might not, be applicable. This is why Schillebeeckx says that "the one real, concrete ethical norm . . . [is] this concrete human person living historically in this concrete society."[71] Every articulated norm is general and abstract because it can do no more than to point inadequately to an aspect of the concrete norm, the person. In effect, what is being said is something with which we have become familiar: The Law, every law, is relative to the good of the humanum. So, if we want to take everything into account in our ethical decision-making which is relevant to the integrated situation of the person here and now, norms can guide but they cannot govern our decision. As we have stressed throughout, norms

> emerge from a concrete experience of life and impose themselves with the clear evidence of experience. Theoretical reflection comes afterward. . . . And so, after the event, such imperatives are put forth as 'generally valid, abstract norms.'[72]

Above all else, negativity and negative contrast experiences indicate without precisely specifying what we ought to do here and now. It is the initial practical response to negativity, by those confronted most directly with it, that leads to the revision, reformulation, reordering, dropping, and adding of norms. Although incomplete and basically inadequate, norms provide us with shortcuts in our moral decision-making. They allow us to generalize from one situation to others and to make efficient use of our heritage. Norms thus help to ensure that a liberationist ethic is neither purely abstract nor entirely situational.

Finally, can we provide concrete examples of old norms which should be replaced or revised or new norms which should be introduced? It would be unhelpful for this ethic, for which a person's whole project counts, to suggest a set of new narrowly behavioral norms to replace those such as not to kill or tell falsehoods. But I will offer a kind of alternative set of guideline 'commandments,' made up both of norms and regulative principles. These will serve to summarize, in part, a liberationist ethic. Such a summary is appropriate here because the next chapter moves to the relationship between ethics and religion.

Norms and guidelines for a liberationist ethic: some examples.

1.   I am your God who brought you out of the place of slavery. You will not have other gods besides me.
     You will not identify me with a given book or rite or place of worship, but with the overcoming of slavery everywhere.

2.   You will honor your father and mother.
     But even more than to the voices of authority—of Parents, Church, Experts, the White Western World . . . You will listen to the voices of experience—of landless peasants and all poor people, battered women and all women, street children and every child, tribal peoples and all people of color. . . .

3.   You will not kill . . . any innocent human directly and intentionally with bullets.
     But neither will you kill any human, however guilty, indirectly and unintentionally by supporting, and by not tearing down, every form of social organization which denies food, shelter, medical attention, protection under the law, education, jobs, a healthy environment. . . .

4.   You will not steal.
     But you will pay a fair wage, support just tax laws, renounce corrupt business practices, distribute land to the peasant, confiscate land to house the urban poor, curb the power of the transnational, cancel the external debt which is crippling poor nations, rewrite trade and aid agreements so they will benefit the poor, and protect the environment for your future generations and for the plants and animals that make it up.

5.   You will not lie.
     But neither will you blind or deafen yourself but will open your eyes and ears to every oppression suffered by other humans, by your own self, by other species and the environment. And you will not hide these things from others. Rather, you will cry to the rooftops of every injustice that you see.

6. You will renounce the arch-sins of dominance, greed, pride, and anger.

    But you will also refrain from a sacrifice that erases yourself, from passivity and denial of your own worth and of that of every exploited group.

7. You will treat your fellow humans equally, treating in a similar way similar sorts of cases.

    You will also seek to bring about equality, treating dissimilar cases differently. Today, you will bring women and minority groups to the front of the queue in sensitive posts such as teaching and policing.

8. Be perfect: be virtuous, be dutiful; have pure intentions and do not indulge in forbidden actions.

    But also, acknowledge and mourn the immersion of your whole human race in structures of oppression; grieve over your inescapable participation in social sin, your fundamental imperfection, impurity. Yet, then, be lifted by the power and freedom invested in every group which joins in solidarity for change.

9. Be guided by Holy Scripture; be a disciple of Christ.

    Yes, if you are Christian, be guided by Jesus and the tradition which follows him in learning what makes life worth living and the skill of living it.

10. Trust in tradition, the wisdom of the past.

    Trust also in your God-given creativity and your power to find new means to make alive, in your context, the ends of human and cosmic flourishment. If you are not afraid of changing your ways of thinking and acting, if you never forget the negativity you want to negate, the oppression you want to liberate, the suffering you want to turn to salvation, if you remember the constancies of your own human nature, its relatedness to other people, culture, the environment . . . , and if you seek flexibility by balancing purposiveness and waiting on chance, you will be effective in creating a world which better reflects your value. If you seek means which resemble your ends you will act from the heart, as an integrated self, and you will have integrity and respect the integrity of others. But, finally, when you are forced to use means which conflict with your ends, if you use restraint, experience uncertainty and regret, you will be healed.

—*When you have done all of this, rest, let go, place your trust in your children and your children's children to take up and reshape your projects in life-giving ways.*

11. Your love will be universal, extending to every human being. *But seek out first those your society shuns, excludes, casts out, the 'eyesore' it sweeps off the streets, the 'useless' it hides away, the idealist it outlaws. . . . But then, make your love truly universal, extending it to all of creation, to dolphins and cedars and ecological systems.*

12. Summing up all the rest, you will seek to obey God's eternal law of order and harmony in all things.
    But you will do so by ordering disorder, mending broken harmony, turning suffering into salvation, oppression into liberation.

CONCLUSION

We have argued from the beginning that our fundamental experience is one of suffering and straining for salvation; we find ourselves an already damaged humanum in an already damaged world. Put more positively, but not capturing the full reality, we find ourselves essentially incomplete in a world which is contingent and open to the future. Both of these experiences demonstrate that we are not given a pre-established order of the universe or a pre-established blueprint for what we ought to do. We must be creative, innovative, in ethics.

Jesus' relationship to the Law brings out more concretely why innovativeness is necessary to ethics. It begins to show how we should go about being innovative. Jesus consistently relativized the established do's and don't's of the Law for the sake of its underlying point and purpose, the value on which it is based—human welfare and flourishment. He exposed the religious leaders who, wittingly or unwittingly, by absolutizing its practical norms, made the Law a tool of oppression rather than liberation. Jesus thus demonstrates that we must find new forms of practice for our changing historical context in order that our practice will reflect and not undermine our permanent moral value. He shows that if our ethic is not innovative it will be oppressive.

While Jesus demonstrates *why* innovativeness is necessary to ethics and *that* it is possible, a non-traditional anthropology and epistemology are necessary to show *how* innovativeness is possible. To make room for genuinely creative decision-making, we must allow for our experience of the external world to extend beyond all our frameworks and challenge those frameworks. We ourselves, in our encounter with that world, must be in movement and must be understood on something of a gestalt or evolutionary model. Creativity must involve allowing and also compelling old, outdated, oppressive forms of practice and thought to disintegrate. By both purposive reflective means and waiting on new forms to emerge, we must seek new, liberating forms of practice and thought. All of this is to say that, not only can we not hang onto old forms, old norms and theories, but we cannot spell out in advance what new forms to put in their place. The tacit dimension of creative learning demonstrates that coming to articulate new structures of practice and thinking, new norms and theories, presupposes practical knowledge, a kind of knowing how. All of this is possible only because new, negative experience reveals a reality which extends beyond our old interpretations and frameworks. Indeed, new experience and exploratory practice are causally, logically, epistemologically, and existentially prior to our frameworks of thought and norms for practice. We can speak of an experiential/practical/hermeneutical circle for which new experience and practice lead to a new interpretation which revises our established ways of practicing and thinking, and which, in turn, opens possibilities for new experience. Thus we see that the liberationist stress on a priority of practice (and experience) over theory must be applied within the ethical realm itself where ethical norms are included as theory.

Because practical know-how is of central importance to innovativeness, so also, paradoxically, is the example of others. We learn how by being shown how. Discipleship to Jesus cannot be understood as imitation of what he did but, as well as accepting his value on the basis of our judgment that his life was utterly worthwhile, discipleship to Jesus involves learning from him how to go on, learning how to determine what we ought to do. We must learn how to integrate our changing practice with our permanent value. We learn values and we can learn how to integrate our practice with our value from more than one model. We can engage in the liberationist project without discipleship to Jesus. By moving into the inner logic of Jesus' story, by creatively transposing from his context to our own, we can gain specific illumination for our time. The basic elements of his story, including his efforts at alleviating suffering, his failure, rejection, execution, and resurrection, fit the general logic of the struggle for liberation where innovativeness inevitably meets resistance and can never at all fully accomplish its ends.

A creative ethic is, ultimately, as responsible as the value it serves. Just as there is a fittingness between the process of liberation and Jesus' story, there is a fittingness between the liberationist value and creativity. A liberationist ethic is responsible in its creativity because it has a multiplicity of guides for creativity and contrary to, for example, traditional natural law theory, Kantianism, and utilitarianism, it does not impose arbitrary or at least unacceptable strictures on our practice. For a liberationist ethic, innovativeness is guided by negativity and anthropological constants, which, because they are permanent, do not yield behavioral norms. It takes both dignity values and welfare values into account, but because it takes our mental/physical character utterly seriously and understands our actions as flowing from who we are, it does not, primarily, weigh dignity values against welfare values but seeks to discern what constitutes both dignity and welfare in a situation. Taking seriously the truly open-endedness of our ethicity, it recognizes that, on occasion, different and even opposing things may be right. It is important that we seek means which resemble our ends, that, for example, we seek peaceful means to achieve peace. But, on occasion, we will have to engage in means which contradict our ends. Behavioral norms are inductively based, grounded in our experience of right practice. The range of issues which thus guide innovativeness and the enormous flexibility this gives to ethics make this a completely responsible ethic.

NOTES

1. I use the terms "creative" and "innovative" interchangeably but I give preference to the latter because it suggests working on material that is already there to produce something new and appropriate, helpful. Sometimes "creative" carries a connotation of mystique associated with creating out of nothing, which I wish to discourage.

2. *God the Future of Man*, pp. 135–37, 153–54.

3. While Schillebeeckx and other liberationists strongly criticize the Pharisees of the gospel stories for their legalistic and oppressive interpretation of the religious law, Schillebeeckx points out that Jesus' renunciation of traditions which made a 'fence around the law' and his insistence that the law serve human need *is also "completely Jewish . . . and in no way goes beyond what was possible for a Jew at that time."* It is acknowledged today that the Pharisees do not

get a fair treatment in the gospels, but our concern does not lie so much with the relationship between Jesus and the Pharisees as with the light shed by liberationists' discussions of Jesus and the Pharisees on the nature of ethics. Comparisons can be made between the New Testament depiction of some Jewish religious leaders of Jesus' time and some Christian religious leaders of our own, the same mechanisms can be seen to be at work, which sacralizes oppression. This adds to the poignancy and urgency of what liberationists say on this issue. Quotation in *Jesus*, p. 232. See also John T. Pawlikowski, *Christ in the Light of the Christian-Jewish Dialogue* (New York: Paulist Press, 1982), chapter four, "Jesus' Teaching: Its Links with and Separation from Pharisaic Judaism," pp. 76–107 for a discussion based on recent biblical and historical scholarship of Jesus' relationship to the Pharisees.

4. Schillebeeckx, *Jesus*, pp. 230–40.

5. Ibid., p. 241.

6. *Faith and Ideologies*, pp. 41–46.

7. For Segundo, faith and ideologies are technical terms representing complementary anthropological constants. They capture the distinction between ultimate end and the system of means of achieving it, our ultimate value and the forms of interpretation and practice we engage in to concretize that value. How we choose or come by faith is associated particularly with affect and our choice of ideologies is associated with reason. Whatever is our faith must be treated by us as absolute, and ideologies must be recognized to be relative. What this means for ethics is that, in order to effectively express permanent values in a changing historical context, we must be prepared to let go of old systems of interpretations and modes of practice and find new ones, create new ideologies. See *Faith and Ideologies*, chapter one, "Towards a New Statement of the Problem," pp. 3–30, especially pp. 15–16, on Segundo's definitions of faith and ideologies.

8. Ibid., pp. 47–49.

9. See *Jesus*, pp. 156–59, 162–65, 169 for Schillebeeckx's discussion of the character of parables and of those parables of particular concern to us. See also *Christ*, pp. 598–99, for his discussion of the Pharisee and the Publican. Quotations in *Jesus*, p. 157.

10. *The Liberation of Theology*, pp. 158–59.

11. *Christ*, pp. 592, 597.

12. Ibid., p. 596.

13. Ibid., p. 593.

14. *The Liberation of Theology*, p. 155.

15. See Schillebeeckx, *Jesus*, p. 248.

16. See Schillebeeckx, *Jesus*, pp. 162–63 and Segundo, *The Historical Jesus of the Synoptics*, pp. 92–94, 96–103. Segundo argues that it is very significant that the "poor" and "sinners" refer to the same people. Poverty was justified because people were sinners and they were sinners because they did not obey the intricacies of the law in which they had not been instructed.

17. Segundo argues that the Pharisees responded so violently to Jesus because they were religious fanatics. But they did not have the power to get rid of Jesus legally and all they had to lose was prestige. The Sadducees, on the

other hand, did have the power to have Jesus executed and had social power and wealth to lose. See *The Historical Jesus of the Synoptics*, pp. 97–102.

18. Segundo expresses this view in *The Humanist Christology of Paul*, p. 53.

19. As we have seen, Schillebeeckx makes the same general point in his discussion of the Sermon on the Mount as a model for ethics.

20. See Thomas S. Kuhn, *The Structure of Scientific Revolutions*, 2nd edition (Chicago: The University of Chicago Press, 1970). It is relevant to note that Schillebeeckx, Gustafson, and Lindbeck have all been influenced by the thought of Thomas Kuhn.

21. Michael Polanyi argues that both empiricist and rationalist fall prey to this, Meno's Paradox. See Michael Polanyi, *The Tacit Dimension* (Garden City, New York: Doubleday and Company, Inc., 1966; Anchor Books Edition, 1967), chapter one, "Tacit Knowing," pp. 3–25.

22. On a physicalist interpretation of natural law, for example, where an action is always immoral if it frustrates the finality of a natural faculty, neither contraceptive technology nor the population explosion can be genuinely taken into account in sexual ethics. In radical contrast to this 'rationalist' view, where what we ought to do can be deduced from what we are and what we are does not change, the empiricist holds both a view of an anthropology built up from a changing experience and insists on such a radical distinction between fact and value that value becomes ungrounded.

23. The inadequacies in traditional rationalism and empiricism are analogous to the inadequacies Segundo sees in Lamarckian and Darwinian evolutionary theories which rely, respectively, on pure purposiveness and pure chance.

24. *Christ*, pp. 31–33.

25. A multiplicity of factors including contraceptive technology and rebellion against established authority by the children of the consumer society led to the 'sexual revolution' that began in the north in the 1960s and which is still playing itself out in terms of the much broader search today for flourishing personal relations. Dissatisfaction with the structure of authority in the Roman Catholic Church, which began with Vatican II in the same decade, leading to a dramatic loss of priests and sisters, has taken a number of directions, such as the development of Basic Christian Communities and experiments in women-church.

26. Liberationists argue that a 'trickle-down' view of responding to poverty is outdated. Feminists point to outdated views of power and ecologists point to outdated views of the individual. All these outdated views are creating untold destruction in our world today.

27. Gilbert Ryle, *The Concept of Mind* (Middlesex: Penguin Books Ltd., 1963), chapter two, "Knowing How and Knowing That," pp. 26–60, especially pp. 28–32. The notion of 'attending from' is Polanyi's. It captures the active element in allowing.

28. David W. Hamlyn talks about blindness to self somewhat along these lines in "Self-Knowledge," Mischel (ed.), *The Self: Psychological and Philosophical Issues*, pp. 170–200.

29. George A. Lindbeck, *The Nature of Doctrine: Religion and Theology in a Post-Liberal Age* (Philadelphia: The Westminster Press, 1984), pp. 114–18, 113, 132. Quotations at pp. 117 and 118, respectively.

30. Ibid. Quotations at pp. 34 and 37, respectively. (My italics.)

31. Ibid., pp. 32, 40–41. Quotation at p. 41.

32. Ibid., p. 39.

33. Ibid., pp. 47–49, 64–65, 68, 128–29. Quotation at p. 49. Throughout, Lindbeck oscillates between a strong position, one which stresses the priority of the cultural-linguistic framework over experience to such an extent as to make it difficult to see how he can avoid the various 'isms' mentioned above, and a weak position, which stresses the interdependence of the framework and experience and makes it difficult to see how his position differs from the experientialist position to which he is opposed. Contemporary experientialists such as Schillebeeckx and Gustafson do not, as Lindbeck claims for the position, base religious practice and belief on a universal private feeling. They fully support the interdependence between the social and personal. But for them, experience has priority over the framework.

34. Lindbeck's view here can be compared with and exemplified by the views of Schillebeeckx and Segundo. We do not learn what to do from scripture but we learn how to decide what to do. Segundo's discussions of creating ideologies and learning to learn are particularly relevant. The topic of the next section, on discipleship, as not imitating but getting in touch with, the inner logic of Jesus' life is relevant to what Lindbeck says here.

35. Segundo discusses this in the context of his objection to David Tracy for placing religious faith, involving a basic trust in existence which can be cashed in contradictory ways, before anthropological faith, the fundamental value in terms of which we live our lives. See *Faith and Ideologies*, pp. 35–40.

36. In each case I mention, first, the position which gives innovative experience and practice priority, and, second, the position which gives priority to the cultural-linguistic framework.

37. See *Faith and Ideologies*, pp. 6–7, 10–15 on learning values from others.

38. Schillebeeckx relates the first story on the first page of *Jesus*, and interprets it on the last page, suggesting that the text in between justifies the interpretation. The second story is told on the last page. As regards Schillebeeckx's own story of Jesus, his depiction is so poignant and lends itself so much to bringing the story alive to people today, that it seems almost to play the same role as the direct experience of suffering and striving against suffering which motivate Latin American liberation theologians.

39. This theme runs throughout Segundo's *Faith and Ideologies*. It also runs through liberationist thought generally, although less explicitly and without the use of technical language. See, for example, Jon Sobrino, *Christology at the Crossroads: A Latin American Approach*, trans. John Drury (London: SCM Press Ltd., 1978), p. 123, where he says that Jesus is the moral standard for his disciples because he turns his value into reality. See Schillebeeckx, *Jesus*, pp. 56–57 where he says that essential to making Jesus the determining factor in our lives is that we take account of a constantly changing situation.

40. *The Humanist Christology of Paul*, pp. 19, 21, 104–05, 115–16, 147. Quotation at p. 116.

41. Segundo mentions learning to learn in *The Liberation of Theology*, pp. 118–20 and in *Faith and Ideologies*, pp. 75–76, 82, 130. While he never develops the notion, see especially p. 130 regarding the present discussion.

42. It is clear that finding new forms of practice and new ways of seeing are interdependent. The very having of a new negative experience, on which new practice is based, involves a new seeing, a new interpretation to some extent. Reflective seeking of new ways of seeing, new interpretations, is a form of theorizing and is preceded by pre-theorizing practice on somebody's part. For example, some people have seen the unhappiness of the protected 'disabled' and have, in practice, tried to respond to this before they and others have come to articulate that, if they are to flourish, the disabled, like everybody else, must be seen in terms of what they can do rather than what they cannot do. Academics, professional theorizers, may not always be aware of the pre-theorizing practice on somebody's part that has provided the stimulus for their interpretations.

43. In the case of the evolutionary key, Segundo denies that he has created a Christology for our time. He sees himself as merely presenting us with some of the concepts, some of the framework for such a Christology.

44. Segundo rightly describes his notion of creating Christologies as a "practical art." It involves knowing how, which we can learn only by being shown how, by practice and by catching on. Segundo's five volumes of *Jesus of Nazareth Yesterday and Today* form an attempt to show us how.

45. *Christology at the Crossroads*, pp. 117–18, 358–62. Quotations at pp. 361 and 118 respectively.

46. This is not something Sobrino stresses but it is crucially important so as not to render meaningless the self-sacrifice he says we are called to. And he does mention this in *The True Church and the Poor*, pp. 155–56.

47. Schillebeeckx, *Jesus*, p. 620.

48. Nothing can preclude the possibility of there being another whose life and death, and whose consequent effect on people, are similar in form to those of Jesus. Discipleship to that person would involve integrating practice to the liberationist value in a context of hope in a very similar way as discipleship to Jesus does. We can learn how to learn from other models. Built into the struggle for liberation from oppression is a kind of crying out for hope that goodness will prevail overall. And the liberationist who is not a disciple of Jesus or someone like him will not have the same, nor, presumably, as good grounds for hope.

The question whether there is something ethically distinctive, or even unique, about discipleship to Jesus comes up in a different context in the next chapter.

49. A teleological view is one for which the rightness of an act is determined by the goodness that the act produces, and a deontological view is one for which the rightness of an act is determined by features intrinsic to the act itself. The latter speaks in terms of intrinsically right and wrong acts and absolute behavioral norms. For more detailed definitions see, for example, William

Frankena, *Ethics* (Englewood Cliffs: Prentice-Hall, 1963), pp. 13–16.

It is worth noting the political dimension of the sexual ethic involved here. A view which takes using contraceptives and masturbation to be seriously evil, rape and incest less so, is profoundly oppressive to women. Taking homosexual acts to be grievously wrong is, of course, oppressive to homosexual people. And, in our social world, in this one instance, it is homosexual men who are more discriminated against than homosexual women. But this is because homosexual men are identified with women and so they are seen to seriously disgrace men. See Richard M. Gula, *What Are They Saying About Moral Norms?* (New York: Paulist Press, 1982), pp. 34–44 on the physicalist interpretation of natural law and its counter-intuitive results. Thomas Aquinas took over the distinction between natural law as based on the orders of nature and of reason from Ulpian and Cicero respectively and used the first, rigid, biological use of human nature in sexual ethics and the second, more flexible use based on reason, in issues of social justice. This may explain why, even today, the social encyclicals of the Roman Catholic Church, which deal with poverty and human rights, are more responsive to human need than its teachings on sexual issues—which are also, in fact, matters of social justice. Indeed, it may explain how, in the very same year, 1968, the same Roman Catholic Church came out with *Humanae Vitae* which reiterated an absolute ban on 'artificial' means of birth control, and the Medellín documents which gave rise to the church's taking up the option for the poor. (Of course, the latter were produced by the Latin American bishops and not the pope and his advisors. But both reflect deep traditions in Catholic teaching.)

50. For a history of the struggle of theologians whose heritage was natural law theory, to find a more flexible ethic, and of the development of proportionalism, see Bernard Hoose, *Proportionalism: The American Debate and Its European Roots* (Georgetown: Georgetown University Press, 1987).

51. A consequentialist ethic is one for which the rightness or wrongness of an act is determined by the goodness or badness of its consequences. Utilitarianism is the major exponent of consequentialism and defines goodness as pleasure or happiness and badness as pain or suffering. I refer only to act-utilitarianism and not rule-utilitarianism for which the rightness of an act is determined, not by its immediate consequences, but in terms of its conformity to rules which are justified on utilitarian grounds. I accept the view that rule-utilitarianism is reducible to act-utilitarianism. See, for example, J. J. C. Smart and Bernard Williams, *Utilitarianism For and Against* (Cambridge: Cambridge University Press, 1973), pp. 9–12.

52. These are seen by proportionalists and liberationists as part of what makes for overall good, connected with dignity values.

53. *The Liberation of Theology*, p. 171.

54. This seems to be implicit in what Segundo says in *The Liberation of Theology*, p. 215.

55. *Faith and Ideologies*, p. 264.

56. Ibid., p. 258.

57. Ibid., pp. 265, 268. Segundo is influenced here by Gregory Bateson, *Steps to an Ecology of Mind* (New York: Ballantine Books, 1972), p. 160 and by

Margaret Mead whom Bateson quotes.

58. The 1986 EDSA Revolution in the Philippines which ousted Ferdinand Marcos marked an *abrupt* change after a long struggle against his regime. But for various complex reasons, including the failure on the part of many of those involved in grassroots organizing to recognize the significance of EDSA when it came, and also the relatively small numbers of the poor having been prepared, the poor have remained desperately poor. Human rights abuses have continued and the 1992 elections demonstrated that the old power structures remain strong. While it was *abrupt*, it seems the EDSA Revolution did not bring about a *radical* change.

59. Ibid., pp. 267–68.

60. Too often, particularly in poor countries, revolutionaries find themselves pointing their guns at "little people" who, for food, protect the powerful. And too often civilians are caught in the crossfire. It is estimated that in the Philippines, between 1986 and 1989, there have been a million internal refugees, people who have been forced to flee the internal conflict. See Ed Gerlock (ed.) *Signs of Hope: Stories of Hope in the Philippines*, (Davao City and Quezon City: Philippine International Forum and Claretian Publications, 1990), p. xii.

61. Ibid., p. 267.

62. See the argument on p. 65 regarding this.

63. Ibid., pp. 285–89.

64. The *barangay* was the only political institution in the Philippines prior to colonialism, a kind of extended family which was self-sufficient and headed by a chieftain. Today, the *barangay* is a neighborhood grouping with an elected captain.

65. Segundo suggests in *Faith and Ideologies*, chapter eleven, "Means and Ends: Our Latin America," pp. 276–303, that the period of fairly large-scale revolutionary violence on that continent is over. See also chapter one, footnote 68. In the Philippines, many groups including Basic Christian Communities, some trade unions, and nongovernmental organizations are helping the movement toward self-determination of the poor.

66. Ibid., p. 264. This is borrowed from Gregory Bateson, *Steps to an Ecology of Mind*, p. 129.

67. Edward V. Vacek, S.J., in "Proportionalism: One View of the Debate," *Theological Studies* 46: 2 (June, 1985), gives a definition somewhat along these lines, pp. 289–90.

68. Schillebeeckx's example of the soldier ordered to shoot an innocent hostage makes this line of argument more convincing. His refusal means that he, rather than others, will die, with the exception of the hostage who will die anyway.

69. "Proportionalism: One View of the Debate," p. 297.

70. See James M. Gustafson, *Protestant and Roman Catholic Ethics: Prospects for Rapprochement* (Chicago: The University of Chicago Press, 1978), pp. 80–94, depicting attempts by recent Roman Catholic theologians to build our historicity into natural law theory.

71. *God the Future of Man*, p. 151.

72. Ibid., p. 153.

5

Religion Has an Ethical Foundation
But Ethics Cries Out for Religion

INTRODUCTION

Development of a liberationist ethic, in terms of even *some* of its fundamental elements and their logic, requires that we discuss the relationship between ethics and religion/theology.[1] The ethic of liberationist
theologians is embedded in their theology. We have made reference to
religious symbols throughout in developing this ethic. Also, in numer-
ous places we have implied, without openly exploring, various things
about the relationship between ethics and religion. We argued, for
example, that the negative contrast experience is foundational for ethics and also that it discloses, for some, God and final salvation. This
implies some sort of priority of ethics over religion and theology. We
pointed out that liberationists take the option for the poor to be the
first principle of both ethics and hermeneutics. This is relevant in
showing that theology logically must have an ethical foundation.[2] The
discussions of Jesus in relation to God's kingdom and the Law demonstrate how, for Jesus, religion is ethically rooted. The general argument
of the last chapter for the priority of ethical practice over norms for
practice parallels the more usual theological argument, relevant to this
chapter, for the priority of orthopractice over orthodoxy, both of which
are forms of the argument for priority of practice over theory. The very
creativity of ethics requires a certain independence of ethics from religion. Finally, however, while all of this indicates a nonreciprocal
dependence of religion on ethics, the logic of this ethic, its aim and raison d'être of liberation, especially for the worst off, cries out for
heaven.

The nonreciprocal dependence of religion on ethics is not
demanded merely by the internal coherence of a liberationist ethic; it is
also demanded by the empirical situation. The already damaged

humanum and cosmos calls for everyone, theist and atheist alike, to take up the ethical imperative to resist suffering and oppression. The ethical imperative rises out of the encounter between our common humanity and our common world. It is not dependent on theology or religious belief. But in order that religion and theology be relevant to the needs of the world they must be rooted in the ethic that responds to the world's needs. However, our experience of the world also makes clear that we cannot bring about more than fleeting moments of salvation; our experience of the world cries out for God and an extra-historical salvation.

This chapter will make explicit how the story of Jesus reflects this relationship between ethics and religion and how our anthropology supports it. It will spell out ways in which ethics is prior to religion and theology. Then, approaching the relationship from the side of religion, it will show why religion is not reducible to ethics. The logic of a liberationist ethic demands completion in an extra-historical salvation and a God with power to bring this about. Content will be given to the "something more" of religious, over and above ethical, experience. Finally, I will ponder what heaven must be like from a liberationist perspective.

JESUS AND THE RELATIONSHIP BETWEEN ETHICS AND RELIGION

It is not necessary to introduce new material here; we can briefly make use of our previous discussions of Jesus, concerning the kingdom and the Law, to indicate how he saw the relationship between the ethical and religious.

We have already stressed the ethical as well as the social character of Jesus' vision of the kingdom of God. He practiced and preached a kingdom of justice and peace, where the hungry have food, the sick are healed, the mournful are consoled, the prisoners are freed. Chronologically speaking, this kingdom is an ethical task before it is an eschatological gift. It is in history that people are hungry and sick. It was in history that Jesus fed the hungry and cured the sick. It was in history that he encouraged others to do likewise. It is this social ethical practice, this attempt to bring about some fragments of the kingdom on earth, which can provide us with a vision of the eschatological kingdom. Our practice of the kingdom can actually disclose, make credible and make meaningful an eschatological kingdom. The disclosure of the latter is a *disclosure* of something more, which provides a new horizon for and lends a qualitative shift to the ethical practice.[3]

It may be objected that while, for Christians, God revealed God's will in a special way through Jesus and his preaching and practice of the kingdom, which has a deeply ethical content, God revealed a vision of the kingdom to Jesus through Jesus' Abba experience, a profoundly religious experience. Indeed, Paul and many others have had radical conversion experiences which would seem to be religious before they are ethical. This is important.[4] While God may be disclosed through ethical experience, an act of altruism say, God may also be disclosed *in the sense of mediated* by a sunset, a polluted river, a discussion with a friend, or anything else in the world that we experience. Although Christians experience a personal God who initiates relationship, this encounter is *always* mediated by experience of the world.[5] While the medium need not, in itself, be ethical, it seems it will always have an ethical as well as religious significance. If one sees in a sunset or in the order of nature a God of pure power, power to do good *and* evil, one sees a God with an ethical significance, one which is inconsistent with the Christian understanding. If one experiences God in a deep feeling of consolation, one experiences a caring and understanding God. If one sees in a polluted river God's call to stop the destruction of the environment, then one is experiencing a central way in which God is revealing Godself today.

Revelation of God is of course contextualized, patterned, and forms part of a personal and, normally, a communal history embedded in a religious tradition. Jesus' Abba experience must have involved an intense encounter with a very personal God but still it would have been a mediated experience, mediated by Jesus' Jewish tradition, in which he was steeped, by his experience of John the Baptist, which Schillebeeckx suggests must have been a conversion experience for Jesus, and by his experience of the marginalized and the religious leaders of his time. Jesus' vision of the kingdom was from God but mediated by Jesus' own experience and interpretation of the world. God's liberating revelation could succeed with Jesus, the gestalt of the kingdom could be formed for Jesus, only because Jesus brought a liberating ethical value to his interpretation of the world—and because he allowed his ethical faith to yield religious faith. This is not to suggest that there need be a chronological move from ethical to religious faith. Jesus, like most religious people, was born into an ethico-religious context. While we are responsible for our ethical faith, we must wait on God for religious faith and for our own experience of God, which we cannot inherit strictly from our tradition. God speaks beyond, and essentially through, our ethicity. Either the religious dimension is disclosed by the ethical dimension or, at least, demands from us an ethical readiness or openness as our contribution to the religious revelation. Any sense we can make of religious experience or a religious dimension to our lives simply evaporates and is found to be contentless if it does not have an ethical root, although the religious surpasses and recontextualizes the ethical.

Finally, we saw from the discussion of Jesus' relationship to the Law that *religious* prescription, the do's and don't's of the Law, ought to be interpreted in terms of, and relative to, the *ethical* value of human welfare. Jesus condemned the religious leaders who defined what is good in terms of religious rules which had become oppressive. In his denial that there can be signs from heaven to 'prove' his authority, and in his lack of concern about a person's credentials in favor of what they do, Jesus stresses that the divine can only be recognized through ethical practice. We cannot first see Jesus as divine and then accept his ethical value; we must have his value in order to see him as divine. Thus we can see in Jesus' own life, in his relationship to the kingdom and the Law, a nonreciprocal dependence of religious meaning and value on ethical meaning and value.

ANTHROPOLOGY AND THE RELATION
BETWEEN ETHICS AND RELIGION

Our discussions of the kingdom of God and the Law indicated that we are fundamentally social and innovative. These are aspects of our anthropology which carry ethical before religious implications. But is there a fundamentally *religious* dimension to our anthropology?

Schillebeeckx talks of a "religious and 'para-religious' consciousness" as an anthropological constant. What he has in mind, minimally, is the hope we must have in order to go on, hope in the power of doing good, hope that, by and large, goodness will come out of our right actions in history. According to Schillebeeckx, this hope is not independent of faith and is incomplete if it does not extend to a religious hope based on a religious faith that goodness will prevail.[6] Indeed, in places he largely agrees with David Tracy, who takes, as a basic human dimension, an experience of a fundamental trust in existence, a trust we have in spite of the evidence and which is an expression of our not accepting our limits. This trust both presupposes and leads us to direct ourselves, in our thinking, feeling, and acting, toward an Absolute.[7]

There are difficulties in affirming this as an anthropological constant both because, as Tracy admits, many people deny a religious dimension to their existence and some make manifest from their behavior that they do not experience fundamental trust that goodness will prevail overall. While our ethical practice may suggest that we have hope for and faith in more than the evidence of experience can bear, psychologically speaking, faith and hope in a religious dimension are not required in order that we go on. But do 'post-moderns' have a tendency to religious commitment which many of them resist? Relevant here is the liberationist view that *whether or not we believe in a transcendent God is not what counts fundamentally, but which god, which ultimate value we believe in, is what counts most. The primary division among people is not to be found in whether they have religious faith but in what is their anthropological faith.*[8] "Fundamental trust in existence" is abstract and can be made concrete only by being rooted in an ethical commitment which may be to liberation or dominance. This important insight lay behind the discussion of Jesus and the Law.

Our anthropology can explain why any content we give to religious trust or the Absolute must be based on a prior commitment to an ethical value which we partly choose. To interact with our world in the ways we described in the last chapter requires not only that we be intending agents, interpreters, actors, and innovators. We do these things out of interests and for values; we are fundamentally valuers. We not only have values and act out of values, which are partly based in our biology and anthropology, partly socially conditioned, and partly chosen in light of our experience, but we also evaluate values. With other species, we can choose, in terms of our desires, between conflicting goals which express different values, between going to a concert with friends or staying home and reading a novel. *We humans can also, within limits, change our desires, purposes, and values. Thus we can, within limits, choose and so become responsible for who we are and what we fundamentally value. Then we can evaluate values not just quantitatively in terms of what we want most, but qualitatively, in terms of their moral worth.*

But on what grounds, according to what criteria, do we determine our ultimate value? *Because all our experience is already interpreted in line with our own value, neither an extrinsic religious authority nor our own anthropology can prove to us what should be our ultimate value.* We are not presented to ourselves as raw data any more than is God or the world. While we can and on occasion must question even our most fundamental value, we cannot have an absolute yardstick or criterion, whether sacred or secular, in terms of which to evaluate it. We can measure our most fundamental value only against our "deepest unstructured sense of what is important," of what it is to be human.[9] In opting for a value, in taking up the option for the poor, for example, we are responding to the quest for the humanum in one particular way, the liberationist way, which cannot be 'proved.'[10] Because we interpret even our religious experience, the "fundamental trust in existence" say, we bring to it a value, one value rather than another, the value of liberation or the value of domination.

Thus we see that interpretation is not value-free but is guided by value, and we partly choose our most fundamental value which can be evaluated and justified but cannot be proved. But if all of our experience is interpreted and we bring our fundamental value for which we are partly responsible to our interpretation, then we cannot avoid evaluating our religious experience, choosing our God, in terms of our fundamental ethical value. This will be expanded below.

WHY THEOLOGY AND RELIGION MUST HAVE AN ETHICAL FOUNDATION; ETHICS AND HERMENEUTICS

Here I shall argue that theology and religion logically must have an ethical foundation. And those who claim to derive ethics from theology and religion are not genuinely doing so but are opting for one ethical position rather than another. This discussion will merge with a discussion of partisanship or why we must take sides or start from a position of commitment in theology as well as in ethics. I shall begin by discussing Gustafson's opposite view, his view that theological ethics derives from religious piety and is not partisan. I shall then raise and respond to his most fundamental objections to the liberationist approach.

Gustafson on the Relationship between Ethics and Theology

In the context of developing a theocentric ethic, Gustafson gives an idealized phenomenological account of how religion develops and how ethics emerges out of piety.[11] He begins with our nonreligious experience of the world, including nature, history, culture, society, and the self, and shows how the experience of these evokes in us various affectivities of which he picks out six 'senses' as central and universal: radical dependence, gratitude, obligation, remorse or repentance, possibility, and direction.[12] These affectivities, which involve a natural piety, further evoke, in some people, religious affections, religious piety, which involves consenting to the religious symbols of a tradition. The classic symbols for Christianity are God as creator, sustainer and governor, judge and redeemer. Theological ethics develops from this.[13] For example, the experience of history evokes a sense of dependence which may in turn evoke the sense of God as governor. Our particular experience of history forces us to understand God's governance in terms of ordering, and not just order, with the consequence that morality becomes the task of discerning what the divine ordering requires and allows in particular circumstances.[14] Science is so important an expression of our experience of the world that our religious belief should not only not be incongruous with scientific knowledge but should be positively indicated by it.[15] Science indicates that we are but a minuscule part and not the 'crowning glory' of the cosmos, that there is no afterlife and that God is not personal, so neither intelligent nor benevolent, but should be identified with nature.[16] All of this serves to displace us as being of central moral concern. The frequent failure of our best efforts to improve the world for ourselves demonstrates that what is in our interest will not always be what is in the interest of the rest of the cosmos.[17] Anthropocentrism is not compatible with theocentrism.

In this phenomenological story, Gustafson moves from a general experience, through natural piety, religious piety, and theology to ethics. He sees liberation theology as starting off from a partisan moral perspective, siding with the poor for their liberation against the rich, and then quoting scripture to lend religious authority to moral opinion. Gustafson objects to both the partisan content and the ethics-to-theology method of the liberationists, and he sees the two as fundamentally connected. In terms of method, he sees rooting religion in ethics as putting religion in the service of ethics, and this he sees as justifying religion for its utility value by using it to rationalize an ethical position already taken. In terms of content, he objects to the partisan position that ethical right and religious authority are placed on the side of one self-interested group pitched against another, which does not take proper account of the sinfulness of all and the ambiguity of every historical situation. He thinks this partisanship on behalf of one's group is but the logical extension of anthropocentrism. Anthropocentrism is inevitable if we start with 'human' ethics and not with objective, 'godly' religion and theology. The move from ethics to theology is thus tied to anthropocentrism and, ultimately, partisanship. Gustafson also objects to a theology for which God takes sides and so becomes 'unitarian,' an instrument in the service of the cause of some human beings and denied to others. While traditionally God has been co-opted by the powerful, this does not justify the liberationists' attempt to co-opt God for the powerless. Both positions conflict with the sovereignty of God. Finally, because Gustafson objects to moving from ethics to theology, he objects to a correlation hermeneutic in theology which starts with contemporary ethical concerns.[18]

Gustafson uses H. Richard Niebuhr's discussions of war in an attempt to demonstrate how scripture and theology should, in the first instance, inform ethics and not vice versa, and to show that God must not be understood to be partisan and that we ought not to be partisan. According to Gustafson, *Niebuhr discerns from scripture and theology that God is judge and redeemer of all, not vengeful but providing a "chastening punishment," where the suffering of the innocent is used for the "remaking" of the guilty.* And while God uses both sides for God's positive purposes, God does not *take* sides with one group rather than another because all groups are sinful. We are called first to repentance and only after that to act for the overcoming of injustice. We must do this without accusing others or treating them as beyond redemption and without holding ourselves and our side up as morally worthy. Neither ethics nor religion give unqualified support to one group over another in a dispute, not even to the oppressed over the oppressor.[19]

Gustafson criticizes directly the liberationists' correlation method for interpreting scripture. He argues, while liberationists have identified themselves with the Israelites of the Exodus to support their political, social, and economic interests, nineteenth-century South African Calvinists used the Israelites' conquest of the land of Canaan to defend their expansion into the lands of black tribes. Whether exodus or conquest, whether liberation from oppression or subjugation of the other is biblically blessed depends for those groups on prior moral convictions. But we must be more critical. For Gustafson, *to the moral conviction that liberation is good and conquest is bad we must add a theological argument to show that liberation is more consistent with the Christian experi-*

ence of God than is conquest, an argument such as Niebuhr gives for God's unvengefulness in war.[20]

A Liberationist Response

Comments on Key Elements of Gustafson's Position

Although, in general, Gustafson is aware that we are conditioned in various ways, he seems to think that if theology informs ethics in the nonreciprocal way that he advocates, both theology and ethics will have an objectivity, a freedom from the biases of human and group concern which the liberationist approach lacks. While God does not and cannot intervene in our history to give us ethical decrees, it seems that our experience of the world places us under an objectively given moral imperative. Morality is directed by an imperfect and apparently imperfectable Nature. However, Gustafson's six "universal senses," on which "natural" piety is based, and which include dependence, gratitude, and repentance, are highly selective in favor of his own neo-Orthodox tradition. This complex of affections, together with the God, symbolized as creator and judge, that they yield is less appropriate to oppressed groups than to middle-class Western men who are likely to see their flaws in terms of power-seeking and pride. It is noteworthy that Gustafson does not mention, as fundamental, our experience of suffering, compassion, or love, or refer to God as Father/Mother or Love.

In fact, the views of Gustafson and the liberationists on the key issue of suffering reflect the differences they see in the relationship between ethics and religion. For liberationists, ethics begins with suffering and as a response to suffering. For Gustafson, concern about suffering follows from concern about what God is requiring and enabling us to do. For liberationists, suffering is a challenge to God as well as to ourselves; for Gustafson, it is strictly God's challenge to us, a way of showing and teaching us what God requires. For liberationists, suffering is negative, an outrage, to be resisted; for Gustafson some suffering is to be taken seriously as an indication from God that something is disordered and needs changing, but it is also natural to the process of ordering a world which is not and cannot be ordered for human ends. To be outraged by it, to see it as a challenge to God, is not to recognize our finiteness. While Gustafson denies that, in cosmic terms, humans are for the sake of the whole, it seems that suffering is to be taken note of and responded to because a part of the whole is weak, something is out of order. The liberationist view that those who are suffering and weak are of special concern and ought to be preferentially treated is firmly rejected.[21]

Finally, regarding the identification Gustafson makes between putting theology and religion *in the service of* ethics and using theology and religion to *rationalize* an ethical position already taken: For theology and religion to play the latter, rationalizing role presupposes that they have an authority which is independent of ethics so that they can be appealed to in order to support or 'prove' the favored ethical position. But this is precisely the opposite to the liberationist perspective, which argues that theology and religion are only as authentic as is the ethic in which they are rooted. However, liberationists do maintain that theology and religion should be in the service of ethics. This means that theology and religion should promote human and cosmic welfare and, if they do not, then, whatever else they promote or accomplish, they fail in their fundamental purpose.

Why Theology Must Have an Ethical Foundation

Contrary to Gustafson, liberationists argue that the genuine doing of theology and engaging in religious practice begin with a partisan commitment to the oppressed—to the poor, to people of color, to women. . . . Theological hermeneutics begins with a demand that theology be engaged in, and scripture be interpreted in light of, the liberation of the oppressed. Segundo argues that a hermeneutical circle in theology

> always presupposes a profound human commitment, a partiality that is consciously accepted—not on the basis of theological criteria . . . but on the basis of human criteria.[22]

Elisabeth Schüssler-Fiorenza is equally outspoken. She says that the basic insight and methodological starting point of all liberation theologies is that

> all theology knowingly or not is by definition always engaged for or against the oppressed. Intellectual neutrality is not possible in a historical world of exploitation and oppression.

She calls this the "advocacy stance" of liberation theology.[23] For Soelle:

> To listen to the howl, to its rage, its despair, its revenge, to listen
> to the offended and raped earth, and to listen to the cry in our-
> selves and in our brothers and sisters is the first step in doing the-
> ology.[24]

Schillebeeckx makes the same point in a general way when he argues
that it is recalcitrant reality that becomes the principle for the interpretation of reality because here we know that the reality experienced is
objective and not mere wish-fulfillment. But how are liberationists to
avoid Gustafson's objections to their blatant partisanship?

Christian theological hermeneutics has an ethical foundation.
Because liberation theology is committed to the view that all experience is interpreted and our frameworks for interpretation change, and
because it is concerned about contemporary suffering and oppression
in light of a promise made in the past and contained in the Christian
scripture and tradition, this theology needs a correlation hermeneutic.
While acknowledging that scripture must be interpreted in light of the
categories and problems in terms of which it was written, we must go
on to insist that, *to be understood as good news for our time, it must also be
interpreted in light of contemporary categories and problems.*[25] This does
not involve an attempt to seek an answer in the text to our contemporary questions nor simply to read into scripture the solutions we think
correct. Schillebeeckx argues that if we understand the Christian message as a promise of salvation and so future-directed, in need of fulfillment, then the truth and correct interpretation of the message is
neither something we find in the text nor something we lay on it but
first something we do.[26]

How then are we to understand the Christian text, the Christian
message as a promise of salvation? What, Schillebeeckx asks, would be
universally recognized as making life meaningful, as salvific? What is
meaningful for the Christian must be meaningful for all. As we discussed in chapter 1,[27] the negation of negation, resistance to every
threat to the humanum, is what is universally recognized to be meaningful, salvific, good news. While our interest in chapter 1 was ethical,
Schillebeeckx's interest in that particular discussion was hermeneutical. *What we took as our first principle of ethics he took as his first principle of
theological hermeneutics, that which, at the most basic level, makes possible a*

correlation between the ancient religious text of a promise of good news and what is relevant to us today.[28] Precisely because resistance to suffering provides the universal preunderstanding for meaningfulness or good news, it provides the universal preunderstanding of talk about God. The first principle of theological hermeneutics is ethical; it is the first principle of ethics, and it is a practice before it is reflective knowledge or a formula for interpretation. We understand the good news of the Christian scripture first by practicing it.[29]

All hermeneutics has an ethical foundation. Christian theology and religion must be rooted in ethical practice because their subject matter centrally involves a promise of salvation. But there is an even deeper reason why not only theology and religion but all the intellectual disciplines, indeed all knowledge and experience, ought to be rooted in and guided by ethical value and practice.

We have argued that all of our experience is interpreted. Implicit in our interpreting experience in terms of images, concepts, and frameworks is that *we also interpret according to interests and values, however implicit, however unconscious.* Humans (and other species) are fundamentally geared toward their world in an intending, evaluating way. Our understanding and knowledge, not only of the external world but of our very anthropology, is not value-free. This is built right into our being interpreters. We must constantly choose from among interpretations and create new conditions for choice. This is to say that the starting point in our experience of the world is not value-free.

This value-base is more obvious in religion and theology than in history and biology, say, because the former involve a proclamation of good news and a promise of salvation. Liberationists stress how history can be interpreted in the interests of the conquerors or the conquered. The critical theorists and many scientists argue that because the sciences and mathematics are not subject-independent, they are not value-free. Helmut Peukert, in line with Jurgen Habermas, argues that, because the scientist is essentially intersubjective and engaged in "communicative practice," in order not to undermine the scientific project, the scientist must respect the implicit values of truth, justice, equality, and solidarity.[30] We can argue more simply, however, that because we are fundamentally interpreters, because all of our experience is interpreted, we are fundamentally evaluators and all of our experience is based on value. *But if our very experience and with it our doing theology is value-laden, then the value with which it ought to be laden is ethical value. So, it is important to make explicit what are the values with which we are operating, not only in theology but in biology and all of our practice, to evaluate those values, and to revise them so that they conform to ethical value.*

We saw in the last chapter that ethics must be hermeneutical, that it must seek new systems of interpretation as well as new norms for right practice in order that our value may come alive in our context. But now we see that, at a deeper level, hermeneutics must be ethical, guided by ethical value and practice. We see why Schillebeeckx, Segundo, and the writers of the Medellín and Puebla documents necessarily take the same founding principle for ethics and hermeneutics, which they articulate as resistance to suffering, response to human need, and the option for the poor, respectively. Because hermeneutics is value-laden, the value with which it ought to be laden is fundamental ethical value.

Although they articulate their basic ethical principle differently, the liberationists are expressing the same fundamental value, the same common faith. But how do they and we know that they are right? How do we evaluate our basic value and adjudicate between values? What standard do we use? As our discussion of ourselves as evaluators brought out, *if we accept that knowledge is based on experience which is always interpreted and value-laden, if our very experience of ourselves, our anthropology, is interpreted and value-laden, and if arguments of reason, including transcendental arguments, cannot be divorced from experience, then we can have no absolute, neutral standard of evaluation. We must be anthropocentric to the extent that we must be the initial 'measurers,' although not 'measures,' of what is the highest value, what is godly. And we cannot prove that what we take to be ethically fundamental is so.*

We cannot prove our value on the basis of an external authority such as religion or theology, nor of the internal authority of our anthropology, because we bring value to all our experience, including our experience of God and ourselves. But again we can see the power of the negative criterion. While the value we bring to experience will influence what we see as negative, negative reality can force us to revise our interpretations and the value we bring with them. From the basic demand that we negate what we are forced to see as negative, we can move on to the argument for the option for the poor, as we did in chapter 2. Thus we have very good grounds for arguing that resistance to suffering and its concretization in terms of the option for the poor not only provide the founding value and imperative for ethics but also for theology and religion—and our engagements in biology and business. . . . Ethics is foundational for theology and religion and all our engagements.

Finally, we can add to the argument of chapter 2 that *because we are fundamentally valuers and must choose our most fundamental values, we cannot avoid being partisan, taking an advocacy stance in ethics and theology, in at least this sense of placing our faith in and opting for, without proof, one value and not another. This gives a general support to the stronger partisanship involved in taking sides with the poor, defended in chapter 2, because it demonstrates the unavoidability of opting for one value rather than another in everything we do, in our very interpreting of experience and in our very experiencing.*[31] Beyond this, there is nothing I can add to the argument of chapter 2 regarding taking sides with the poor. We need not explicitly choose between the option for the poor and the option for the rich but implicitly we must do so. Not to support changing the structures of poverty and oppression is, consciously or unconsciously, to support the structures that are in place. And some of the structures that are in place, together with the actual values that they embody, are very largely responsible for poverty and oppression. Therefore, *if* it is most important, as liberationists argue from their experience, that massive numbers of people not be dehumanized, deprived of even the barest material, psychological, intellectual, and social needs, deprived of all control over their lives and their children's lives, and deprived at an early age of life itself, *then* it is most important that we take up the option for the poor. This must be at the core of ethics. And if the option for the poor is at the core of ethics, then the argument of this section shows that it must be the founding value for theology and religion, the value in terms of which we interpret scripture, structure our theology, engage in religious practice, and articulate religious experience and belief.

WAYS IN WHICH ETHICS IS PRIOR TO THEOLOGY AND RELIGION

In effect, we have just argued that ethics, as it involves interpreting, or acting out of, a value which we partly choose and for which we are responsible is logically prior to religion, theology, and all the disciplines. Thus they logically cannot go on except in the context of ethics. Because in religion and theology we must interpret an ancient tradition for our time, and because the content of that tradition is a promise of salvation, its interpretation requires our ethical practice and understanding.

Here we shall describe a variety of ways in which ethics is prior to or foundational for theology and religion, ways in which theology and religion are rooted in ethics. We should note, however, that to say that theology and religion are rooted in ethics is not to suggest that God and a suprahistorical eschaton are so rooted. Theology and religion are human projects or forms of life. And while God and the eschaton may be influenced by us and our projects, they are not reducible to our frameworks and projects. God and the eschaton have the role in theology and religion of objective referents.[32]

Autonomy of Ethics vis-à-vis Theology and Religion

It has become self-evident that being ethical is independent of being religious for the good reason that millions of people who deny any religious commitment demonstrate an ethical commitment which is as deep and as sensitive as that of religious believers. It is recognized that they are not doing something which is unintelligible or irrational. In recent writing, Schillebeeckx argues that God is a "useless, superfluous hypothesis" and, for post-moderns, a luxury.[33] He explicitly denies that we need God to establish ethics or anthropology and warns that if we use God for this purpose, when we find that we do not need God, we will lose God.[34] Segundo demonstrates that he supports the autonomy of ethics by subordinating religious faith to anthropological faith.[35]

It may be argued, however, that while ethics is autonomous from the point of view of the atheist, it is only relatively autonomous from the point of view of the religious person because, for the religious person, God is the ultimate source and foundation of ethics. And for the religious person, the atheist has no satisfactory answer to the question, Why be ethical? We may respond, It is true that for the religious person God is the ultimate source and foundation of everything that is good; God thus makes ethics possible. But for the atheist there is a perfectly good answer, *the primary answer, to the question Why be ethical? Because people are suffering and that is bad for them. If the acting, choosing, feeling, and thinking other does not call forth our ethical response, no religious belief will authentically do so.* The theist's picture is clearly more inclusive than the atheist's. But the atheist's picture is not inconsistent nor is it incomplete in such a way as to make it clearly wrong. A person may believe that there is something fundamentally unfinished and unfinishable, even perhaps absurd, about reality, and yet go on to make meaning and bring about the good where possible.

While ethics is thus autonomous vis-à-vis theology and religion, theology and religion are not similarly autonomous. Rather ethics is epistemologically, logically, existentially, causally, and in terms of human responsibility, prior to or foundational for religion and theology.

Five Ways in which Ethics Is Prior to Religion and Theology

Epistemological Priority

While most of us inherit a particular religious and theological as well as ethical perspective, there are important ways in which our genuine and justified ethical knowledge must precede that of religion and theology. In chapter 4 we argued that it is only on the basis of some people's right practice that we can justify, and so know, behavioral norms and ethical theory. Indeed, we argued that ethical knowledge is primarily practical knowledge, knowing how, and not propositional knowledge, knowing that. We thus applied the liberationist insistence on the epistemological priority of practice over theory to the ethical sphere itself. We argued even further that, in general, practical knowledge precedes propositional or theoretical knowledge; knowing how precedes knowing that. Now we shall argue, more directly in line with what liberationists actually mean when they talk about priority of practice over theory, that ethical practice must guide our understanding of religious doctrines and practices and must ground religious experience and belief. Orthopractice is epistemologically prior to orthodoxy.

Against the essentially extrinsicist view that ethics is something we learn and ought to accept on religious authority, Schillebeeckx argues:

> The understanding of good and evil logically precedes understanding God and doing God's will. That means that we cannot define our moral obligations primarily in terms of God and God's will.[36]

Segundo says something similar when he insists that Jesus can be recognized as God's revelation only by those who already have the same values as Jesus.[37] We can learn values and how to decide on right practice from others. Jesus' disciples learned and continue to learn from him. But we do not learn and come to accept these values because we recognize Jesus as Christ or because we recognize the Mosaic Law as coming from God. We can recognize the authority of God and of Jesus only because they conform to our deepest sense of what is worthwhile. It is intrinsic to our being ethical that we are free and responsible in determining what is ethical. It is intrinsic to God and knowledge of God that God is good and knowable through our ethical understanding and practice.

For liberationists, revelation is not fundamentally propositional or doctrinal, but experiential and practical. We can come to believe and adequately understand such central Christian notions as resurrection, salvation, and Jesus as Christ only through our experience of these things. This experience is tied to right practice. Only by experiencing the godliness of others and moments of salvation, and only by responding by way of godly practice ourselves and contributing to others' experience of salvation, can we come to know God and salvation and Jesus as Christ. Persons, including God and Jesus Christ, we know primarily experientially. To know propositions about them is not to know them and is only inadequately to understand the propositions about them. The same holds for phenomena such as salvation, poverty, and war. But tied to experiential knowledge is practical knowledge. Knowing a person involves knowing how to relate to that person. Knowing war is knowing how to survive in war, psychologically if not physically. While we can learn creeds and narrowly religious practices from our religious tradition and independent of ethical practice, these will be empty and not fully understood if they are not rooted in right practice and experience. In this sense, each social group and each individual must discover God, salvation, and religious doctrines and practices anew. These things cannot *merely* be handed down by a tradition.[38]

Logical or Conceptual Priority

When I speak of ethics as epistemologically prior to religion and theology, I mean that knowledge of the latter is nonreciprocally dependent on knowledge of the former. When I say ethics is logically or conceptually prior to religion and theology, one thing I mean is that, *not just the knowledge of but the very meaning of* religious experience, practice, and propositions is, to a significant extent, nonreciprocally rooted in ethics. We do not just come to recognize that Jesus is Christ and salvation-bringer through his and our ethical practice, but his ethical practice and his influence on our ethical practice are central to what we mean when we speak of Jesus as Christ and salvation-bringer. Similarly, central to what we mean by the kingdom of God is that it involves a set of social relations among people where there is no hierarchy and there are no outcasts but wherein all flourish. The only meaning we can give to final salvation is as an extension of the partial salvation we bring about and experience. Whatever sense we can make of God and God's goodness must come from our experience of goodness in history.

We can look at the conceptual priority of ethics over religion from another perspective. It is not only the case that authentic religion is disclosed by authentic ethics but also what is one's religion is founded in what is one's ethic. Segundo stresses this by emphasizing what is, in effect, a conceptual priority of anthropological faith over religious faith. For him, we do not determine what is our religion by looking at the forms of ritual in which we engage or the creed to which we pay lip service. Rather, we determine what is our religion, who is our god or idol, by looking first at the structure of our moral values made manifest in our ethical practice. We cannot agree in our religion and theology if we do not agree in our fundamental ethics.[39]

Existential Priority

If our religion and theology are to be honest, authentic, and existentially true, then they must be grounded in right practice. *Existential priority is related to conceptual priority, but while the latter concerns public meaning the former concerns lived truth.* Precisely because religion and theology must be grounded in right practice in order to be meaningful, they must be grounded in right practice in order to be authentic. Authentic theology and religious belief presuppose and must cohere with authentic value and ethical practice. But also, whatever will be the existential force of our theology and ethics will depend on where our value lies and what our practice is. Again, the issue is not so much *whether* we believe in a transcendent God and a suprahistorical salvation but which god, which is to say which structure of salvation, which system of values, do we subscribe to?

Theology and religion are inauthentic, not expressive of a lived truth, when, rather than being grounded in ethics, they claim to ground ethics.[40] Then ethics is extrinsic to us, apparently laid on from the outside, a set of formulae which we do not consciously choose but to which we must give obedience. The relationship between ethics and theology as a relationship of practice to theory is relevant here. Authentic theory must be based on practice and experience, not the other way around. Our belief in doctrines and creeds, our orthodoxy, must gain their authenticity from our right practice and value and not the other way around.[41]

Causal Priority

From the point of view of most theists, God is ontologically prior to ethics; God is the source and foundation of our ethical life. But, from this perspective, God is ontologically prior to everything, including human religion and theology, and is the source and foundation of all that is not evil. From a liberationist point of view, ethics is causally prior to religion and theology, and this in no way reduces God, religion, or theology to ethics or to our ethical life. Schillebeeckx and others argue that ethical experience and practice, such as the experience and practice of social solidarity of and with those who are oppressed, can give rise to a religious experience including hope for a suprahistorical salvation in God. Because religion and theology are brought about and engaged in by human cultures, because they essentially involve states of consciousness and human practice, because they are not objects to be known that are independent of human consciousness and choice, there is a close connection between the epistemological priority of ethics to religion and theology and its causal priority. The ethical form of life, by disclosing a religious dimension, causes religious experience for some.[42]

Also, while our ethical practice does not cause a suprahistorical salvation any more than it causes God, liberationists argue that what we do in history, the moments of salvation we do or do not bring about, will affect the shape of the eschaton, will causally affect its content. Meaning, including eschatological meaning, is not simply something we find but something we help to bring about. For liberationists, we are co-creators with God.[43]

Priority in Terms of Importance for Us as Responsible Agents

Here I have in mind the question concerning what is it to which we ought to give priority or our first attention? As we saw in the discussions of Jesus and the Law, Jesus consistently demonstrates that human welfare must come before religious obligation. But, also, human welfare is the fundamental religious obligation, the point of the Law. So there should be no conflict between ethical and religious claims on us. When there is conflict, it is almost inevitably because our religious obligation is distorted and does not reflect right practice. Then, right practice should have priority and, indeed, should change the shape of our religious commitment.

Relevant to this, the Christian tradition has consistently maintained that love is more important than knowledge, that doing good to the other is more important than believing what is true about God and the universe, even though the tradition has often mistakenly thought that knowledge must be prior to love, that orthodoxy must be prior to orthopractice, in order that we know how to love and what to do. Connected with this, modern theists would argue that ethics is prior to religion and theology in terms of our responsibility because we cannot opt out of being ethical, and we cannot completely choose whether to be religious.

It is misleading, however, to argue that it is more important to be ethical than to be religious. This is only really true when we separate the two, either in terms of setting up a conflict between religious obligation and ethical demand, or setting up a choice between engaging in right practice and right belief. Authentic religion is rooted in ethics but is more than ethics. *It takes our ethicity up into itself and offers a transformed and more embracive experience and understanding of reality than being ethical alone can.* Here the theist and atheist must part ways. From a religious point of view, to be ethico-religious is more meaningful and true and valuable than to be simply ethical. From a nonreligious point of view, there is something illusory and untrue, even if meaningful and subjectively authentic, about the ethico-religious experience.

WHY RELIGION AND THEOLOGY ARE NOT
REDUCIBLE TO ETHICS

In this chapter, I have stressed the importance of ethics and how religion and theology must be rooted in ethics in order to be meaningful and authentic. Therefore, we may wonder why we should bother with religion and theology at all. Surely these are but superfluous additions to ethical life. The short answer to this is that being religious is not something we entirely choose. Ordinary experience, particularly ethical experience, discloses, for some, God and what we might call religious meaning, a significance of history which extends beyond itself. In this section, I will discuss how ethical experience can disclose a religious dimension and what are the significant differences between the theist and the atheist with an aim to showing that God and a suprahistorical eschaton are not unfitting or redundant additions to a liberationist ethical perspective. Rather, this ethic logically and morally cries out for God and heaven, although it does not logically or practically necessitate them. I will conclude with a discussion of ways in which Christian ethics is and is not distinctive.

Ethical Experience Can Disclose a Religious Dimension of Reality

Liberationists agree with virtually all theologians of our time that God does not intervene directly in history. They also think that arguments that attempt to prove God or an afterlife are not convincing. If we are to experience God or have grounds for God and for a final salvation, these must be rooted in and revealed through our experience of the world, what Schillebeeckx calls a disclosure experience. As we have mentioned,[44] this involves an ordinary empirical experience opening up, for some, a deeper dimension, eliciting an experience which goes beyond the original one, transforming the original experience and relocating it against a horizon which gives it a fuller meaning. While the new experience is not completely private, neither is it completely empirically verifiable,[45] and although it affects the whole person, including emotions, commitment, and sense of integratedness, it can be false or illusory.

The Negative Contrast Experience Discloses
God and Final Salvation

The very experience of partial salvation amidst suffering calls forth the imagined possibility of and desire for a full salvation without suffering. By means of a disclosure experience this desire can become hope for and faith in full salvation. Partial salvation is then experienced as part of a whole, a moment of a total salvation for which a gestaltist but not an empiricist view of perception and knowledge forms a theoretical background. On a gestaltist view, *we do not merely infer from part to whole but we see, experience, the part as part of a whole.* We see the door as having another side; we experience humans as having inner feelings and so on. This is very different from, for example, inferring that an ambiguous drawing can represent an old woman from the parts that are pointed out to us when the gestalt refuses to form for us. Schillebeeckx himself explicitly subscribes to the gestaltist distinction between seeing and inferring in order to explain how the religious person lives in a different world and does not just interpret the world differently from the nonreligious person.[46] The gestaltist perspective helps to explain *how some* people can *experience* partial salvation as *of* something more, a full salvation; we need not make an inference from the one to the necessity of the other.

Not only the experience of partial salvation but also the effort to bring about partial salvation in the ethical practice of resistance to suffering can disclose God and final salvation. We cannot really talk about resistance to suffering without talking about suffering for the sake of overcoming suffering, and this involves agape, altruism. Altruism captures the human capacity to be ethical but in its extreme and also paradigmatic cases, so contradicts our ordinary ways that we experience it as transcendent and as gift. As we have said before, it can have an incalculably salvific effect, erasing in a moment a lifetime of suffering. The altruism involved in concrete struggles against oppression most often involves solidarity and even mutuality, the project of a group. An experience of salvation is found in the struggle of the group. Altruism, and with it the solidarity and mutuality that are based on altruism, must provide the fundamental disclosure that goodness will prevail—in spite of the quantity of evil.

Jesus: Paradigm Source of Disclosure of God and Final Salvation

In chapter 1 we described in some detail how Jesus is an ethical paradigm, a paradigm of one who experienced and responded to the negative contrast. We described how his experience of the suffering of others juxtaposed against his Abba experience, itself a disclosure experience issuing into his vision of the kingdom of God, led to his agapeic response. The failure of that response to touch very deeply the people to whom it was directed, including Jesus' own disciples, culminating in his own torture and death, must have profoundly deepened his experience of suffering. But, by all accounts, it also deepened his Abba experience and his belief that God's kingdom would come, that goodness would prevail. The Christian religious experience of Jesus as risen and, with it, of God and final salvation, must come as a disclosure from the experience of this story of Jesus' agapeic living out of the negative contrast.

While Schillebeeckx stresses the forgiveness experienced by those disciples who abandoned Jesus as the paradigm Easter experience, we have seen that he describes Mary Magdalene's experience as one of loving assurance that Jesus lives. In fact, we can include all of Jesus' disciples in this more general description of an Easter experience. We can see it as disclosing that Jesus and Jesus' value live; goodness and God's kingdom prevail. Segundo argues that the resurrection stories described by the evangelists point to this.[47] Jesus appears only to his disciples, only to those who have the same values as he. They have trouble recognizing him, and they do recognize him only when he says or does something which reminds them of their past experience of him. *Coming to see, with effort, Jesus as risen, the same and yet transformed, involves coming to see, with effort, that Jesus' value is risen, that Jesus' project of God's kingdom which failed in history succeeds in heaven.* Jesus' first disciples would not have been able to see this, to glimpse the eschaton, if what they saw was not an integration, the forming of a gestalt, of fragments which they had experienced during Jesus' lifetime. Their Easter experiences disclosed to them what they had already had an intimation of, yet had not seen. Also, by forming the starkest contrast with their fear, confusion, isolation, and despair following Jesus' death, the disciples' Easter experience led them to act with fearless solidarity and hope in carrying on Jesus' project of alleviating suffering in God's name. Their Easter experience was not just a salvific feeling but formed part of a negative contrast propelling them to salvific practice which would itself reinforce their religious experience.

The story of Jesus, told through the Easter experience of his first disciples, discloses God and salvation even today.

The Poor and Oppressed: Paradigm Source of Disclosure of God and Final Salvation

Schillebeeckx argues that, if the fundamental symbol of God is the living person, then the place where the person is

> dishonoured, violated and oppressed . . . [is] the preferred place
> where religious experience become[s] possible in a way of life
> which seeks to give form to this symbol, to heal it and give it its
> own liberated existence.[48]

God is in the oppressed, in the closest solidarity with them, as the
power of goodness and life, saying "no" to their plight and demanding
that all humans act to overcome their suffering. The place of deepest
negativity is, from a religious perspective, where we should locate ourselves because it is where salvation has to go on, where the God of
Jesus is needed, where the negation needs most to be negated.

But God is especially located in the poor and oppressed not only
as a protest but because "again and again it will be the oppressed
themselves, of all languages and colours, who hold high the vision in
their humiliation."[49] Again and again in history, just as we have
recently seen in southern Africa, the oppressed rise up against their
oppression. They know best, broadly speaking, how to give form to the
living person, the primary symbol of God, how to heal and liberate it,
because they are in the place where it is dishonored, violated,
oppressed. Like Jesus, they act out of the negative contrast in a radical
way.

More phenomenologically speaking, theologians, social activists,
religious, and people from every walk of life who have made an effort
to rub shoulders with the poor have expressed the experience of being
closest to God when they are with the poor. And they can never say
just why. Certainly, it has something to do with being in direct contact
with acute human need and the meaningfulness of acting to overcome
that need. But there is more. Liberationists rightly stress that God calls
us to take up the option for the poor just because they are poor and not
because they are good. There are many very bad poor people. Yet, generally speaking, to experience the poor is a profoundly moving, hum-
bling experience. Again, it is hard to say why. But it is related to the
striving of the poor, their enormous effort and creativity in finding
ways of surviving—and enjoying. Granted there is the need, but also
there seems to be a tendency, among the poor, to support one another
and share what they have, even with the sympathetic outsider. Consider sitting in a McDonald's restaurant in Manila. Inside, the mostly
upper-middle-class children are cheerful enough, but demanding the
latest McDonald's gimmick. But if you turn your gaze outside to the
parking lot, you might see street children creating games with pebbles
and disposed cups. At the doors, between the two, stand heavily

armed guards. It makes one ponder. The poor can reveal God to the nonpoor but we must look in their direction.

Finally, the poor do not disclose God to the rest of us simply through their situation and their own response to it any more than Jesus reveals God simply through his life and story. We have to respond, take up the option for the poor, Jesus' value, if Jesus and the poor are, in a profound way, going to disclose God and salvation. This will involve our locating ourselves in the place of greatest negativity, being persecuted, made to suffer for the sake of overcoming suffering.

Liberationist Ethics, Atheism, and Theism; Why Liberationist Ethics Cries Out for Heaven

It is impossible, in general terms and in such a way that all would agree, to define the distinction between theist and atheist. Followers of at least some forms of Buddhism do not fit comfortably into either category. How theists characterize the deity they believe in is as varied as are the values and metaphysical structures humans can conceive. For many theists God is personal and benevolent, but, for some, including Gustafson, God is neither of these. Also, while for large numbers of religious people, belief in an afterlife is central, Gustafson and many others see this as self-interested, wishful thinking. But for liberationist theists, experience of the world discloses a good God who is 'located' especially in the places of greatest need, protesting oppression and encouraging resistance to it. And, for most,[50] the experience of partial salvation discloses a final full salvation. My interest here is not to try to explore the difference between theism and atheism in general, but only between liberationists who are theists and those who are atheists. *So I shall take belief in a transcendent God who is good and belief in a final salvation made possible by God's power, to distinguish the liberationist who is a theist from the one who is an atheist.* My aim is to show that, while we can coherently be a liberationist and be either a theist or an atheist, the inner logic of a liberationist ethic, its value and goal and forms of practice, do not tend toward atheism but cry out for a fully blown theistic interpretation.

Regarding God and final salvation, Schillebeeckx argues that the theist can challenge the atheist to look at the implications of liberationist practice: "Judge me by the way in which I live!"[51] The point is not that there will be something better about the practice of theist than atheist but that the practice of *both* indicates a trust that goodness will prevail which the atheist denies. The atheist can reply, however, that the need of this hungry person, today, or of this landless group, this year and this decade, compels me to act in the hope that my action, together with theirs and that of many others, will help to alleviate suffering and oppression. But this may or may not happen; the world may or may not become a better place in which to live. Indeed, it is coherent and even imaginable that, say, Schillebeeckx's soldier,[52] ordered to shoot an innocent hostage, might forfeit his life, even though it would save no one, in a context where this soldier believed that humanity was in a humanly inspired hell, was becoming demonic and would not come out of it—and that there was nothing more. *The soldier's act may create a context for hope, but it need not presuppose nor be motivated by hope, conscious or unconscious, on the part of the soldier.* Finally, while I can, by empathizing with the theist, take on, as it were, the experience of the theist, I do this in order to understand the theist. It is not how I authentically experience and integrate my experience and belief.

The theist may respond that the story of a soldier who forfeits his life so as not to harm another, in a context of cosmic hopelessness, is so extreme as to be *almost* incoherent. Surely, at the very least, it depends on the soldier's *having* lived in a context of hope. So we can still ask where does the meaning and hope in history come from? Whence comes the human power to oppose evil against all odds? Indeed, from where does the recognition of evil as evil derive? Whence comes ethics? The atheist can reply, My explanation of my experience and practice is not as lengthy as that of the theist and it may be perceived to be incomplete. I cannot explain the source of human caring and altruism and the capacity to resist suffering against all odds, except by reference to our social anthropology. And while I must admit that partial experiences of salvation cannot help but lead to a yearning for an end to all suffering, I see this yearning as stimulating me to go on trying to bring about partial changes. I do not see it as disclosing a promise of an end to suffering and death—although it would be wonderful if it were true! Indeed, the liberationist theist leaves as many questions unanswered as I do. The liberationist's experience of God, in the protest and action of the poor and those in solidarity with the poor, provides only a partial answer to the problem of evil. If this God can transform the moments of salvation that we create into a total salvation, then it would seem that this God can stop the horrendous suffering and oppression that is experienced by masses of people in every period of history. Why does this God allow the suffering to go on?

The conversation between theist and atheist seems to have met a stalemate, both in terms of their differing experience and explanations of their experience. However, liberation theologians sometimes seem to suggest that whether we are theists or atheists makes little difference. What matters is our ethics, the values by which we live and out of which we act. Latin American liberation theologians of the poor have been explicit that it is not atheism, *whether* God, but idolatry, *which* god, that threatens them. For Segundo, it is the value we live by and not the creed we mouth which demonstrates who or what we worship. 'Being religious,' affirming a transcendent as such, is not what is most important, but the anthropological faith, on which any given religious faith may or may not be based, is what is most important.[53] Indeed, the Christian must risk atheism by judging Jesus in terms of the contribution he makes to humanization, before considering whether he is the bearer of something transcendent.[54] Schillebeeckx explicitly seeks as first principle of ethics and of theological hermeneutics something which will be meaningful and acceptable to *all* humans, theist and atheist alike, and he finds this in the negative contrast experience.[55] He maintains that the atheist is neither less rational nor less moral than the theist.[56] In fact, in our time, nonreligious movements even more than religious movements have taken up the cause of the poor.[57] In recent writing, Schillebeeckx argues unabashedly that, relative to what happens to us in history, "God is a useless, superfluous hypothesis. For us, God as a remedy for the human condition has completely disappeared from sight." Thus, for the 'post-modern' who does not need God's intervention for the control of nature and history, the question of God becomes free and gratuitous. The way to God no longer involves a manipulative 'obedience' for reward, where we decide the rules and, in effect, control God. Rather, God must be experienced as "pure gift," the "supreme luxury."[58]

Liberationist theologians sometimes suggest, however, that their position is importantly different from the atheist's because it has an eschatological perspective in terms of which it can and must relativize history, particularly our achievements and utopian dreams. By our policies and actions, the most we can do is bring about partial salvation, and only for a time before they become outmoded. But this is not to say that we should do nothing. Rather, we must criticize present negativities and attempt to bring our situation as much as possible in line with our (mainly negatively understood) vision of the kingdom.

Schillebeeckx sometimes suggests that atheists, without an eschatological perspective, think that they can find final this-worldly humanly achieved solutions—or that they can find no solutions at all.[59] Recently, however, he has argued that "the denial of God no longer calls into being the boastful divinization of humanity . . . ; on the contrary, it leaves men and women in their *condition humaine*, sometimes in a down-to-earth way, sometimes bravely or humbly."[60] *Many atheists fully recognize the contingency of history and the limitedness of humans in overcoming suffering but also that humans do have a limited capacity to overcome suffering.* Even without God and a suprahistorical eschaton, people can integrate their experience in the way of an 'as it were' eschatological proviso. Their thought is not inconsistent.[61]

In spite of all these apparent suggestions to the contrary, however, whether there is God and final salvation matters profoundly, both personally to individuals and structurally in terms of the inner logic of a liberationist ethic. Considering the individual first, God and the promise of final salvation provide the horizon for the liberationist theist's experience of and practice in history. These impinge and pervade this person's experience of history itself. God is seen especially where there is need and where there is response to need; the promise of salvation without suffering is seen in the salvific moments which are a relief from suffering. Humans are seen as utterly valuable because of the kind of being they are, because of the kinds of things they can and sometimes do. Humans are also seen as valuable because they are co-creators with God of a better world, and because they help to shape the eschaton. Theists can be encouraged by the hope that failures of human efforts in history will be fruitful in the eschaton. Humans, and the entire cosmos, are seen, not only as each connected in every other, but as united in a caring God. Liberationist atheists do not see humans as merely objects but also as subjects. They do not see history and the life of the individual in history as meaningless but as including partially successful attempts to make meaning. They see humans as connected in one another and in the cosmos. But their world view is governed by the contingency of historical existence. The world view of the theist is conditioned by the experience of God and final salvation which transcends historical existence. Theists and atheists integrate their whole experience differently; they see a different significance in it. *And it matters utterly to the theist and to the atheist that she or he is a theist or atheist. It is a matter of integrity, a matter of living what one experi-*

ences and believes to be the way things truly are ultimately. Theists' ethical lives are taken up into, located, and redefined in terms of, and so transformed by the religious dimension of their lives. But atheists too have a world view in terms of which they integrate their lives, including their ethical lives.[62] And, of course, what is transformation for the theist is illusion for the atheist. Finally, while it matters utterly to both theist and atheist that they are theists and atheists, they may go on to say that it does not matter all that much whether *another* is a theist or atheist. But what matters a great deal is another's fundamental value and practice.

Whether we are theists also matters structurally to a liberationist ethic. Schillebeeckx's rather flamboyant statements concerning the uselessness, luxury, and gratuitous gift that God is for humans may appear to suggest the contrary, that the structure of a liberationist ethic is indifferent to whether we are theists. However, these statements are but colorful ways of expressing the prominent view that humans must come of age, we must take responsibility for our lives, and not treat God as a stopgap. Post-moderns do not need a stopgap God because they can make their lives meaningful without God. Our relationship to God must move from one of dependence, manipulation, and 'loving' for what we can get out of it, which the atheist finds objectionable, to a relationship of free and gratuitous giving. Only when we do not need God in the way of a stopgap can we be sure our belief in God is authentic. Only because, in this way, there has become so little difference between the theist and atheist, can there be the deep and profound difference between having something like a personal relationship between ourselves and God, and not having such a relationship. And only because there has become so little difference between what we see as our aim in history and our understanding of final salvation can the theist experience the enormous gap between the world we aim at and the world we experience, and can theist and non-theist alike experience the unfathomable gap between a perspective for which there is final salvation and for which there is not.[63] However, *Schillebeeckx also expresses a persistent concern for the vast numbers of people who have lived and continue to live a life of suffering, oppression, and deprivation and who have died and who continue to die, not as martyrs for a cause, but meaninglessly and without hope. He asks, "Are they the chaff in our history that we throw away?"*[64] He asks whether the middle-class view, that it is more honest and respectful of human dignity to recognize life's limitations and not engage in wishful thinking about an afterlife, takes proper account of the worst off. Indeed, he asks this on behalf of, not only the very worst off, but also the vast majority of humans down through the ages who have not been able to make a genuinely meaningful life for themselves, who, at best, have experienced but moments of salvation in a history weighed down by suffering.

Those who live and die wretchedly need God, not primarily as recompense or repayment for their having suffered, but in order that their oppression may turn to liberation, their suffering may turn to salvation, their deprivation may turn to flourishment. Indeed, we all need such a God. No one, however, needs a stopgap God. Those who are alive need human solidarity. We need a God who grounds solidarity and encourages the overcoming of suffering, a God who allows and requires that humans be God's co-creators. It is such a God with whom we can relate as co-creators, whom we can see as superfluous—but also gratuitous. It is such a God and not a stopgap God who relates to a history where there is no practical difference between the action of atheist and theist, who can transform history so that suffering will end and flourishment will abound for all.

A liberationist ethic does not logically or practically presuppose God and final salvation; it is neither logically incoherent nor practically self-defeating without these things. Whether or not there is God and final salvation, we are ethically called to resist suffering and to put the worst off first. However, a liberationist ethic logically and practically cries out for God and a suprahistorical eschaton, not just to add a finishing touch as it were to what we can accomplish in history, not just so that the liberationist value can be realized ultimately and eternally. *The liberationist ethic restricted to history fails to realize its value at its heart because it fails those who are its first concern, the very worst off—those who live and die wretchedly.*[65] Also, secondarily, a liberationist ethic cries out for heaven for all our sakes, because we cannot overcome some of the most fundamental sorts of suffering and deprivation, the suffering and deprivation that come, for example, from death and old age, guilt, rejection, and severe disability. *A gearedness to a final salvation made possible by God is built into the raison d'être of this ethic; it is built into its primary aim.* There is no question, then, of liberation theology reducing religion to ethics, reducing theism to a humanistic atheism, or reducing out the eschatological dimension in favor of history. This ethic cannot succeed where it counts most if there is no God and no final salvation. In its logic and value it is not at all reductionist in the direction of this world and of our history.

Christian Ethics and Human Ethics

It is appropriate to ask at this stage what is and can be the difference between Christian ethics and human ethics. Most of what we have said would lead us to believe that Christian ethics is not other than universal human ethics. But our consideration of the differences between theist and atheist suggests that we can develop the discussion touched on in the last chapter[66] of how religion influences ethics.

Christian Ethics Is not Other than Universal Human Ethics

That Christian ethics is not other than universal human ethics has been implicit in almost everything that has been said. This does not mean, of course, that we start with Christian ethics, derived from Christian sources, and argue that, on grounds of Christian religious authority, Christian ethics ought to be universalized. Rather than arguing that religion and theology provide the foundations for ethics, we have argued that, in various ways, ethics grounds religion and theology. A plurality of religions, each with its own salvation figure, may be rooted in a *fundamentally* similar ethical experience. But neither does ethics derive from abstract human nature. It is not first a theory but a practice in response to an experience based on a fundamental value, a response by way of resistance to particular sorts of cases of concrete suffering. We have used Schillebeeckx's notion of the negative contrast experience to articulate this experience and its emergent practice.

Throughout, we have attempted to maintain a balance between a commitment to historical consciousness which recognizes the essentially contextual character of our moral decision-making as regards practice, and a commitment to the view that there is a unity of the human race, a common humanity, which looks out onto a common world and responds to that world in a fundamentally similar or at least analogous way. If this were not the case, Christians could not be followers of Jesus; those of us who are Christian would not find meaning and relevance in our ancient scriptures. But we do.[67] Indeed, the transmission of knowledge in any of the disciplines, our very communicativeness, presupposes a basic commonness of humanity interacting with a common world.

As we have seen, Schillebeeckx explicitly seeks what is universal in determining what is, in effect, the founding value and first principle for Christian ethics. The Christian answer to the question of human meaningfulness cannot be other than the human answer. What can be universally agreed upon is that every threat to the humanum should be resisted. And this agreement is based on a common experience of a reality which confronts and shatters our false interpretations. Not everyone agrees with this line of thought and with the option for the poor to which it leads. Schillebeeckx and other liberationists justify their views by appealing to the evidence of recalcitrant reality, the consequences of their proposals, and witnesses, including the witness of Jesus, history, anthropology, and social science. While liberationists must be open to discussion, it would make no sense if they did not argue that their grounded ethical position is right for all and should be accepted by all.[68] Finally, not only does Schillebeeckx argue for a fundamental value and goal which is universal, but he also articulates a set of anthropological constants which must always be taken into account in determining how to effect this value. These constants can do no more than guide; we cannot deduce from them universal norms for right behavior because these must change with our changing context.

Segundo's distinction between faith and ideologies helps to articulate the formal relationship between what is constant and what changes in ethics. Anthropological faith is constant and involves our fundamental value, which we choose on the basis of worthwhile lives already lived. Christians recognize in Jesus' example the value which is worth living by, the value of resistance to suffering which Schillebeeckx argues can be universally agreed upon. But ideologies, our systems of means for attaining goals, must change with our changing historical context. We interpreted this, for ethics, as the requirement to find new forms of practice and interpretation in new circumstances which will reflect our permanent value. We discussed ways of finding right practice by reference to learning to learn, engaging in a practical hermeneutical circle, and for Christians, creating ideologies that are Christologies. But we argued that first attempts at new right practice are made at least partly by a trial-and-error method in response to new experience and guided by the negative criterion which expresses our fundamental value. New practice is prior to new norms for and theories of right practice. The faith-and-ideologies distinction is thus useful in capturing what is universal in the relationship between what is constant and what must change in ethics. And it is useful in helping to demonstrate a permanent strategy for decision-making in ethics.

Thus, on these views, Christianity has no other ethics than universal human ethics in its fundamental value, in its need to find new practices so that its practice will be integrated with its value through a changing history, and in some basic strategies for finding new practices. But our dialogue between atheist and theist suggests that there is something distinctive about Christian ethics not captured in earlier discussions.

The Distinctiveness of Christian Ethics

In the first chapter we demonstrated that Jesus' story provides a paradigm example of one who lived according to the negative contrast experience, of one for whom the experience of the poor and marginalized was in sharp contrast to his Abba experience, and who responded by resisting suffering with all his strength and to death. This is a liberationist interpretation of the more general Christian view that Jesus shows us our humanity. Jesus' distinctiveness and, perhaps, his contingent uniqueness lie in revealing in such a paradigmatic way this central, foundational aspect of what is meaningful and ethical for humans.

We also argued, in showing us our humanity and the value of what is good for the humanum, Jesus showed us God's will for us, the will of a God who is utterly good and on the side of humanity. And by his resurrection and our Easter experience, the story of Jesus provides Christians with hope for final salvation. But whatever our Christology, experience of and belief in Jesus as Christ cannot open up for the Christian a content of ethic which is different from that which is meaningful to and available for all humans whether they hold Christian beliefs or not. Jesus cannot be an ethical model for us in any other way than by showing us our humanity because we cannot follow him except in our humanity. Yet our worldview forms a horizon or context within which we locate our ethics. And whether that horizon is restricted to contingent history or includes a benevolent transcendent realm will affect the quality of our ethicity. But we must make some distinctions here.

Schillebeeckx argues that, because Christianity has no ethic of its own, it is open to the humanum sought by all.[69] What he means is that *ethics is autonomous vis-à-vis religion and theology in terms of its fundamental value, to resist suffering; in terms of what we ought to do, to seek forms of practice appropriate to our context which will reflect this value; and in terms of the fundamental motivation and reason for doing it, to act for the sake of the other. In this sense, Christian ethics is not other than universal human ethics,* and discipleship to Jesus is discipleship to one who in a poignant and paradigmatic way showed us our humanity. But, while *what* should be our fundamental value, practice, motive, and reason for acting will not be affected by our broader worldview, their *quality* and *significance* will be. While the Christian dimension does not change the ethical *practice* of the Christian, it changes the quality of practice utterly. We see the good that we do as not our own but God acting in us. While people who are not Christian have as strong a *motivation* to act against suffering as Christians, for many Christians, the hope implicit in their Easter experience and the sense that God acts in them strengthen the propelling force of their negative contrast experience, making it possible for them to do what, otherwise, they could not. While the plight of the other remains the necessary and sufficient *reason* for being ethical, seeing God in the poor, in their protest and in their struggle, and seeing humans connected not only in one another and with the cosmos but seeing all as connected in God, reshapes and provides a new dimension to our fundamental reason for being moral. God wills that we act for the sake of the other, and in acting for the sake of the other we act in accordance with God's will and God acts in us. But none of this should lead us to replace the plight of the other with something like God's will as the reason for being moral. There is something immature, extrinsicist, and contractual about acting morally in the world primarily for such specifically religious reasons as that I must repay the creator or even the loving God or that I must give obedience to God the judge. It would be schizophrenic to deny that in acting in accordance with the will of a loving God whom we see as on our side we should move into acting for the sake of that God as well as for the sake of the other in need. The quality of our reason for acting for the sake of the other is transformed by the Christian dimension. But we can speak too of the quantity of reasons for acting as being increased by the Christian experience. Finally, the Christian dimension does not replace the fundamental *value* of resistance to suffering but transforms that value. The humanum and cosmos do not become more valuable by being related to God and a final salvation, so that it becomes more important and more urgent to act on their behalf in history. To see ourselves as co-creators with God, who help to shape the eschaton, to see ourselves and the cosmos as having a godly, eschatological value, ironically, does not add to as much as it transforms our value and the value of resistance to every threat to the humanum and cosmos.

Discipleship to Jesus involves not only Jesus' showing us value and showing us how to go on, things which others can show us as well. But also it involves coming to know the God Jesus reveals and coming to experience the hope Jesus had. Not only will the atheist's worldview and quality of ethicity be different from the Christian's but the Christian's will be somewhat different from the world views, and so quality of ethicity of members of other religions. In chapter 4 it was argued that in creating ideologies which are Christologies, we attempt to *transpose* the logic of Jesus' way into our context; we seek an analogous way. This suggests that there really is something unique in discipleship to Jesus. While the view of God and humanity which Jesus reveals through his particular history are to some extent revealed by others through their history, history seems to tell us that it is inevitable that Jesus will have more influence on some groups, Mohammed or Hare Krishna on others, and that one of the 'great' religions will not replace any or all of the others. It is an empirical question in what measure these other witnesses are also distinctive in their living according to the contrast experience. But it seems that to be a disciple or follower of one person rather than another will make for *some* difference not only to one's worldview but to one's style and forms of practice. And this makes sense because different salvation bringers and their followers live their lives in the context of different cultures and traditions. Indeed, different salvation bringers contribute to forming different traditions with their disciples. And what is one's culture and tradition is ethically relevant, as Schillebeeckx's anthropological constants indicate. Thus, to some extent, there will be a "family resemblance" in the forms of life of a salvation bringer and that person's disciples.[70]

Finally, none of what I have said precludes the possibility that other salvation figures and other members of the Christian tradition may stress aspects of our humanity and God's will for us which Jesus does not. The entire direction of our argument suggests, however, that what is of fundamental ethical significance in Christianity will not be very different from what is of fundamental ethical significance in the other religions because the phenomenon we have articulated in terms of the negative contrast is fundamental to all. But if this is so, and even if it is not so, dialogue among the religions and with the secular society will be most fruitful when it starts with discussion of massive global sufferings. Our claim is that whether or not there is fundamental ethical agreement among the religions, Jesus captures what is fundamental to human ethicity.[71]

A LIBERATIONIST CONCEPTION OF HEAVEN

Because a liberationist ethic cries out for heaven and because the view one has of heaven bends back and affects one's entire perception of history and ethics, it is fitting that we should consider a liberationist view of heaven. First, I shall allow the liberationists we have featured, Soelle, Segundo, and Schillebeeckx, to speak for themselves about their eschatologies and I will discuss their somewhat surprising disagreements. Then I will make use of the ethic we have been developing in order to build a truly liberationist description of the eschaton. This will allow me to collect the central features of a liberationist ethic into a holistic description.

What Theologians Say

Soelle

Soelle is deeply concerned about those who have suffered utterly deprived and pain-ridden lives and who have not had the experience or energy to make their suffering productive. It is these, who have not died for a cause but whose death has been as meaningless as their lives, who make us cry out for a powerful and loving God, but who also force us to question the existence of such a God. Soelle argues that if we are not to see God as a sadist and executioner, then we cannot understand God as an independent and all-powerful creator and ruler of the world who stands above us and demands our obedience.[72] Rather than executioner God is in the victim, giving consolation and strength—and God is the victim.[73] Rather than independent and all-powerful creator, God's loneliness and need for others are at the beginning of creation;[74] God is in the process of becoming as is everything we love.[75] Rather than God's being over and above us, the more we are creative and liberative, the more God is God.[76] God has no other hands but ours. Indeed, God is what occurs between people when they love, and is our capacity to love.[77]

Thus, for Soelle, we are co-creators with God in the strongest sense. God can do nothing without us just as we can do nothing worthwhile without God. Her God seems to be purely immanent, not having power for a suprahistorical eschaton. To ensure God's goodness, God's power is restricted. But also, more positively, this gives us a role and responsibility in creation and a maturity made possible by a sort of mutuality we can enjoy with God.

In response to the plight of those who live and die wretchedly, she stresses that they must be remembered and their senseless suffering must be a stimulus to us to overcome senseless suffering. These people can thus live on in us and their lives can be given meaning by us. Salvation is found in wholeness, which is not only the integratedness of the individual life but the wholeness which comes by our binding together, forming a connectedness with one another and with the cosmos. "Solidarity is the Christian answer to the human wish not to be destroyed."[78] It provides the sense in which no one dies in vain and the meaning of the Christian belief in resurrection.[79] Finally and importantly, Soelle recognizes that none of this offers anything personally to those who live and die wretchedly. She admits that we use them for the sake of the living and that, perhaps, we owe them a debt we cannot repay—but this is the best we and, it seems, God can do.[80]

Segundo

In *The Historical Jesus of the Synoptics*, Segundo argues that, for Jesus, the kingdom is for the poor; they are its objects. And because they are not yet truly human, not yet subjects, they do not have to do anything to attain it.[81] Yet in his discussions of eschatology, which unfold largely in his interpretation of Paul and his treatment of evolution, Segundo's entire stress is on our being co-creators with God. The 'Christ-figures' seem to come to the fore and the worst off seem to be forgotten.[82]

For Segundo's Paul, free, creative, altruistic action is essential to our being mature, integrated humans. However, we rarely succeed in the integrative project, partly because Sin, a mechanism of self-deception, enslaves us to our desires and redirects our conscious intentions so that we give up the creative integrating effort and give in to the law of the members, the course of least resistance. External laws of nature contribute as well to undermining our projects.[83] By imitating the evolutionary process, however, by combining chance and purposiveness so as to maximize flexibility, we can succeed somewhat in the task of creative integration. But this means we must make use of the law of the members as well as our creative energies by not only acting purposively but also by allowing the mechanisms that are already in place to play a part. The effort evolution itself makes, to bring about integration, has the consequence of survival and permanence, and so a touch of immortality. Among humans this effort constitutes love and, contrary to some ecological views, must be particularly directed toward including the excluded, the 'weak' and the poor.[84]

Many of our projects fail due to lack of effort, poor judgment, or because others refuse to cooperate. And even when they succeed, it is only temporarily. Liberating projects and structures become oppressive over time. Worse than this, because the evolutionary project requires nonreusable energy, which is only in finite supply, it is ultimately doomed to failure. However, as has been mentioned before, Segundo thinks that it does not make sense that all the effort involved in evolution, the effort that led even to the appearance of human minds that have consciously and freely joined the evolutionary struggle, should come to nought.[85] Indeed, we can experience in an unverifiable way a qualitative disproportion between those works which we can recognize as our own, performed in freedom and love, even when they are ineffective, and those projects which are under Sin's control. Our experience of good and evil does not allow us to measure them equally. Works done in freedom and love carry infinitely more weight with us than those under Sin's control. The experience of this disproportion, fundamentally a negative contrast experience and a disclosure experience, allows us to see eschatological success in historical failure. Indeed, this is given expression in our faith in the resurrection of Jesus.[86]

Our creative efforts to alleviate suffering and to bring about liberation in history make us co-creators with God *in history*. But that these efforts are transformed by God so as to last forever, to form the eschatological kingdom where love succeeds so that goodness prevails, make us co-creators with God of God's and our *heaven*. *What we do, by God's transforming power, causes the eschaton to have the character it does.* Segundo stresses with Segundo's Paul that *what gets saved and lasts forever is "not only or mainly . . . individuals, but . . . the future of their projects."*[87] We seek immortal life not only for our soul and body but for our "tent," our "whole existence with its values and projects."[88] Indeed, it is not the person *with* her or his work but the person's *work* which will be tested by fire. And only that work will last which was, in history, aimed at building up the brothers and sisters; the rest will be burnt off.[89]

Like Soelle, Segundo stresses the importance of our efforts as co-creators with God but, unlike Soelle, Segundo's God has transcendent power. God makes us to be God's co-creators, takes a risk with us, gives us "something immensely worthwhile to do." *But if our loving acts usually succeeded in history and were cumulative so that we could talk of progress, then there would be nothing left for some of us to do.* Segundo speaks of Paul's Jesus as leaving his kingdom

> at the mercy of the powers that corrupt human projects. . . . Otherwise he would have no further need of collaborators, and human beings would be mere spectators of his victory. . . .

God takes a risk with us which God decides a priori to be worthwhile. Emphasizing the importance of our efforts even more, Segundo goes on to argue:

> In the building up of God's kingdom, *not even God will supply the results that were not procured in a creative, realistic way by God's co-workers seeking to be as effective as they could be.*

It is not simply that what we do will last forever but, just as important, what we fail to do will not be compensated for by God. Everyone has something to contribute to the liberating project; no one is completely useless.[90]

Segundo's eschatology combines three factors: First, people's efforts and projects which are for the good of the humanum are stressed as what will last; second, this seems to be arranged by God so that our efforts will not be cumulative in history; third, God will not compensate for what we do not attempt. *This combination supports his view that what we do in history really counts eschatologically but brings into question the extent to which what we do in history really counts historically and how much the eschaton can offer the worst off.* It forces us to ask whether Segundo's eschatology is not more fitting to saints and heroes, that is, to Christ-figures, than to the victims of history? Also, because it seems God not only allows but assures that there will continue to be suffering, it leaves Segundo open in an acute way to the challenge of those who argue that all of heaven is not worth the torture of a single child.[91]

Schillebeeckx

Like the other liberationists, Schillebeeckx stresses the importance of our seeking salvation in history, particularly by way of alleviating the sufferings of the worst off. And like Segundo, he thinks our success is very limited; he stresses the illusoriness of this-worldly utopias. But Schillebeeckx's God is opposed to all suffering and does not arrange things so that we will fail. The fragments of joy, the moments of salvation we experience in the context of the negative contrast make our very failure in history cry out for its overcoming in heaven—especially for those whom history fails most deeply. We may repeat Schillebeeckx's haunting question to the middle-class secular society concerning those who live and die wretchedly: "Are they the chaff in our history that we throw away"?[92]

Like Segundo, Schillebeeckx sees us as co-creators with God, not only in history but for the eschaton. He argues that what we do in history, in particular, what we achieve in love and as salvation for our fellow humans, will shape the eschaton which he describes as something to be achieved and not cashed in on.[93] But while Segundo stresses that it is Jesus' kingdom which will last, Schillebeeckx points out that, in spite of the fact that Jesus always preached God's kingdom and not himself, God vindicated not only the kingdom Jesus preached but the person Jesus was.[94]

Generally speaking, *while Segundo stresses our action in his discussion of eschatology, Schillebeeckx stresses the consequences, the salvation that will be brought about for persons.* Just as Schillebeeckx thinks our salvific experiences in history must be understood primarily negatively, he thinks our understanding of the eschaton must be negative, involving "neither mourning nor crying nor pain any more."[95] This stress on the negative is important because it speaks directly to the needs of the worst off. But it also embraces the suffering we cannot overcome and which we all experience, the suffering from guilt, rejection, failure, and mortality. Put positively, final salvation for Schillebeeckx has to do with human wholeness, including the physical, social, and thinking elements of the person, a wholeness which cannot be achieved by pursuing this-worldly utopias.[96] Final salvation has to do with "the consummation of the undamaged 'ecological milieu' which human beings need to live in."[97] Due to our social connectedness, final salvation must be for all.[98]

While Schillebeeckx's God does not arrange things so that there will always be suffering to be overcome, his God has transcendent power and creates us free so that we may create meaning and salvation—and also unmeaning, suffering.[99] Schillebeeckx does not escape the challenge of those who think our freedom is not worth all the suffering we create. However, contrary to Segundo, who claims that God will not make up for what we do not do, *Schillebeeckx warns that we cannot set limits on the eschaton because, to do so, would be to set limits on God's freedom and forgiveness.*[100] Thus, because Schillebeeckx thinks the eschaton must be understood primarily negatively, because he emphasizes the resurrection of persons, and because he thinks God can contribute to the eschaton where we failed in history, *his eschatology is not in danger of leaving out the worst off* who are most in need of a suprahistorical salvation, as Segundo's eschatology is in danger of doing. However, *we may be concerned that, unlike Segundo, Schillebeeckx puts into question the eschatological, as distinct from the historical value of our practices and projects precisely because God may make up for what we do not do.*[101]

Schillebeeckx points out that talk of an afterlife is virtually always found in a religious and not a secular philosophical context. And this is because final salvation must be seen, ultimately, as a gift of God.[102]

An Attempt to Resolve the Problems and Disagreements in Liberationists' Eschatologies

We have seen throughout that liberation has both objective and subjective dimensions. It involves both the alleviation of material suffering, oppression, and deprivation, and also the emergence of the freedom to resist these things and so to grow in human dignity and autonomy. The negative contrast experience combines these by showing that, first, we need a partial experience of salvation amidst all our suffering in order that we will be able to act against suffering and, second, the very action against suffering produces a partial experience of salvation. However, in our discussion of Segundo's and Schillebeeckx's eschatologies, a gap seems to have been created between these two. Segundo stresses that in the eschaton our practices and intended projects that are done in love will survive, and Schillebeeckx stresses that in the eschaton every negation will be negated.[103] Segundo seems to ensure the eschatological value of our attempts to produce good at the expense of ensuring that the worst off will flourish. Schillebeeckx seems to ensure the latter at the expense of the former. Furthermore, both can be challenged by the view that a good and powerful God would not allow the suffering that people endure in history.

Segundo's stress on the eschatological significance of projects over persons lends itself to the view that we last to the extent that our works do; we last through our 'tent.' We can suggest, for example, that our social relations last to the extent and intensity that, in history, they were participated in with love. Totally negative relationships simply will not exist eschatologically. So we can ask ourselves: Do we genuinely want the colleague or neighbor with whom we do not get along not to exist for us eschatologically? If we do not want this other literally not to exist for us, then we must build a positive relationship. This suggestion is enormously meaningful within the framework of the social life of people who have every opportunity to give to others. Perhaps within that framework, it should be taken seriously. But we do not want to restrict our eschatological relatedness with one another to our positive attempts in history. And even more importantly, we have to offer something more to those who lived and died wretchedly than what they contributed in history. Whether Segundo intends it or not, *we must insist that, independent of who contributed what, all are included equally in the eschatological fruits of our co-creating with God.* And those fruits first involve including the worst off. For Segundo himself it is what we do for our sisters and brothers, especially those who are most in need, which will last. But those who our *intended* acts and projects do not reach must be taken up with the rest of us.

But is this enough? Should we agree with Segundo that God's contribution to the eschaton is to make the good we attempt in history to be effective everlastingly but not to 'add' to it? In one way, we have just admitted that God 'adds' by including those we do not reach even in our attempts. But should we restrict at all God's power to express God's love and compassion and forgiveness, for the sake of ensuring the eschatological value of our projects?

The primary value of our actions and projects in history must be found to lie within history. We should attempt to alleviate suffering and overcome oppression because people need liberation from these things in order that they can flourish and join in the liberative project. Because this world really matters, because what we do and what happens to us in this world really matter, we must not look for the primary value of our actions beyond this world in an eschatological dimension. *Fundamentally, history is our concern and the eschaton is God's concern.* "God has no other hands but ours" in history; but if there is a beyond-history, then God must have "other hands," a power which transcends that which lies behind our efforts in history. So, is it necessary to restrict God in God's eschatological domain in order to ensure the secondary, eschatological value of our actions in history?

I do not want to diminish the significance of Segundo's and Schillebeeckx's view that what we do in history will shape the eschaton. Because we are fundamentally creative, innovative, and free, it is essential that, if there is heaven for us, we participate in its creation. Otherwise, our freedom will be ultimately frustrated and our human dignity and value will be ultimately denied. Also, if the eschaton is to have any meaning for us, it must be continuous with history in roughly the way Segundo and Schillebeeckx suggest. Our only grounds for hope of final salvation, and the only meaning and value we can give to it, come from the moments of salvation we experience in history. I do not want to deny that we should be encouraged to go on in history by the belief that our efforts which fail in history should be raised in heaven. Those who do have hope for heaven cannot help but to allow this hope to affect their lives in history. And it is right and important that they should. But we must respect the gap between history and heaven. We must understand heaven as, fundamentally, gift, as in the distance and not what we are straining for in history. Perhaps God will not compensate eschatologically for what we fail to do in history. Perhaps God's mercy and forgiveness will do no more eschatologically than to let us know we are loved and forgiven, and perhaps that will be enough. Traditionally, some have argued that the individual's communion with God in heaven is proportionate to the efforts at goodness that person made in history so that different individuals would have a different degree of fulfillment in God. Those with 'less' would not be lacking because they would be filled to their capacity. An analogous suggestion could be made with respect to the liberationist's social salvation, such that we all share equally and fully but in proportion to the efforts we made as a community in history. This is meaningful and perhaps true. But, as well as acknowledging the possibility of God's power to transform what we do, we should not preclude the possibility of God's contributing to the shape of the eschaton in ways which will surprise us. God can do this without forfeiting, as a part of a larger experience, the eschatological value of our efforts made in history. If, in the eschaton, we are not to be concerned about who has contributed what among humans, does it make sense to be concerned about who contributes what between God and humans?

Segundo's view, that the good we do in history is not cumulative[104] because God arranged things thus in order that we will always have something of eschatological significance to do, implies that God wills that there will always be victims in order that there will always be Christ-figures who will take on suffering to alleviate suffering—but with little success. *But insofar as God arranges things so that, in order that our efforts may accumulate for the eschaton, our good works will not accumulate in history, then our actions acquire eschatological significance but lose historical significance. Insofar as Segundo's view moves in this direction, it is not taking history seriously. And it raises the problem of evil in a most acute way.* As we have seen, Soelle rejects a suprahistorical eschaton because she thinks a good God could not allow the terrible suffering of the innocent victims of wars and famines and so could not have the power to stop it. The implication seems to be, if God cannot stop suffering, God cannot eschatologically transform our efforts. Schillebeeckx denies that God wills suffering and argues rather that God "transcends these negative aspects in our history, *not so much by allowing them as by overcoming them*, making them as though they had not happened."[105] However, he accepts from Thomas Aquinas that God makes us free, and we choose to liberate or oppress.[106] For Schillebeeckx as well as for Segundo, God can be seen as taking a risk in making us free. Both can be challenged by the person who thinks all of heaven is not worth the torture of a single child.[107]

I cannot embark on anything but the briefest discussion of the problem of evil here, suggesting not a solution to that problem but a strategy for facing it. A liberationist perspective provides a partial response by its paradoxical argument that, instead of massive human suffering's demonstrating that there is no God, it demonstrates where God is especially 'located.' God is especially in the poor and in those suffering in solidarity with them, in their protest and resistance. God's revelation in Jesus, the poor, and in all our experiences of negative contrast is not to explain evil but to show us that we must resist evil.[108] But this does not explain why, if God can transform our efforts so they will last forever, God cannot or will not stop the terrible suffering now. The traditional reply, which seems to be that of Schillebeeckx, is to say that God does not will or want us to suffer but, while respecting our freedom, encourages us to resist suffering. The response to those who argue that all of heaven—or human freedom—is not worth the torture of a single child, would be to say, simply, that it is. A heaven God creates by transforming our altruistic efforts is worth all the suffering in history. A difficulty with this view, however, is that often, concretely speaking, it is one group of people who are co-creators and another group who are oppressed victims. Certainly, some of the latter group will not evaluate things in the same way as Schillebeeckx—but some of them will.[109]

While there is a certain coherence and even completeness in the responses of Soelle, Segundo, and Schillebeeckx, all their views are ultimately unsatisfactory. For Soelle, there is no final salvation and no hope for the worst off; for Segundo and Schillebeeckx, God could stop the suffering in the world but, because God has given us free reign in history, God does not. I cannot put the data together in a better way than these others. But rather than to systematize vis-à-vis the problem of suffering and evil, I suggest that we affirm all and only the things which, on the basis of experience and all the evidence, we believe to be true, even though we recognize that what we say is not complete and may even contain apparent or real inconsistencies. While, ultimately, real inconsistencies are not acceptable, before we can distinguish real from apparent inconsistencies, we must take the risk of including the latter. What follows is appropriate to a liberationist view: God is utterly good and the power of all goodness. God is opposed, not only to unjust suffering and all moral evil, but to all suffering. Human history is weighed down by debilitating suffering which God does not want or allow. God encourages us to resist suffering in history and God can transform our efforts and eradicate suffering in the eschaton. We are partly free and co-creators with God not only in history but for a suprahistorical eschaton. It may not be possible to know how all these things can be held together. To suggest that God is in process makes it unclear how God can transform our efforts. To suggest that God did not create from nothing but encourages evolution toward greater and greater complexity and richness, and therefore with greater and greater capacity for good and evil, joy and suffering, involves God in risk-taking not unlike that contained in the traditional story: God creates, out of nothing, humans with free will. It seems preferable to think that God does not decide that freedom is worth the risk of evil, that God cannot stop the suffering in history, but that God, as power of goodness, does encourage the flourishment of all in history and can and will transform our efforts and bring about flourishment eschatologically. But this is to say too much. In conformity with the suggested strategy, we should let experience guide us. Let us take seriously the liberationist experiential and methodological starting point in terms of the "already damaged humanum" and cosmos, the experience of salvation mixed with much more suffering, and the experience of God, the power of goodness, as empowering us into liberation and co-creation both in history and beyond it. Then we may remain agnostic concerning how God relates to the coming about of suffering while affirming that God is opposed to suffering, encourages us to resist it, and promises a final transformation into flourishment.[110]

A Liberationist Description of Heaven

A liberationist ethic does not logically or practically require that there be a suprahistorical eschaton. We ought to embrace a liberationist ethic whether we have hope for something beyond history or not. Humans, other species, and the whole cosmos strain for liberation, salvation, and flourishment. While we cannot deduce heaven from our anthropology, humans cry out for heaven because they cannot help but wish for, although some do not hope for, ongoing salvation without suffering. A liberationist ethic cries out for heaven because, restricted to history, the liberationist ethic fails to realize its value at its heart; it fails those who are its first concern, those who live and die wretchedly—the worst off. Also, secondarily, a liberationist ethic cries out for heaven so that the deprivation that all of us suffer in history will be overcome and so that the altruistic efforts made in history will be, not rewarded, but vindicated eschatologically. But how can a liberationist characterize heaven?

From the discussion of the negative contrast experience, we can argue that *the eschaton can be understood by us in history primarily in negative terms*, as the ultimate negation of every negativity. It promises joy and justice and peace and fulfillment which we best understand as its wiping away whatever is our experience of sorrow and oppression and dissension and deprivation. The same reasons Schillebeeckx gives for seeking salvation in history, primarily through negating concrete negations, also hold for understanding the eschaton, primarily negatively. We can understand the eschaton as the negation of every negation whereas we can barely begin to imagine what it will involve positively. Also, just as seeking historical salvation by negating negation makes our action concrete, relevant, and effective and ensures against falling prey to the illusion that we can produce a this-worldly utopia, all the more is it the case that our understanding of a suprahistorical eschaton should be primarily negative so that it will play a constructive and critical and not deceptive role in our lives. All of this implies that just as a liberationist ethic, founded on the negative contrast experience, aims at effecting results for people in terms of the alleviation of suffering, so too the eschaton provides people with lasting concrete salvation. Finally and importantly, if the eschaton involves the negation of *every* negation, of every suffering and oppression *and deprivation*, then it will involve a *total, complete, full, no longer partial, salvation*.

We argued in chapter 2 that, in history, partisanship in favor of the poor is justified by the intensity and urgency of their need and by the fact that, inevitably, if we try to be impartial, we will favor the status quo, and the poor will be left out. Connected with this, as we saw in the present chapter, it is especially for the sake of the worst off that a liberationist ethic cries out for heaven. For those whom a liberationist ethic fails, those who live and die wretchedly, there is nothing without heaven. The heavenly kingdom must be shaped to include especially the outcasts, the marginalized, the powerless and deprived in history. We could speak of the worst off as gaining more eschatologically than those who were better off in history, but only in the sense that the negation of their negation will be greater. Just as the liberationist aim is not to reverse the situations of people in history, making the powerless powerful and vice versa, neither does it promote an eschatological reversal. Rather, the eschaton will erase these differences we have created in history, will erase every hierarchy in erasing every oppression, will erase every ill-gotten pleasure in erasing every suffering. The eschaton does not involve something like a redistribution of wealth and power, some gaining and some losing for the sake of equalization. Rather, it erases the quantitative measurements such a vision implies. It does not need such measurements because there is plenty. But, also, they are irrelevant because what will be valued and what will constitute salvation will be a mutuality which must be based on equality.

In chapter 3 we argued that, due to our social connectedness, we are conditioned by the history created by others which can be oppressive or liberating, and, as subjects of history, we can transform our history and social conditions, both for ourselves and others. But because we are thus fundamentally historical, what happens to us in history and what we do in history matter utterly, and must matter as much to those with hope for heaven as to those without. Thus, given that we are fundamentally historical and that life in history is so valuable, it only makes sense that there should be a continuity between history and the eschaton, that what we do in history should contribute to shaping the character of the eschaton.

Our solidarity with every other human and our connectedness with the entire cosmos imply that the eschaton should involve *universal* salvation, inclusive of all humans, and also in some sense, other species and the cosmos. Schillebeeckx emphasizes both the continuous character of his eschatology and the universal character of final salvation when he speaks of "the consummation of the undamaged 'ecological milieu' which human beings need to live in. . . ."[111] Segundo does not explicitly suggest that everything, including the cosmos, will last forever. But the character of his evolutionary theory, wherein 'mind' performs the task of integration at every level, each of which is 'analogous' to every other, lends itself to the uplifting of history and nature into a suprahistorical eschatological dimension.

But does this take sin seriously enough? Segundo argues that those who reject the kingdom's values exclude themselves from the kingdom. And, because for him everything which is not done in love will be 'burnt off' as it were, then wrong, oppressive connections will simply cease to be. Those whose every relationship was to dominate would simply have no place in the eschaton and would not be missed. We must respond that it is not up to us to decide how personal sinfulness will be dealt with eschatologically. But it is relevant to recall that, although restrictedly free, we are also socially conditioned; all of us are immersed in social sin. And virtually everyone, in different contexts, both oppresses and is oppressed.

If all humans equally enjoy final salvation, then the eschaton cannot involve rewarding good and punishing evil. *It is not governed by anything we normally mean by justice but by generous and gratuitous love*; it is gift which involves "mercy and compassion at the very heart of reality."[112] There need be no measuring out because there is plenty; there can be no measuring out because our connectedness demands that your salvation cannot be other than my salvation. In this sense individual identity breaks down. However, finally, it is because, in history, we are social *individuals* that a liberationist ethic cries out for heaven for the worst off. It is only fitting that we should maintain that, in the eschaton, we flourish as social individuals.

The stress on human innovativeness in chapter 4 reflects the liberationist view that our starting point in history is with the already damaged humanum and cosmos, that there is not a blueprint which reflects a past golden age or a future utopia. In history, we must be co-creators with God, innovatively finding new structures, policies, and practices which will serve the worst off. For Soelle it seems this can be cumulative, and we can make real headway in building God's kingdom in history. But, for her, there is no beyond-history into which this can be taken up. For Segundo and Schillebeeckx, however, while the evil we do will die, *the good that we attempt, those practices and projects we do in love for the sake of the liberation of the other, will be raised up, transformed, made everlastingly effective; they will shape the eschaton.* In God, we have the freedom and the responsibility to contribute not only to making a history that is worthy of us but a heaven that is worthy of God. However, as we argued above, it is people, social individuals, who, together with God and the cosmos which God will raise, will enjoy the fruits of all our labors. *And God may contribute not only to transforming our efforts but to shaping the eschaton in surprising ways.*

In chapter 5 we argued that religion and theology are only meaningful and authentic if they are closely related to, and in certain ways rooted in, ethics. This suggests that the liberationist view of the eschaton will be primarily ethical or will be the fulfillment of our fundamental ethical value. And, of course, the present discussion has drawn an ethical picture of the eschaton by considering how the different elements of a liberationist ethic provide us with insights into it. But while our ethical practices and projects contribute to shaping the eschaton, and while ethical value governs its character, there is clearly a mammoth gap between what we can do and accomplish and what the eschaton is or will be.[113] Only by God's heavenly power will ethical value truly prevail and reach all the way to the worst off. As Schillebeeckx rightly says, talk of an afterlife is virtually always found in a religious and not in a 'merely' ethical and anthropological context. It responds to humanity's deepest desire for salvation without suffering. But it is neither something we can achieve by our right practice, nor is it something we can deduce from our anthropology and ethics, as something we are owed; it is gift.

NOTES

1. There is a linguistic difficulty here because, while "ethics" refers both to our ethical life and the discipline of ethics, "religion" refers to our religious life and "theology" refers to the discipline pertaining to religion. My concern throughout has been to develop a liberationist ethic, to develop ethical theory. But when I have talked about ethics, I have virtually always been talk-

ing about our ethical life and particularly our ethical practice and value. My central concern in this chapter is to consider how our ethicity, our being ethical beings who live ethically, relates to both our religious life and our theology. But, to avoid awkwardness, I will normally use "religion" to refer to both our religious life and its expression in theology.

2.   When I speak of ethics as foundational as regards theology and religion I am referring to the various ways in which ethics is prior to theology and religion. See pp. 183–87 of this chapter.

3.   This will be discussed on pp. 188–92 and 200–201 of this chapter.

4.   This issue was raised by Paul Lakeland in the summer of 1990 in response to an earlier draft of this chapter.

5.   For a discussion of how our experience of God can be one of personal yet mediated encounter, see Roger Haight's *Dynamics of Theology* (New York: Paulist Press, 1990), pp. 73–78.

6.   *Christ*, pp. 740–41.

7.   See David Tracy, *Blessed Rage for Order: The New Pluralism in Theology* (New York: The Seabury Press, 1975), 92–94, 100–04.

8.   *Faith and Ideologies*, pp. 25, 36–40, 50–54.

9.   Charles Taylor, "What is Human Agency?", in Mischel ed., *The Self*, pp. 103–35. My discussion of evaluating values relies heavily on this article, although I do not treat the relationship between our evaluating values and our being interpreters in the same way as does Taylor.

10.   Discussion of other species and the environment have made us see the inadequacy of Schillebeeckx's "already damaged humanum" as the criterion for ethics. The most fundamental criterion of the liberationist perspective that I have been developing is that we should be guided by negativity in order to resist negativity. But Gustafson, land ethicists, and some feminist theologians want to be guided, primarily, by a vision of harmony or a sense of the whole in connection. MacIntyre contrasts Plato and Aristotle by arguing that if we begin in ethics with an account of goodness which is compatible with the good person suffering torture and injustice, as Plato does, then the whole perspective of our ethics will be different from an ethic in which we begin by asking in what way of life doing well and faring well may be found together, as Aristotle does. This involves the difference between how to endure a society in which the just are crucified and how to create a society in which this no longer happens. For MacIntyre, the first perspective will lead to an ethic which is irrelevant to the task set by the second perspective. A liberationist ethic must question itself in face of the views of all these thinkers. See MacIntyre's *A Short History of Ethics*, p. 60.

11.   *Ethics from a Theocentric Perspective*, Volume 1, chapter five, "God in Relation to Man and the World": 195–279.

12.   Ibid., pp. 196–225.

13.   Ibid., pp. 235–51.

14.   Ibid., p. 242.

15.   Ibid., p. 257.

16.   Ibid., pp. 251, 258, 270.

17.   Ibid., p. 202.

18. *Can Ethics Be Christian?*, pp. 124–44; *Ethics from a Theocentric Perspective*, Volume 1: 3–7, 22–25, 53–55, 202, 251.

While Gustafson objects to these positions, in *Ethics from a Theocentric Perspective*, Volume 1: 73–74, he expresses some uncertainty as to whether they can all be fairly ascribed to liberation theology. But they are important objections to which a liberationist approach must respond.

19. *Can Ethics Be Christian?*, pp. 124–27; *Ethics from a Theocentric Perspective*, Volume 1: 53–55.

20. *Can Ethics Be Christian?*, pp. 131–44; *Ethics from a Theocentric Perspective*, Volume 1: 3–7, 22, 251, 202.

21. It could be argued that Gustafson's entire theology is directed toward solving the problem of suffering by its interpreting God as Nature which relates to us by pointing out where there is suffering or any analogue of suffering in the cosmos. Gustafson himself explicitly rejects this interpretation, however, saying that *the conclusions he draws with respect to suffering follow from his theology and not vice versa.* See James M. Gustafson, "A Response to Critics," *Journal of Religious Ethics* 13:2 (Summer, 1985): 203.

22. *The Liberation of Theology*, p. 13.

23. See Elisabeth Schüssler-Fiorenza, "Toward a Feminist Biblical Hermeneutics: Biblical Interpretation and Liberation Theology," Mahan and Richeson, eds., *The Challenge of Liberation Theology*, p. 93.

24. Dorothee Soelle, "Thou Shalt Have No Other Jeans Before Me," Mahan and Richeson, eds., *The Challenge of Liberation Theology*, p. 14.

25. My aim in this discussion is to locate liberationist hermeneutics vis-à-vis ethics and not to explore the very complex topic of hermeneutics. This discussion is connected with that in chapter 4 of creating ideologies and Christologies which involves finding *new interpretations* and forms of practice. See pp. 140–43. But here we are locating the permanent hermeneutical *value* which ought to be the fundamental criterion in our attempts to create ideologies.

26. *The Understanding of Faith*, pp. 59, 66–68.

27. See pp. 6–7 of chapter 1.

28. *The Understanding of Faith*, pp. 91–95.

29. Ibid., p. 92. See also, pp. 97, 100, and *God the Future of Man*, p. 37, footnote 41, p. 38, and p. 184, for statements by Schillebeeckx that theological hermeneutics is first a "hermeneutics of praxis" or "of doing." We may recall Schillebeeckx's story of the paralyzed man who must leap and dance when telling the story of his mentor to show how his mentor had done it. See page 140.

30. For Peukert's description of his project, see, especially, "Introduction: On Political Theology," pp. 1–15 of *Science, Action and Fundamental Theology*.

The general theme of the value base of all knowledge runs through several essays in Max Horkheimer's *Critical Theory: Selected Essays*, trans. Matthew J. O'Connell and others (New York: The Continuum Publishing Com-

pany, 1982). See also Michael Polanyi, *Personal Knowledge: Towards a Post-Critical Philosophy* (Chicago: The University of Chicago Press, 1962) and Maurice Merleau-Ponty, *The Structure of Behaviour*, trans., Alden L. Fisher (Boston: Beacon Press, 1963).

31. Strong partisanship involves, for example, taking sides with the oppressed against the powers of oppression and, if necessary, against those who support oppression. This is the partisanship we talked about in chapter 2. Gustafson is opposed to this kind of partisanship, but I offer no new arguments, as such, for it in this chapter. Weak partisanship involves opting for, and placing faith in, a value which must be chosen and for which we are responsible but which cannot be 'proved' correct. In this section, I argue that in theology and religion we must opt for a value, take an advocacy stance and, at least in this weak sense, be partisan. Gustafson is also opposed to this. He thinks that if we are partisan in the weak sense, if our choice of value is not guided by one kind of objective and universal experience, interpreted by many in religious terms, then we will inevitably be anthropocentric in the sense that we will side with humans and even with one group of humans at the expense of another. We will be partisan in the strong sense. Ironically, this can only be true if we accept what Gustafson rejects and liberationists argue for, that we cannot but take sides with one group or another, that in choosing 'all humans' say, we are choosing the status quo. Otherwise, we could opt, without an objective standard, for 'all humans.' Finally, however, I see the argument of this section, the logical necessity of partisanship in the weak sense, as providing a general support for partisanship in the strong sense advocated in chapter 2. At the deepest level, which underlies all our knowledge and even experience, we cannot but opt for a side on value, and so we cannot object to opting for a side in general.

32. This means that the atheist cannot simply give a reductionist *interpretation* of religion and theology in the direction of ethics but must say the theist is *mistaken* in believing in God and a suprahistorical eschaton.

33. *Jesus in Our Western Culture*, pp. 4–6. Quotations at pp. 4 and 6 respectively.

34. *Christ*, pp. 59, 774–75.

35. *Faith and Ideologies*, pp. 25–26, 37–38.

36. *Christ*, p. 59. (Exclusive language replaced.)

37. *Faith and Ideologies*, p. 64.

38. Paradoxically, while practical knowledge is prior to propositional knowledge in the ways discussed in the last chapter, we can have a propositional grasp of what we have not experienced or practiced. Otherwise, as Schubert Ogden points out, we could not disbelieve, so neither could we believe, the Christian witness. See *On Theology* (San Francisco: Harper and Row Publishers, 1986), pp. 17–19. And, through empathy and imagination, we can have *some* experiential and practical understanding of things we have never directly experienced or practiced, even which, as in the case of a religion, we may think

to be illusory. But all of this presupposes *somebody's* having direct experiential and practical knowledge of these things.

39. See, for example, *The Liberation of Theology*, p. 43.

At an even more basic level, the argument of pp. 177–81, especially pp. 179–81 of this chapter, showed that ethics must be logically prior to theology and religion.

40. My objection here is not to the Christian belief that God ontologically grounds ethics but to the view that religion and theology, human forms of life, provide us, from outside our context of decision-making, with first ethical knowledge. While many people are raised in a religious context and 'learn ethics' through that context, the argument of the last section showed that we must come to choose, at least in the sense of taking responsibility for, which religion and god we will have faith in, on the basis of value. And making this choice is an ethical action. Only then is our ethic and our religion authentic, truly our own.

41. According to the argument of the last section, putting theory before practice, accepting a set of religious formulae and seeking what we ought to do as coming out of these, are things we choose to do according to a value we choose, usually the value of the status quo.

42. I do not wish to deny that a genuine encounter with God partly depends on, and is caused by, God.

43. See, for example, Segundo, *The Humanist Christology of Paul*, pp. 75, 124; Soelle, *Suffering*, p. 149; Schillebeeckx, *Christ*, p. 792.

44. We briefly discussed how ordinary experience can disclose a religious dimension before, especially at pp. 21–27. While I stressed there the power of *ordinary* experience and particularly *ethical* experience to reveal God and final salvation, what I want to get across here is the compelling power of the *religious* experience, more so than ethical experience, and how ethical experience cries out for a religious dimension.

45. Schillebeeckx formally defines disclosure experience in *Jesus*, p. 742.

46. *Christ*, pp. 53–54.

47. *The Historical Jesus of the Synoptics*, "Appendix I: The Resurrected Jesus," pp. 166–77.

48. *Christ*, p. 837.

49. Ibid., p. 649.

50. Soelle seems to be an exception. See pp.203–204 of this chapter.

51. *Christ*, p. 800.

52. See *Jesus in Our Western Culture*, pp. 58–63. There Schillebeeckx argues that the atheist may forfeit his own life out of a hope in the triumph of the humanum in history. I push the example further.

53. *Faith and Ideologies*, pp. 34–40.

54. *The Historical Jesus of the Synoptics*, p. 11.

55. *The Understanding of Faith*, pp. 91–101.

56. *Christ*, pp. 59–61.

57. Ibid., p. 651.

58. *Jesus in Our Western Culture*, pp. 4–6. Quotations at pp. 4 and 6 respectively. Schillebeeckx thinks that God as luxury is a necessary counterbalance to the technological world's instrumental mentality.

59. We can think of atheist liberationists as tending toward the former category, atheist existentialists as tending toward the latter.

60. *Jesus in Our Western Culture*, p. 5. See, for example, *God the Future of Man*, p. 186, for Schillebeeckx's former view. And see *Christ*, pp. 661–69 for Schillebeeckx's criticism of this-worldly utopias and pp. 770–89 for his discussion of how the eschatological proviso relates to politics.

61. I think Schillebeeckx's recognition of this, that an 'as it were' eschatological proviso does not depend on religious belief, is an important reason why in his recent writing he talks of God as a useless hypothesis and a luxury.

62. H. Richard Niebuhr argues that while revelation imparts no new beliefs concerning natural or historical facts, it involves "the radical reconstruction of all our beliefs" so that they are seen as connected, as forming a "rational pattern," as having an ultimate meaningfulness, as transformed. This may be compared with what the religious perspective imparts to our ethicity, not new information about right practice and value but a new gestalt-horizon. We must add to what Niebuhr says, however, that everyone has a worldview which extends beyond and bends back and influences their ethicity. In this sense everyone experiences a sort of 'faith in revelation.' And the worldview of the liberationist atheist sees humans as subjects and sees contingent connectedness and meaningfulness in history. See H. Richard Niebuhr, *The Meaning of Revelation* (New York: The Macmillan Co., 1960), pp. 93–94, 96, 172, 182.

63. We can see the remarkable similarities between the worldviews of liberationists who are theists and atheists. Both make meaning and connectedness vis-à-vis our lives and history. Indeed, neither can do any more than this. We can, to some extent, put ourselves in the position of each and experience the two perspectives from the inside. Where God is something like the power of goodness in us, but does not have transcendent power, and where there is no final salvation, perhaps we have a transitional position. I feel, however, that a gap opens up between this and the atheist position on the one hand and the 'fully blown' theist position on the other. It seems to me that ultimately we can experience only two separate perspectives, not a transition from one to the other. There is a difference in kind between a perspective for which there is only contingent and partial meaningfulness and one for which there is also ultimate and embracive meaningfulness. This is formally, although not, of course, in content, somewhat comparable to our experience of the difference between life and death. In both cases, attempts at comparison ultimately must give way to a sense of an unfathomable, inarticulable gap.

64. *Christ*, p. 764.

65. I have been arguing throughout that, as a group, the materially destitute are the worst off and our first option should be for them. But, the very worst off are those our ethic does not reach, those who *die* still wretched.

66. See chapter 4, pp. 143–46.

67. See Segundo, *The Historical Jesus of the Synoptics*, p. 31. Even John Hick, who, in the context of his discussions of dialogue among the religions, stresses that we are formed and restricted by our varying cultures, admits that there seems to be universal agreement that what is morally bad is harming people and what is morally good is preventing or benefiting people. He points out that what counts as benefit and harm and who counts as a person or object of concern will both vary. He is saying that not, for example, the Kantian categorical imperative, but the liberationist value of resistance to every threat to the humanum, and *through this*, seeking salvation is fundamental across cultures. See John Hick, "On Grading Religions," *Religious Studies* 17 (1981): 458.

68. Expanding on this, Haight argues that "the *inner dynamic of truth*, however truth is defined, leads in *the direction of universality*," that if we believe we have grasped something fundamentally true we cannot but see it as relevant to all, that "the idea of 'truth merely for me' is inherently self-contradictory." See Roger Haight, "Towards an Understanding of Christ in the Context of Other World Religions," *East Asian Pastoral Review* XXVI (Nos. 3 & 4, 1989): 260.

69. *Jesus in Our Western Culture*, p. 50.

70. This does not contradict but merely nuances my claim in the last paragraph that the ethical practice of the Christian should not be different from that of the atheist. My stress there was on the differences and similarities between the liberationist theist and atheist, who I have assumed to be Christian or coming out of a Christian context. But we have been arguing throughout that ethical practice is relative to context, and one's religious tradition connected with culture is part of one's context. While the significance of ethics will be different for liberationist atheist and theist, if they both come out of the same cultural context, their practice will not be very different.

Also, none of this is to suggest that we are ethically 'locked' into the demands of culture or tradition. These need to be regularly revised so that they will be liberating. This is what engaging in a hermeneutical circle is about. It is why ethics must be hermeneutical *and* why hermeneutics is ethical.

71. This is to say that Christians should enter dialogue already holding some views that they would think should be universally acknowledged, not that they should not be prepared to revise those views in face of counter-evidence and counter-argument.

72. *Suffering*, pp. 141–50, especially pp. 142, 147–49, 102; *The Strength of the Weak*, pp. 29–30.

73. *Suffering*, pp. 102, 147.

74. Dorothee Soelle with Shirley A. Cloves, *To Work and to Love: A Theology of Creation* (Philadelphia: Fortress Press, 1984), p. 14.

75. *Suffering*, p. 92.

76. *To Work and to Love*, p. 39.

77. Dorothee Soelle, *Death by Bread Alone: Texts and Reflections on Religious Experience*, trans. David L. Scheidt (Philadelphia: Fortress Press, 1978), p. 134; *Suffering*, pp. 92, 149; *The Strength of the Weak*, pp. 136, 138.

78. *Death by Bread Alone*, pp. 73, 135–39. Quotation at p. 135.

79. *The Strength of the Weak*, p. 73.

80. *Suffering*, p. 149.

81. *The Historical Jesus of the Synoptics*, pp. 139–40.

82. Segundo himself points out that Paul does not show Jesus' sensitivity to structurally caused injustice and oppression which, together with his heavy use of Paul in his discussion of eschatology, may help to explain why the poor suddenly seem to be left out. But this does not make Segundo's position less problematic. See *The Humanist Christology of Paul*, p. 139.

83. Ibid., pp. 69, 116.

84. This describes, in evolutionary language, Soelle's aim of our creatively bringing about a more and more embracive connectedness among humans and with the cosmos. It even supports her view that we will, in a sense, overcome death through our connectedness.

85. *An Evolutionary Approach to Jesus of Nazareth*, pp. 93–105.

86. Segundo does not think in terms of 'evidence' for a suprahistorical eschaton and sometimes, but not always, says that, on the basis of our faith in the resurrection, we must *assume* that good and evil cannot be measured equally and that goodness will 'rise.' I would argue that it is the experience of the disproportion between good and evil, which I have discussed in the context of altruism, that gives grounds for belief in the resurrection. See p. 98. See also *The Humanist Christology of Paul*, pp. 122–24 and 129 on Segundo's view.

87. Ibid., p. 74. (My italics.)

88. Ibid., p. 75. Segundo quotes from Paul: "We who are in this tent . . . do not want to have it taken off but to have the other put on over it, so that what is mortal may be absorbed by life." (2 Cor. 5:2, 4.)

89. Ibid., p. 130. Segundo thinks that when the emphasis is placed on the eschatological result of action rather than on personal survival, reward and punishment are ruled out as reasons for action. As I will argue, however, Segundo's view easily lends itself to the interpretation that those with 'more in their tent,' the Christ-figures, will have a fuller, richer eschatological survival.

90. Ibid., quotations, p. 124. (My italics running into Segundo's in second quotation.) See also pp. 137, 160, and *An Evolutionary Approach to Jesus of Nazareth*, pp. 114–16.

91. For a sympathetic, constructive, and also creative account of Segundo's eschatology, see Frances Stefano, *The Absolute Value of Human Action in the Theology of Juan Luis Segundo* (Lanham, MD: University Press of America, Inc., 1992).

92. *Christ*, p. 791. Quotation at p. 764.

93. Ibid., p. 792; *The Understanding of Faith*, p. 10; *God the Future of Man*, p. 156.

94. *Christ*, p. 796.

95. *The Understanding of Faith*, p. 11, from Rev. 21:4.

96. *Christ*, p. 764.

97. *Jesus in Our Western Culture*, p. 29.

98. *Christ*, p. 801.

99. Ibid., p. 728.

100. Ibid., p. 793. As we have seen, Schillebeeckx argues that central to the resurrection experience of the first disciples was the sense of having been forgiven by Jesus. This gives forgiveness an important place in Schillebeeckx's theology and eschatology and supports his referring to it now in the context of God's contribution to the eschaton.

101. Most likely Segundo stresses the eschatological value of our practices and projects partly in order to ensure their historical value, that what we

do in this world really matters. But to show that this world really matters by showing it matters for the eschaton is not satisfactory. Alleviating suffering now matters utterly because the fact that people are suffering and deprived *now* matters utterly and quite independently of whether there is or is not an eschaton.

102. *Christ*, pp. 798–99.

103. Ironically, some comparison can be made here between the Kantian value of good intentions and the utilitarian value of good consequences. Segundo, who stresses that we must attempt to be efficacious in history to the point where he argues that the end justifies the means, also argues that it will be our attempts, our good intentions if these are understood as issuing in attempted action with attempted good consequences, which will last forever. Schillebeeckx, who is outspokenly against utilitarianism in history, sees the eschaton as where there will be the negation of every negation, the effecting of the most far-reaching good consequences.

104. The good we do in history must be cumulative to some extent even if we restrict cumulativeness to a particular kind of liberation for a society, as for example, respect for human rights in Western society. If we could not build on what we have accomplished, we would truly be in a Sisyphus situation. Of course, Segundo does not have to deny *all* cumulative effect of the good we do in order to be assured that we will always have plenty to do. He may be concerned to deny an evolutionary view that progresses to a utopia, a view which conflicts with the evidence and with our understanding of how liberating social conditions inevitably become oppressive. However, for the reasons I give, there is something seriously inadequate in the way Segundo puts these issues together.

105. *Christ*, p. 729. (My italics running into Schillebeeckx's.)

106. Ibid., p. 728.

107. I have in mind the sort of person represented by Ivan in the *The Brothers Karamazov*. He challenges the religious faith of his brother Alyosha by reciting stories of atrocities against children, culminating in the story of a landowner who sets his dogs on a young peasant child, forcing his mother to look on as the dogs tear the child to pieces. Ivan rejects the 'harmonizing' that comes from the Christian response of forgiveness. He concludes, "We cannot afford to pay so much for admission. . . . It is not God that I do not accept, Alyosha. I merely most respectfully return God the ticket." See Fyodor Dostoyevski, *The Brothers Karamazov*, Volume I, trans. and introd. David Magarshack, 2 vols. (Middlesex, Penguin Books Ltd., 1958): Part Two, Book Five, "Rebellion": 276–88. Quotation at p. 287. (Exclusive language replaced.)

108. Schillebeeckx thinks that we should not attempt to explain suffering or evil because to do so is to justify and therefore neutralize them. They are incomprehensible and the only appropriate response is to resist them. However, while it would be completely misguided to spend our time pondering the problem of suffering and evil rather than acting against them, there are places, like right here, where it is appropriate and even necessary to raise these issues. Schillebeeckx himself does so when he brings in Thomas Aquinas to explain how God is not responsible for the evil we do. See *Christ*, pp. 704, 721, 728.

109. In his novel, *The Wars*, Timothy Findley describes the perspective of one victim. Robert Ross had experienced the worst of the depravity of World War I. He was lying on a stretcher still on the front line in agony from the burns covering most of his body, almost unable to speak, knowing he would never walk or see again, and knowing that a court-martial awaited him. As told by Marian Turner: "'I'm a nurse. I've never offered death to anyone . . . that night, I thought: *I am ashamed to be alive* . . . "I will help you, if you want me to." And I knew he understood—because he said: "Not yet," *Not yet*. Do you see? He might have said "No." He might've said "never." He might've said "yes." But he said, "Not yet." There, in those two words, in a nutshell—you have the essence of Robert Ross. And perhaps the essence of what it is to be alive.'" See Timothy Findley, *The Wars* (Markham, Ontario: Penguin Books Ltd., 1978), pp. 188–89. (Findley's italics.)

110. If we take seriously finding ourselves in an already damaged, already suffering world, then the only appropriate and meaningful thing to do is not to give back the ticket as Dostoyevski's Ivan does, to a God who is over and above us, for a play we have merely come to observe. Rather, we must direct ourselves to a God who is in the suffering and who calls us to participate in overcoming suffering as Alyosha does. This is the only response Alyosha can make to Ivan. And, finally, if we are genuinely to give up attempting to see the whole and offer a total answer to the problem of evil as both Schillebeeckx and Soelle recommend, then we can affirm God's promise of final salvation and remain agnostic about whether God can, except through God's encouragement, stop the suffering in history. Soelle discusses the above aspect of the encounter between Ivan and Alyosha in *Suffering*, pp. 174–78.

111. *Jesus in Our Western Culture*, p. 29.

112. Schillebeeckx, *Jesus*, p. 20.

113. Only because there is this gap between ethics and our anthropology on the one hand, and heavenly existence on the other, can we truly respect the positions of both theist and atheist.

Conclusion

This book has not proceeded by a linear argument to a set of conclusions but, when taken as a whole, forms a single picture or description of a liberationist ethic. I shall conclude by highlighting the outstanding features explored in the various chapters which, together, involve a sort of paradigm shift in ethics.[1] While all of these features are now familiar, and some of them accepted outside a liberationist perspective, *it has been important to locate them in an integrated ethic so that we may see that this new vision should not be at the periphery but at the center of ethics—and so that we may see how far we are from having located it there in our ethical lives.*

THE NEGATIVE STARTING POINT OF A LIBERATIONIST ETHIC

The ethic we have been developing takes as its starting point the experience of an already damaged humanum in an already damaged world, that is, the experience of dis-order, dis-harmony, indeed of too much and too severe suffering and oppression. We have argued: What ethics is primarily about is responding to this situation. This will not come about by seeking a pre-existent order in existence or by operating, ethically, out of a view of a universal positive human nature; it will not come about by seeking harmony or the whole-in-connection directly.

There are the most urgent ethical reasons for taking negativity as our starting point in ethics: Debilitating deprivation and degrading oppression, on a massive scale, cannot wait. There are also sound epistemological reasons for taking negativity as our starting point. The suffering we resist is concrete, particular, already there in existence; the harmony we aim at does not exist even as an idea, and every group's

226

and every individual's dreams will be different. So we can be certain of and come to common agreement about negativity in a way in which we cannot about our positive visions. This epistemological priority of negativity over positivity is built right into the nature of experience because it is only where reality resists or negates our interpretations and our practice that we can be sure we are in touch with a reality that extends beyond our frameworks and our wishes. Taking negativity as our guide captures the particularity and concreteness that ethics requires to be relevant to human and cosmic need. And also it captures the universal agreement of a common humanity confronting a common world that ethics requires to be meaningful. If we do not take negativity as our guide, the particular, concrete need of the worst off will remain to haunt the privileged and to belie every attempt at positivity made by those of us who can enjoy the luxury of dreaming up utopias.

THE NEGATIVE CONTRAST EXPERIENCE AS FOUNDATIONAL FOR ETHICS

Our experience is not only one of suffering with an implicit imperative to resist suffering. Our experience is one of suffering and striving against suffering, of suffering and seeking salvation, an experience which seems to constitute the fundamental force and rhythm of human history and of life itself. Not the suffering but the struggling against suffering for the sake of salvation seems to constitute the very *raison d'être* of existence.

Schillebeeckx's negative contrast experience articulates this fundamental phenomenon, pointing out as well that to struggle against suffering, to seek salvation, requires that we already have some, however minute, experience of salvation. The negative contrast experience is not foundational for ethics in the sense of its being a starting point of a deductive or semi-deductive system. It does not, even indirectly, yield universal norms for right practice. Indeed, it undermines their possibility. The negative contrast experience is foundational for ethics because it captures the starting point of ethics in the experience of suffering and struggling against suffering for the sake of salvation. Also, it captures what is at the core or center of ethics, and yields its fundamental value, imperative, and criterion for right practice—to resist suffering for the sake of salvation. It is foundational because, while suffering makes ethics necessary, the negative contrast experience makes ethics possible.

Because the negative contrast experience is an occurrent experience, the ethic it yields is concrete, contentful, respectful of our historical character, and historically relevant; because it is an anthropological constant and thus a universal tendency and value, the ethic it yields is universally relevant, respecting that we belong to a common humanity, encountering a common world. Also, because the negative contrast experience respects the epistemological priority of negativity, the ethic it yields has all these same characteristics of concrete relevance and universal acknowledgment. Because it insists on the ontological priority of positivity, the ethic it yields affirms that life is fundamentally and positively valuable and not reducible to a search for mere nonsuffering, for nothingness. That the productive force of the negative contrast experience, the imperative to resist suffering, is a practice before it is linguistic knowledge ensures that this ethic will respond to suffering by innovative practice and not by blindly applying outdated rules. An ethic for which the negative contrast experience is foundational thus has a balance which defies the impracticability of an ethic which begins with a positive, abstract, and universal view of human nature. It also defies the anarchical character of an ethic which begins merely with the situation.

THE OPTION FOR THE POOR CONCRETIZES THE GENERAL IMPERATIVE TO RESIST SUFFERING

We have claimed that the power of this ethic is that it is concrete and responds to need. But the imperative of resistance to suffering is incomplete as it stands. It must be concretized and instantiated or the ethic for which it is first principle will be abstract and ineffective. The reason for this is that we all suffer, and an ethic of resistance to suffering will be neutralized if we do not insist that first concern be given to the worst off—and that they be named. Liberation theologians capture this in their call to take up the option for the poor. This notion has a both generic and specific sense. Generically, it refers to the option for the victims of all structurally caused oppression, such as the materially poor, women, and people of color. Specifically, it refers to the option for the worst off, the materially destitute who do not have even the means of survival, whether they be women or men, black, brown, or white. The option for the materially poor is the first, paradigmatic concretization of the imperative to resist suffering. The option for the poor in both its generic and specific sense is foundational for ethics. A part of what this means concretely is that, whether or not our personal vocation is explicitly directed toward the needs of the poor and other oppressed groups, the social institutions of which we are a part ought to be reshaped to respond to the needs of the worst off—and we must see that they do. Our lifestyle, and, in a real sense, our life's commitment, including how we steer our vocation, must be geared to this end. For Christians, this is to participate in bringing about God's reign, God's kingdom.

The option for the poor involves a paradigm shift in ethics which recognizes that we are essentially embodied and socially conditioned. Liberation and salvation in history become central to ethics and joining with others to transform oppressive social structures is a central means. This is an appropriate response to the acknowledgment of our social sinfulness, our forced participation in structures of oppression. Most people belong both to groups which are oppressed and to groups which are dominant and all, even the worst off, are called by this ethic to take up the option. It is crucial that oppressed groups take up their own cause in order that they/we achieve subjective liberation. Central to the paradigm shift involved in the option for the poor is taking sides with the poor and oppressed both in the way we interpret the world and how we act in it. This involves partisanship and potential conflict with those who want to maintain the status quo, but it cannot be avoided. Contrary to the tradition's view that a partisan outlook is untrue because it is not objective, and a partisan practice is unjust because it shows favoritism, this ethic argues that if we do not take sides with the poor, if we attempt to be neutral, not to take sides at all, we will support the status quo and those who benefit from the way things are. Thus, the option for the poor must be the first principle of both hermeneutics and ethics. But, while this ethic demands that we take sides with the poor and oppressed, it is not *essentially* divisive. All are included in the call. It is the only means to universal love.

AN ETHIC OF SOCIAL SOLIDARITY

As has already been indicated, presupposed in the paradigm shift involved in the option for the poor is the move from a personal ethic of the autonomous individual to an ethic of social solidarity. The shift to social solidarity is very connected with the more general shift from an ahistorical to a historical perspective because both centrally involve our fundamental relatedness. On the traditional model, the individual moral agent is not conditioned by body, social structures, or the relativities of history but, in the moral sphere, can be completely knowing, free, powerful, and responsible. An ethic of social solidarity, an ethic which stresses our social conditionedness and connectedness, acknowledges limitations in our personal knowledge, power, freedom, and responsibility not recognized by the tradition. But it also gives ethics a much broader scope. Conditions which were thought to be 'natural' or 'divinely ordained' and outside the sphere of our moral concern are now recognized as humanly caused, revisable, and at the center of moral concern. But this is to extend our knowledge, free our freedom, exercise our power to liberate, and take responsibility for our context. It is to recreate our conditions for existence which is, in part, to recreate our humanity.

Because we are essentially relational and conditioned by social structures and institutions, and because these are so central to causing poverty and oppression, the ethics of transforming oppressive structures, social structural ethics, must be moved to the very center of ethics. And our understanding of personal ethics must be revised in light of this. The latter must be understood to involve, primarily, our personal attempt to relate to others in nonoppressive, nonhierarchical ways, acknowledging that these attempts will be restricted by oppressive structures even when we understand them and are struggling to transform them. But personal ethics also, in part, unfolds within a framework of understanding, belief, and norms that are commonly acknowledged by members of a community, so that personal ethics has a relative stability, certainty, and doability that structural social ethics does not.

Mutuality, a relationship of reciprocity based on equality, is the only appropriate form of relationship between sexes, races, religious groups, and classes; it is our goal. But mutuality is always based on altruism. And, in our world which is profoundly dis-ordered, inegalitarian, oppressive, and where few will make the effort for change, there is great need for altruism or agape, indeed for eros/agape, a felt love for the worst off which issues in action. Stewardship is the only appropriate relationship between humans and the nonhuman world that we affect. And while it involves recognizing that everything has its own worth and is not a mere means to our ends, it also involves a scale or hierarchy of values. But while we cannot avoid conflict in our relations with humans and hierarchy in our relations with the world, the emphasis of an ethic of social solidarity must be one of exploring our connectedness and encouraging integratedness.

AN INNOVATIVE ETHIC FOR WHICH PRACTICE IS PRIOR TO NORMS FOR PRACTICE

Because the starting point of this ethic is the experience of an already damaged humanum in an already damaged world which is disordered and has no blueprint for right order, this ethic must be fundamentally creative, innovative. More concretely, because it is an ethic for which the option for the poor and social solidarity are central, so that it brings into question and attempts to transform the very structures and frameworks in terms of which rules for right practice are applicable, it must be innovative. Creativity in ethics forms part of the paradigm shift we have been describing. It replaces a view of ethics for which there are universal rules of right practice of which we can be certain and which call us to obedience. By contrast, a liberationist ethic insists that in order that our fundamental value remain alive in our history, in order that we genuinely seek the good of the humanum, we must creatively seek new forms of interpretation and practice for new contexts. Norms are derived from experience and must be revised in light of new experience.

Because practice must be prior to norms for practice, we can understand this ethic on the model of a skill, a kind of knowing-how where practical knowledge precedes the knowledge of formulae. Because being shown how is important to learning how, this ethic much more than a rule ethic is one for which human models are important. Jesus showed us how to relativize practice to fundamental value in the attitude he took to the Mosaic Law. And the tradition after him showed how we can transpose from his situation to our own, how we can attune ourselves to the inner logic of his life. Human models, by their example, are also important in helping us to decide what will be our fundamental value. They provide an extension to our personal experience and, in their lives and stories, they show us their value integrated in a living project, so that we can see concretely what we are giving assent to. This ethic, then, encourages, for Christians, a new nonimitative ethic of discipleship.

A creative liberationist ethic can respond to any fears the tradition may have of its being anarchical. In moral decision-making it does not choose arbitrarily and in a vacuum but, on the contrary, accepts guidance from every source and takes all the relevant data into account. For this reason, unlike Kantian, utilitarian, and a rigid form of natural law ethics, it does not lead to counterintuitive results. It takes account of the criterion of negativity and anthropological constants. It encourages us to find means which resemble our ends but recognizes that this will not always be possible. It concerns itself with values, actions, and consequences, but also, with intentions, motives, and virtues. It takes both dignity and welfare values, both the subjective and objective demands of liberation, to be of central importance. This ethic is flexible enough to recognize that there may be occasions on which different and even opposing actions may be right. Finally, more generally, an innovative ethic is a paradigm of responsibility because it acknowledges our creative capacity and the need to make meaning in our broken world. It insists that we be morally adult, which is the only way in which we can be truly moral.

ETHICS, RELIGION, AND SUFFERING

An ethic which starts with the experience of an already damaged humanum and cosmos and with no blueprint for making things right, and which, in face of this, demands creativity, is not an ethic which derives what we ought to do from an extrinsic religious authority. Indeed, a liberationist ethic is both autonomous vis-à-vis religious commitment and, in important ways, foundational for theology and religion. Hermeneutics involves the choice of a fundamental value, and insofar as theology and religion are hermeneutical, they are based on that value. We see why the first principle of hermeneutics must be the first principle of ethics. Because we cannot avoid choosing our fundamental value, we cannot avoid choosing who or what will be our god in accordance with that value. A god who lays on values or rules from the outside is a god we choose. But it has been the argument of this book that the value that is worthy as first principle of ethics and hermeneutics is the liberationist value of resistance to suffering, concretized in terms of the option for the poor. This is the founding value of an authentic and meaningful theology and religion for our time and, with the nuances that have been expressed elsewhere, for any time.

While a liberationist ethic need not involve religious commitment, its central concern, response to suffering, has much in common with almost every religion. Indeed, because resistance to suffering and to the suffering of the worst off is its first and overriding concern, it cannot avoid religion. It is an ethic, *the ethic* which responds to the threat and challenge that massive world suffering makes to our ethicity today. But, because it fails to bring even temporary salvation to the very worst off, to those who live and die wretchedly, this ethic fails at its heart. It does not necessitate but, logically and ethically, cries out for God and final salvation.

But also, there are a number of positive reasons why a liberationist ethic encourages a merging of its ethical vision with a religious vision. The experience of partial salvation which results from and is found in our efforts to bring about liberation in history calls forth, in some, the hope for a full salvation without suffering. The experience of the poor, by the rich and the poor, calls forth, for some, a God who reveals Godself in the poor protesting their plight and demanding their uplifting. For Christians, the experience of Jesus as a radical example of one who lived and died out of the negative contrast experience and who was raised provides a particularly strong impetus for hope. While we cannot opt out of our ethicity, and while we cannot completely choose whether to be religious, liberationist ethics, from every angle, draws us toward a religious experience and vision. *Ethics can face the threat and challenge of excessive suffering only when it places at the center of its concern what has been historically the religious concern for suffering and especially the suffering of the worst off. Religion can face the threat and challenge of excessive suffering only when it roots itself in a liberationist ethic.* The experience of God in the poor, in Jesus, and in our own negative contrast experience alleviates, for religion, the problem of evil. We are born into an experience of an already damaged humanum and cosmos, of suffering and struggling against suffering. God reveals Godself in that experience, not to explain suffering but to show us how to resist it, and to give us hope of a heaven that we participate in creating, a heaven in which suffering will be turned to salvation.

NOTE

1. I do not draw out in detail, as I have not throughout the book, from what vision this ethic is a paradigm shift. We have not had a homogeneous vision, but the ethics rising out of the Enlightenment, particularly a Kantian ethic of autonomy, Roman Catholic manual ethics based on a static view of nat-

ural law, and secular utilitarianism are all relevant. In general, I am concerned with a shift in ethics from what is positive, universal, abstract, personal, and ahistorical, and which issues into the giving of obedience to an extrinsic or intrinsic authority, to what is negative, particular, concrete, social, historical, and innovative.

Selected Bibliography

Works by Edward Schillebeeckx

Schillebeeckx, Edward. *God the Future of Man*. Translated by N. D. Smith. London: Sheed & Ward, 1969.

_____. "Critical Theories and Christian Political Commitment." In *Political Commitment and Christian Community. Concilium* 84 (1973): 48–61. Edited by Alois Muller & Norbert Greinacher. Translated by N. D. Smith.

_____. *The Understanding of Faith: Interpretation and Criticism*. Translated by N. D. Smith. New York: The Seabury Press, 1974.

_____. *Jesus: An Experiment in Christology*. Translated by Hubert Hoskins. London: Wm. Collins Sons Co. Ltd., 1979; Fount Paperbacks, 1983.

_____. *Interim Report on the Books Jesus and Christ*. Translated by John Bowden. New York: The Seabury Press, 1981.

_____. *Christ: The Experience of Jesus as Lord*. Translated by John Bowden. New York: The Crossroad Publishing Co., 1983.

_____. "Ideology and Ideology Critique as Hermeneutics." In *The Schillebeeckx Reader*, pp. 113–15. Edited by Robert J. Schreiter. New York: The Crossroad Publishing Co., 1984.

_____. *Jesus in Our Western Culture: Mysticism, Ethics and Politics*. Translated by John Bowden. London: SCM Press Ltd., 1987.

_____. *Church: The Human Story of God*. Translated by John Bowden. London: SCM Press Ltd., 1990.

Books and Articles on Schillebeeckx

Dupré, Louis. "Experience and Interpretation: A Philosophical Reflection on Schillebeeckx' *Jesus* and *Christ*." *Theological Studies* 43 (1982): 30–51.

Fackre, Gabriel. "Bones Strong and Weak in the Skeletal Structure of Schillebeeckx's Christology." *Journal of Ecumenical Studies* 21:1 (Spring 1984): 248–77.

Galvin, J. P. "The Uniqueness of Jesus and His *Abba* Experience in the Theology of Edward Schillebeeckx." *Catholic Theological Society of America* Proceedings 35 (1980): 309–14.

George, William P. "The Praxis of the Kingdom of God: Ethics in Schillebeeckx's *Jesus* and *Christ*." *Horizons* 12 (1985): 44–69.

Lefébure, Marcus. "Schillebeeckx's Anatomy of Experience." *New Blackfriars* 64 (June 1983): 270–86.

O'Donovan, Leo. "The Ethical Implications of Schillebeeckx's Christology." *Catholic Theological Society of America* Proceedings 38 (1983): 119–22.

Portier, William L. "Schillebeeckx' Dialogue with Critical Theory." *Ecumenist* 21 (1983): 20–27.

_____. "Edward Schillebeeckx as Critical Theorist: The Impact of Neo-Marxist Social Thought on his Recent Theology." *Thomist* 48 (1984): 341–67.

Schreiter, Robert J. & Mary Catherine Hilkert, editors. *The Praxis of Christian Experience: An Introduction to the Theology of Edward Schillebeeckx.* San Francisco: Harper & Row Publishers, 1989.

Works by Juan Luis Segundo

Segundo, Juan Luis. *The Liberation of Theology.* Translated by John Drury. Maryknoll, New York: Orbis Books, 1976.

_____. *Jesus of Nazareth Yesterday and Today.* Volume 1: *Faith and Ideologies.* Translated by John Drury. Maryknoll, New York: Orbis Books, 1984. Volume 2: *The Historical Jesus of the Synoptics.* Translated by John Drury. Maryknoll, New York: Orbis Books, 1985. Volume 3: *The Humanist Christology of Paul.* Translated by John Drury. Maryknoll, New York: Orbis Books, 1986. Volume 5: *An Evolutionary Approach to Jesus of Nazareth.* Edited and translated by John Drury. Maryknoll, New York: Orbis Books, 1988.

_____. *Theology and the Church: A Response to Cardinal Ratzinger and a Warning to the Whole Church.* Translated by John W. Diercksmeier. Minneapolis: Winston Press, 1985.

Books and Reviews on Segundo

Baum, Gregory. "The Theological Method of Segundo's *The Liberation of Theology.*" *Catholic Theological Society of America* Proceedings (1977), pp. 120–24.

Haight, Roger. Review of *Faith and Ideologies. Cross Currents* 34 (Spring, 1984): 106–09.

_____. "A Political Interpretation of Jesus." *Cross Currents* 36 (Spring, 1986): 85–90.

_____. "Segundo's Pauline Anthropology." *Cross Currents* 37 (Spring, 1987): 99–104.

Stefano, Frances. *The Absolute Value of Human Action in the Theology of Juan Luis Segundo.* Lanham, MD: University Press of America, Inc., 1992.

Works by Dorothee Soelle

Soelle, Dorothee. *Beyond Mere Obedience: Reflections on a Christian Ethic for the Future.* Translated by Lawrence W. Denef. Minneapolis: Augsburg Publishing House, 1970.

_____. *Political Theology*. Translated by John Shelley. Philadelphia: Fortress Press, 1974.

_____. *Suffering*. Translated by Everett R. Kalin. London: Darton, Longman & Todd, 1975.

_____. *Death by Bread Alone: Texts and Reflections on Religious Experience*. Translated by David L. Scheidt. Philadelphia: Fortress Press, 1978.

_____. "'Thou Shalt Have No Other Jeans Before Me' (Levi's Advertisement, Early Seventies) The Need for Liberation in a Consumerist Society." In *The Challenge of Liberation Theology: A First World Response*, pp. 4–16. Edited by Brian Mahan & Dale Richeson. Introduced by David Tracy. Maryknoll, New York: Orbis Books, 1981.

_____. *The Strength of the Weak: Toward a Christian Feminist Identity*. Translated by Robert & Rita Kimber. Philadelphia: The Westminster Press, 1984.

Soelle, Dorothee, with Shirley A. Cloves, *To Work and to Love: A Theology of Creation*. Philadelphia: Fortress Press,1984.

Books on Liberationist Ethics/Liberationist Fundamental Theology

Andolsen, Barbara Hilkert, Christine E. Gudorf, & Mary D. Pellauer. *Women's Consciousness, Women's Conscience: A Reader in Feminist Ethics*. San Francisco: Harper and Row Publishers, 1985.

Boff, Clodovis. *Theology and Praxis: Epistemological Foundations*. Translated by Robert R. Barr. Maryknoll, New York: Orbis Books, 1987.

Dussel, Enrique D. *Ethics and the Theology of Liberation*. Translated by Bernard F. McWilliams. Maryknoll, New York: Orbis Books, 1978.

_____. *Ethics and Community*. Theology and Liberation Series. Translated by Robert R. Barr. Maryknoll, New York: Orbis Books, 1988.

Fourez, Gerard. *Liberation Ethics*. Translated and adapted by David Morris, Barbara Hogan, & Gerard Fourez. Philadelphia: Temple University Press, 1982.

Harrison, Beverly W. *Making the Connections: Essays in Feminist Social Ethics*. Edited by Carol Robb. Boston: Beacon Press, 1985.

Kammer, Charles L., III. *Ethics and Liberation: An Introduction*. Maryknoll, New York: Orbis Books, 1988.

Lamb, Matthew. *Solidarity with Victims: Toward a Theology of Social Transformation*. New York: The Crossroad Publishing Company, 1982.

Lane, Dermot A. *Foundations for a Social Theology: Praxis, Process and Salvation*. New York: Paulist Press, 1984.

Metz, Johann Baptist. *Faith in History and Society: Toward a Practical Fundamental Theology*. Translated by David Smith. New York: The Seabury Press, 1980.

Mieth, Dietmar & Jacques Pohier, editors. *The Ethics of Liberation—The Liberation of Ethics. Concilium* 172 (1984).

Moreno, Francisco. *Moral Theology from the Poor: Moral Challenges of the Theology of Liberation*. Quezon City: Claretian Publications, 1988.

Moser, Antonio, & Bernardino Leers. *Moral Theology: Dead Ends and Alternatives*. Translated by Paul Burns. Maryknoll, New York: Orbis Books, 1990.

Planas, Ricardo. *Liberation Theology: The Political Expression of Religion*. Kansas City: Sheed and Ward, 1986.

Welch, Sharon D. *Communities of Resistance and Solidarity: A Feminist Theology of Liberation*. Maryknoll, New York: Orbis Books, 1985.

Chapter 1

Adorno, Theodor W., & Max Horkheimer. *Dialectic of Enlightenment*. Translated by John Cumming. New York: The Continuum Publishing Co., 1972.

Bernstein, Richard J. *Beyond Objectivism and Relativism: Science, Hermeneutics, and Praxis*. Philadelphia: The University of Pennsylvania Press, 1988.

Chopp, Rebecca S. *The Praxis of Suffering: An Interpretation of Liberation and Political Theologies*. Maryknoll, New York: Orbis Books, 1986.

Gerlock, Ed, editor. *Signs of Hope: Stories of Hope in the Philippines*. Davao City and Quezon City: Philippine International Forum and Claretian Publications, 1990.

Habermas, Jürgen. *Theory and Practice*. Boston: Beacon Press, 1974.

Held, David. *Introduction to Critical Theory*. Berkeley: University of California, 1980.

Horkheimer, Max. *Critical Theory: Selected Essays*. Translated by Matthew J. O'Connell and others. New York: The Continuum Publishing Co., 1972.

Jay, Martin. *The Dialectical Imagination*. Boston & Toronto: Little, Brown & Co., 1973.

MacIntyre, Alasdair. *A Short History of Ethics*. Fields of Philosophy Series. New York: The Macmillan Co., 1966.

Schüssler Fiorenza, Francis. "Political Theology as Foundational Theology." *Catholic Theological Society* Proceedings 32 (1977): 142–77.

Taylor, Charles. "What Is Human Agency?" In *The Self: Psychological and Philosophical Issues*: 103–35. Edited by Theodore Mischel. Oxford: Basil Blackwell, 1977.

Chapter 2

Adriance, Madeleine. "Whence the Option for the Poor." *Cross Currents* 34 (Winter 1984–85): 500–507.

Antoncich, Ricardo. *Christians in the Face of Injustice: A Latin American Reading of Catholic Social Teaching*. Maryknoll, New York: Orbis Books, 1987.

Baum, Gregory. "Class Struggle and the Magisterium: A New Note." *Theological Studies* 45 (1984): 690–701.

_____. *Compassion and Solidarity: The Church for Others*. CBC Massey Lectures Series. Montreal: CBC Enterprises, 1987.

_____. "Faith and Liberation: Development Since Vatican II." In *Theology and Society*, pp. 3–31. New York: Paulist Press.

Chittister, Joan. *Job's Daughters: Women and Power*. New York: Paulist Press, 1990.

Clarke, Thomas E. "Option for the Poor: A Reflection." *America* (January 30, 1988), pp. 95–99.

Doran, Robert M. *Theology and the Dialectics of History*. Toronto: University of Toronto Press, 1990.

Dorr, Donal. *Option for the Poor: A Hundred Years of Vatican Social Teaching.* Maryknoll, New York: Orbis Books, 1983.

Eagleson, John, & Philip Scharper, editors. *Puebla and Beyond: Documentation and Commentary.* Translated by John Drury. Maryknoll, New York: Orbis Books, 1979.

Elizondo, Virgil, & Leonardo Boff, editors. *Option for the Poor: Challenge to the Rich Countries. Concilium* 187 (1986).

Ferm, Deane William. *Third World Theologies: An Introductory Survey.* Maryknoll, New York: Orbis Books, 1986.

Freire, Paulo. *Pedagogy of the Oppressed.* Translated by Myra Bergman Ramos. Middlesex: Penguin Education. Penguin Books Ltd., 1972.

Geremia, Peter, editor. *Church Persecution: A Test Case: Kidapawan Diocese. Nagliliyab,* Series no. 13. Quezon City: Claretian Publications, 1988.

Gutiérrez, Gustavo. *A Theology of Liberation: History, Politics and Salvation.* Translated and edited by Sister Caridad Inda & John Eagleson. London: SCM Press, 1974.

_____. *The Power of the Poor in History.* Translated by Robert R. Barr. Maryknoll, New York: Orbis Books, 1983.

Haight, Roger. *An Alternative Vision: An Interpretation of Liberation Theology.* New York: Paulist Press, 1985.

_____. "The Origins and Relevance of Liberation Theology." Series of 4 articles: "From Vatican Council II to Liberation Theology," "Liberation Theology in the Language of Vatican II," "God and Jesus Christ," "God's Spirit and the Human Response." *PACE/Professional Approaches for Christian Educators* 17. Edited by Mary Perkins Ryan, 1987: 12–17, 59–64, 92–96, 119–25.

Kuhn, Thomas S. *The Structure of Scientific Revolutions.* 2nd edition. Chicago: University of Chicago Press, 1970.

Lonergan, Bernard. *Method in Theology.* New York: The Seabury Press, 1972.

Mahan, Brian, & Dale Richeson, editors. *The Challenge of Liberation Theology: A First World Response.* Introduced by David Tracy. Maryknoll, New York: Orbis Books, 1981.

Sacred Congregation for the Doctrine of the Faith. "Instruction on Certain Aspects of the 'Theology of Liberation,'" Vatican City: 1984.

_____. "Instruction on Christian Freedom and Liberation." Vatican City: 1986.

Second General Conference of Latin American Bishops (1968). *The Church in Present-Day Transformation of Latin America in the Light of the Council: II, Conclusions.* 2nd Edition. Washington D.C.: Division of Latin America— USCC, 1973.

Sobrino, Jon. "Jesus' Relationship with the Poor and Outcasts: Its Importance for Fundamental Moral Theology." Translated by Paul Burns. In *The Dignity of the Despised of the Earth,* pp. 12–20. Edited by Jacques Pohier and Dietmar Mieth. *Concilium* 130 (1979).

_____. *The True Church and the Poor.* Translated by Matthew J. O'Connell. Maryknoll, New York: Orbis Books, 1984.

_____. "Poverty Means Death to the Poor." *Cross Currents* 36 (Fall, 1986): 267–76.

Torres, Sergio & John Eagleson, editors. *Theology in the Americas*. Maryknoll, New York: Orbis Books, 1976.

_____. *The Challenge of Basic Christian Communities: Papers from the International Ecumenical Congress of Theology, February 20–March 2, 1980, São Paulo, Brazil*. Translated by John Drury. Maryknoll, New York: Orbis Books, 1981.

Chapter 3

Andolsen, Barbara. "Agape in Feminist Ethics." *The Journal of Religious Ethics* 9 (Spring 1981): 69–83.

Bateson, Gregory. *Steps to an Ecology of Mind*. New York: Ballantine Books, 1972.

Berger, Peter L., & Thomas Luckmann. *The Social Construction of Reality: A Treatise on the Sociology of Knowledge*. New York: Doubleday Anchor Books, 1967.

Birch, Charles, William Eakin, & Jay B. McDaniel, editors. *Liberating Life: Contemporary Approaches to Ecological Theory*. Maryknoll, New York: Orbis Books, 1990.

Callicott, J. Baird. "Animal Liberation: A Triangular Affair." *Environmental Ethics* 2 (1980): 311–38.

Clark, Stephen R. L. *The Moral Status of Animals*. Oxford: Clarendon Press, 1977.

Fletcher, Joseph. "Give If It Helps But Not If It Hurts." In *World Hunger and Moral Obligation*, pp. 103–14. Edited by William Aiken & Hugh La Follette. Englewood Cliffs, New Jersey: Prentice-Hall, Inc., 1977.

Gustafson, James M. *Ethics from a Theocentric Perspective*. Volume 1: *Theology and Ethics*. Chicago: The University of Chicago Press, 1981. Volume 2: *Ethics and Theology*. Chicago: The University of Chicago Press, 1984.

Hardin, Garrett. "Lifeboat Ethics: The Case Against Helping the Poor." In *World Hunger and Moral Obligation*, pp. 11–21. Edited by William Aiken & Hugh La Follette. Englewood Cliffs, New Jersey: Prentice-Hall, Inc., 1977.

Harrison, Beverly W. "The Power of Anger in the Work of Love: Christian Ethics for Women and Other Strangers." *Union Quarterly Review* 36 (1981): 41–57.

Hutchinson, Roger C. "Mutuality: Procedural Norm and Foundational Symbol." In *Liberation and Ethics: Essays in Religious Social Ethics in Honor of Gibson Winter*, pp. 97–110. Edited by Charles Amjad-Ali & W. Alvin Pitcher. Chicago: Center for the Scientific Study of Religion, 1985.

Leopold, Aldo. *Sand County Almanac*. New York: Oxford University Press, 1981.

Lonergan, Bernard. "The Transition from a Classicist World View to Historical Mindedness." In *Law for Liberty*, pp. 123–33. Edited by James E. Biecher. Baltimore: Helicon Press, 1967.

Merleau-Ponty, Maurice. *The Phenomenology of Perception*. Translated by Colin Smith. London: Routledge and Kegan Paul, 1962.

Midgley, Mary. *Beast and Man: The Roots of Human Nature*. Hassocks, Sussex: The Harvester Press, 1978.

Niebuhr, H. Richard. *The Responsible Self: An Essay in Christian Moral Philosophy.* Introduced by James M. Gustafson. New York: Harper and Row Publishers, 1963.

———. "The Center of Value." In *Radical Monotheism and Western Culture: With Supplementary Essays,* pp. 100–13. New York: Harper and Row Publishers; Harper Torchbooks, 1970.

Pawlikowski, John T. *Christ in the Light of the Christian-Jewish Dialogue.* New York: Paulist Press, 1982.

Rauschenbusch, Walter. *A Theology for the Social Gospel.* Nashville: The Abingdon Press, 1946.

Regan, Tom, & Peter Singer, editors. *Animal Rights and Human Obligations.* Englewood Cliffs, New Jersey: Prentice-Hall, Inc., 1976.

Ruether, Rosemary Radford. *Sexism and God-Talk: Toward a Feminist Theology.* Boston: Beacon Press, 1983.

Stone, Christopher D. *Earth and Other Ethics: The Case for Moral Pluralism.* New York: Harper and Row Publishers, 1987; Perennial Library, 1988.

Strawson, P. F. *Individuals: An Essay in Descriptive Metaphysics.* London: Methuen & Co. Ltd., 1964.

Wittgenstein, Ludwig. *Philosophical Investigations.* Translated by G. E. M. Anscombe. Oxford: Basil Blackwell, 1958.

Chapter 4

Cahill, Lisa Sowle. "Teleology, Utilitarianism and Christian Ethics." *Theological Studies* 42 (1981): 601–29.

Curran, Charles E. "Utilitarianism and Contemporary Moral Theology: Situating the Debates." In *Readings in Moral Theology No. 1: Moral Norms and Catholic Tradition,* pp. 341–62. Edited by Charles E. Curran & Richard A. McCormick. New York: Paulist Press, 1979.

Davis, Charles. "Theology and Praxis." *Cross Currents* 23 (1973): 154–68.

———. "From Inwardness to Social Action." *New Blackfriars* 67 (March, 1986): 114–25.

Frankena, William. *Ethics.* Englewood Cliffs: Prentice-Hall, 1963.

Fuchs, Josef. "The Absoluteness of Behavioral Moral Norms." In *Personal Responsibility and Christian Morality,* pp. 115–52. Washington, D.C.: Georgetown University Press, 1983.

Gula, Richard M. *What Are They Saying About Moral Norms?* New York: Paulist Press, 1982.

Gustafson, James M. *Protestant and Roman Catholic Ethics: Prospects for Rapprochement.* Chicago: The University of Chicago Press, 1978.

Hoose, Bernard. *Proportionalism: The American Debate and Its European Roots.* Washington, D.C.: Georgetown University Press, 1987.

Jackson, Timothy P. "Against Grammar." Review of George Lindbeck's *The Nature of Doctrine. Religious Studies Review* 11 (July, 1985): 240–45.

Lamb, Matthew. "The Theory-Praxis Relationship in Contemporary Christian Theologies." *Catholic Theological Society of America* Proceedings 31 (1976): 149–78.

Lindbeck, George A. *The Nature of Doctrine: Religion and Theology in a Postliberal Age*. Philadelphia: The Westminster Press, 1984.

McCormick, Richard A. "Reflections on the Literature." In *Readings in Moral Theology No. 1: Moral Norms and Catholic Tradition*, pp. 294–339. Edited by Charles E. Curran & Richard A. McCormick. New York: Paulist Press, 1979.

_____. "Notes on Moral Theology." *Theological Studies* 44 (1983): 71–122.

_____. "Notes on Moral Theology." *Theological Studies* 46 (1985): 50–64.

Polanyi, Michael. *Personal Knowledge: Towards a Post-Critical Philosophy*. Chicago: The University of Chicago Press, 1962.

_____. *The Tacit Dimension*. New York: Anchor Books, 1967.

Ryle, Gilbert. *The Concept of Mind*. Middlesex: Penguin Books Ltd., 1963.

Smart, J. J. C., & Bernard Williams. *Utilitarianism For and Against*. Cambridge: Cambridge University Press, 1973.

Tracy, David. "Lindbeck's New Program for Theology: A Reflection." *Thomist* 49 (July, 1985): 460–72.

Vacek, Edward V. "Proportionalism: One View of the Debate." *Theological Studies* 46 (1985): 287–314.

Wood, Charles M. "Review of George A. Lindbeck's *The Nature of Doctrine: Religion and Theology in a Postliberal Age*." *Religious Studies Review* 11 (July, 1985): 235–40.

Chapter 5

"Focus on the Ethics of James M. Gustafson." *The Journal of Religious Ethics* 13:1 (Spring, 1985): 1–112.

Gustafson, James M. *Can Ethics Be Christian?* Chicago: The University of Chicago Press, 1975.

_____. *Ethics from a Theocentric Perspective*. Volume 1: *Theology and Ethics*. Chicago: The University of Chicago Press, 1981.

_____. "A Response to Critics." *The Journal of Religious Ethics* 13:2 (Summer 1985): 185–209.

Haight, Roger. "Towards an Understanding of Christ in the Context of Other World Religions." *East Asian Pastoral Review* XXVI (Nos. 3 & 4, 1989): 248–65.

_____. *Dynamics of Theology*. New York: Paulist Press, 1990.

Hick, John. "On Grading Religions." *Religious Studies* 17 (1981): 451–67.

Hick, John, & Paul F. Knitter, editors. *The Myth of Christian Uniqueness: Toward a Pluralistic Theology of Religions*. Faith Meets Faith Series. Maryknoll, New York: Orbis Books, 1987.

James, William. "Is Life Worth Living?" In *The Will to Believe and Other Essays in Popular Philosophy*, pp. 52–62. New York: Dover Publications, 1956.

Knitter, Paul F. *No Other Name? A Critical Survey of Christian Attitudes Toward World Religions*. Maryknoll, New York: Orbis Books, 1985.

_____. "Towards a Liberation Theology of Religions." In *The Myth of Christian Uniqueness: Toward a Pluralistic Theology of Religions*, pp. 178–200. Edited by John Hick & Paul F. Knitter. Faith Meets Faith Series. Maryknoll, New York: Orbis Books, 1987.

Kroger, Joseph. "Prophetic-Critical and Practical-Strategic Tasks of Theology: Habermas and Liberation Theology." *Theological Studies* 46 (1985): 3–20.

Min, Anselm. "Critique of Schubert Ogden." *Journal of the American Academy of Religion* LVII (Spring, 1989): 83–102.

Niebuhr, H. Richard. *The Meaning of Revelation*. New York: The Macmillan Co., 1960.

Ogden, Schubert M. *Faith and Freedom: Toward a Theology of Liberation*. Nashville: Abingdon Press, 1979.

_____. *On Theology*. San Francisco: Harper and Row Publishers, 1986.

Peukert, Helmut. *Science, Action and Fundamental Theology: Towards a Theology of Communicative Action*. Translated by James Bohman. Cambridge: MIT Press, 1986.

Schüssler-Fiorenza, Elisabeth. "Toward a Feminist Biblical Hermeneutics: Biblical Interpretation and Liberation Theology." In *The Challenge of Liberation Theology: A First World Response*, pp. 91–112. Edited by Brian Mahan & Dale Richeson. Introduced by David Tracy. Maryknoll, New York: Orbis Books, 1981.

Sobrino, Jon. *Christology at the Crossroads: A Latin American Approach*. Translated by John Drury. London: SCM Press Ltd., 1978.

Taylor, Charles. "What Is Human Agency?" In *The Self: Psychological and Philosophical Issues*, pp. 103–35. Edited by Theodore Mischel. Oxford: Basil Blackwell, 1977.

Tracy, David. *Blessed Rage for Order: The New Pluralism in Theology*. New York: The Seabury Press, 1978.

_____. *Plurality and Ambiguity: Hermeneutics, Religion, Hope*. San Francisco: Harper and Row Publishers, 1987.

Index